T0211870

Communications
in Computer and Information Science 1115

Editorial Board Members

Joaquim Filipe ⓘ
Polytechnic Institute of Setúbal, Setúbal, Portugal
Ashish Ghosh
Indian Statistical Institute, Kolkata, India
Raquel Oliveira Prates ⓘ
Federal University of Minas Gerais (UFMG), Belo Horizonte, Brazil
Lizhu Zhou
Tsinghua University, Beijing, China

More information about this series at http://www.springer.com/series/7899

Maria Fazio · Wolf Zimmermann (Eds.)

Advances in Service-Oriented and Cloud Computing

Workshops of ESOCC 2018
Como, Italy, September 12–14, 2018
Revised Selected Papers

 Springer

Editors
Maria Fazio
University of Messina
Messina, Italy

Wolf Zimmermann
Martin Luther University Halle-Wittenberg
Halle (Saale), Germany

ISSN 1865-0929   ISSN 1865-0937   (electronic)
Communications in Computer and Information Science
ISBN 978-3-030-63160-4   ISBN 978-3-030-63161-1   (eBook)
https://doi.org/10.1007/978-3-030-63161-1

© Springer Nature Switzerland AG 2020
This work is subject to copyright. All rights are reserved by the Publisher, whether the whole or part of the material is concerned, specifically the rights of translation, reprinting, reuse of illustrations, recitation, broadcasting, reproduction on microfilms or in any other physical way, and transmission or information storage and retrieval, electronic adaptation, computer software, or by similar or dissimilar methodology now known or hereafter developed.
The use of general descriptive names, registered names, trademarks, service marks, etc. in this publication does not imply, even in the absence of a specific statement, that such names are exempt from the relevant protective laws and regulations and therefore free for general use.
The publisher, the authors and the editors are safe to assume that the advice and information in this book are believed to be true and accurate at the date of publication. Neither the publisher nor the authors or the editors give a warranty, expressed or implied, with respect to the material contained herein or for any errors or omissions that may have been made. The publisher remains neutral with regard to jurisdictional claims in published maps and institutional affiliations.

This Springer imprint is published by the registered company Springer Nature Switzerland AG
The registered company address is: Gewerbestrasse 11, 6330 Cham, Switzerland

Workshop Editors

Cloudways and OptiMoCS

Claus Pahl
Free University of Bozen-Bolzano
Italy
Claus.Pahl@unibz.it

Zoltan Adam Mann
University of Duisburg-Essen
Germany
zoltan.mann@paluno.uni-due.de

WESOACS

Andreas S. Andreou
Cyprus University of Technology
Cyprus
andreas.andreou@cut.ac.cy

Luciano Baresi
Politecnico di Milano
Italy
luciano.baresi@polimi.it

ESOCC PhD Symposium

Vasilios Andrikopoulos
University of Groningen
The Netherlands
v.andrikopoulos@rug.nl

Massimo Villari
University of Messina
Italy
mvillari@unime.it

ESOCC EU-Projects Track

Federico Facca
Martel Innovate
Switzerland

Dumitru Roman
SINTEF
Norway
dumitru.roman@sintef.no

Preface

The European Conference on Service-Oriented and Cloud Computing (ESOCC) is the premier event on advances of the state of the art in services and cloud technologies. It serves as an important venue for scientist as well as practioners from industry. The main objective is to provide a forum for an exchange of ideas. In this respect, the workshops are an important part of the conference. They contribute to an intensive exchange in special fields of service-oriented and cloud computing. In addition, ESOCC organized a PhD symposium where PhD students can present their ideas and results, ranging from early ideas to almost completed work. The EU projects track discusses recent developments from European Projects. The workshop proceedings of ESOCC 2018 contains contributions from the following workshops and events:

- 14th International Workshop on Engineering Service-Oriented Applications and Cloud Services
- Joint Workshop on Optimization in Modern Computing Systems and the 4th Workshop on Cloud Migration and Architecture
- PhD Symposium
- EU Projects Track of ESOCC

We are grateful to Flavio de Paoli and his team for the great organization in a nice location. Pierluigi Plebani supported us in the administration and organization of this volume – thank you very much. We thank the organizers of the workshops and the Program Committee members of the workshops. Their work enabled an attractive program. Finally, we thank the authors who submitted their work to the workshops, the presenters, and the attendees. Without their support, active and fruitful workshops would be impossible.

March 2020

Maria Fazio
Wolf Zimmermann

Organization

General Chair

Flavio di Paoli   University of Milano-Bicocca, Italy

Program Chairs

Kyriakos Kritikos   ICS-FORTH, Greece
Pierluigi Plebani   Politecnico di Milano, Italy

Workshop Chairs

Maria Fazio   University of Messina, Italy
Wolf Zimmermann   Martin Luther University Halle-Wittenberg, Germany

Steering Committee

Antonio Brogi   University of Pisa, Italy
Schahram Dustdar   TU Wien, Austria
Paul Grefen   Eindhoven University of Technology, The Netherlands
Kung Kiu Lau   The University of Manchester, UK
Winfried Lamersdorf   University of Hamburg, Germany
Frank Leymann   University of Stuttgart, Germany
Flavio de Paoli   University of Milano-Bicocca, Italy
Cesare Pautasso   University of Lugano, Switzerland
Ernesto Pimentel   University of Malaga, Spain
Ulf Schreier   Hochschule Furtwangen University, Germany
Stefan Schulte   TU Wien, Austria
Massimo Villari   University of Messina, Italy
John Erik Wittern   IBM T.J. Watson Research Center, USA
Olaf Zimmermann   HSR FHO Rapperswil, Switzerland
Wolf Zimmermann   Martin Luther University Halle-Wittenberg, Germany

Contents

ESOCC 2018 EU Projects Track

Joint Cloudways and OptiMoCS Workshop

CloudWays/OptiMoCS 2018
Abstract/Summary

Joint CloudWays/OptiMoCS 2018 Workshop:

- 4th International Workshop on Cloud Migration and Architecture (CloudWays 2018)
- First International Workshop on Optimization in Modern Computing Systems (OptiMoCS 2018)

Regardless of the benefits of cloud computing, many organizations still rely on business-critical applications in the form of legacy systems that have been developed over a long period of time using traditional development methods. Despite often serious maintainability issues, (on-premise) legacy systems are still crucial as they support core business processes. Therefore, migrating legacy systems towards cloud-based platforms allows organizations to leverage their existing systems deployed and provided (using publicly available resources) as scalable cloud services.

CloudWays 2018 brought together cloud architecture experts from both academia and industry; to promote discussions and collaboration amongst participants; to help disseminate novel cloud adoption, migration, and software architecture practices and solutions; and to identify future cloud architecture challenges and dimensions.

OptiMoCS 2018 served as a platform for discussing recent work on optimization in modern computing systems (e.g., service-oriented computing, cloud computing, edge and fog computing, mobile computing, network function virtualization). Such systems must satisfy several goals regarding performance, consumption of computing and network resources, energy consumption, and financial costs. Optimization of these goals is an important concern in the design and operation of many systems, leading to challenging optimization problems. Improved algorithms for these problems directly translate to more effective and more efficient systems.

CloudWays/OptiMoCS 2018 Preface

Cloud computing has been the focus of attention of both academic research and industrial initiatives. From a business point of view, organizations can benefit from the on-demand and pay-per-use model offered by cloud services rather than an upfront purchase of costly and over-provisioned infrastructure. From a technological perspective, the scalability, interoperability, and efficient (de-)allocation of resources through cloud services can enable a smooth execution of organizational operations.

Regardless of the benefits of cloud computing, many organizations still rely on business-critical applications in the form of legacy systems that have been developed over a long period of time using traditional development methods. Despite often serious maintainability issues, (on-premise) legacy systems are still crucial as they support core business processes. Therefore, migrating legacy systems towards cloud-based platforms allows organizations to leverage their existing systems deployed and provided (using publicly available resources) as scalable cloud services.

This fourth edition of the CloudWays workshop – the 4th International Workshop on Cloud Migration and Architecture (CloudWays 2018) – was held in Como, Italy, on September 12, 2018, as an ESOCC satellite event. The first edition was held in September 2015 in Taormina, Italy, the second in September 2016 in Vienna, Austria, and the third on September 12, 2017, in Oslo, Norway, all as a satellite events of ESOCC. The workshop's goals were to bring together cloud migration and cloud architecture experts from both academia and industry; to promote discussions and collaboration among participants; to help disseminate novel cloud adoption, migration, and architecture practices and solutions; and to identify future cloud challenges and dimensions that help software applications to be architectured for and deployed in the cloud.

In this fourth edition, three full CloudWays papers were accepted for presentation during the workshop, out of a total of six submissions.

The First International Workshop on Optimization in Modern Computing Systems (OptiMoCS 2018) served as a platform for discussing recent work on optimization in modern computing systems. Modern computing paradigms (e.g., service-oriented computing, cloud computing, edge and fog computing, mobile computing, and network function virtualization) allow the construction, deployment, and operation of systems of ever larger scale and complexity. Such systems must satisfy several important, often contradicting, quantifiable goals. Metrics of interest include performance, consumption of computing and network resources, energy consumption, and financial costs. Optimization of these goals is an important concern in the design and operation of many different systems, leading to challenging optimization problems. Improved algorithms for these problems directly translate to more effective and more efficient systems.

OptiMoCS 2018 was organized as a special track of CloudWays 2018. From two submissions, one paper was selected for presentation during the workshop.

The first CloudWays paper "Model-Driven Simulation for Performance Engineering of Kubernetes-style Cloud Cluster Architectures" by Federico Ghirardini, Areeg Samir, Ilenia Fronza, and Claus Pahl looked at performance engineering for container environments. Here Kubernetes was the target for which a model-driven simulation tool has been developed.

The second CloudWays paper "On enhancing the orchestration of multi-container Docker applications" by Antonio Brogi, Claus Pahl, and Jacopo Soldani also had container architectures as a concern. Raising the abstraction level through standardized languages such as the orchestration language TOSCA was the starting point to enhance the orchestration of Docker containers.

The third CloudWays paper "Transactional Migration of Inhomogeneous Composite Cloud Applications" by Josef Spillner and Manuel Ramírez López targeted interoperability of cloud applications.

The final OptiMoCS paper "Secure Apps in the Fog: Anything to Declare?" by Antonio Brogi, Gian-Luigi Ferrari, and Stefano Forti provided a declarative way of specifying security capabilities of Fog infrastructures and security requirements of Fog applications, as well as a probabilistic reasoning strategy to determine application deployments and to quantitatively assess their security level.

We take this opportunity to thank all authors, members of the Program Committee, and workshop attendees, whose participation was invaluable to the success of the event. We also acknowledge the support provided by the Free University of Bozen-Bolzano, Italy.

March 2020

Vasilios Andrikopoulos
Nane Kratzke
Claus Pahl
Zoltan Adam Mann

CloudWays/OptiMoCS 2018 Organization

CloudWays Program Committee

Aakash Ahmad	University of Hail, Saudi Arabia
Vasilios Andrikopoulos (Co-chair)	University of Stuttgart, Germany
Thais Batista	Federal University of Rio Grande do Norte, Brazil
William Campbell	Birmingham City University, UK
Fei Cao	University of Central Missouri, USA
Nicolas Ferry	SINTEF, Norway
Sören Frey	Daimler TSS, Germany
Vinicius Garcia	Universidade Federal de Pernambuco, Brazil
Wilhelm (Willi) Hasselbring	Kiel University, Germany
Abbas Heydarnoori	Sharif University of Technology, Iran
Pooyan Jamshidi	University of South Carolina, USA
Ali Khajeh-Hosseini	RightScale, Inc., UK
Nane Kratzke (Co-chair)	Technical University of Applied Sciences Lübeck, Germany
Xiaodong Liu	Edinburgh Napier University, UK
Paulo Henrique Maia	Ceará State University, Brazil
Nabor Mendonça	University of Fortaleza, Brazil
Claus Pahl (Co-chair)	Free University of Bozen-Bolzano, Italy
Dana Petcu	West University of Timisoara, Romania
Alessandro Rossini	EVRY, Norway
Américo Sampaio	University of Fortaleza, Brazil
Bruno Volckaert	Ghent University, Belgium

OptiMoCS Program Committee

Vasilios Andrikopoulos	University of Groningen, The Netherlands
Steffen Becker	University of Stuttgart, Germany
Luiz Bittencourt	University of Campinas, Brazil
Pascal Bouvry	University of Luxembourg, Luxembourg
David Breitgand	IBM Research, Israel
Antonio Brogi	University of Pisa, Italy
Rajkumar Buyya	The University of Melbourne, Australia
Emiliano Casalicchio	Blekinge Institute of Technology, Sweden
Noel Crespi	Institut Mines-Telecom, France
Schahram Dustdar	TU Wien, Austria

Marco Guazzone	University of Piemonte Orientale, Italy
Odej Kao	TU Berlin, Germany
Gabor Kecskemeti	Liverpool John Moores University, UK
Francesco Palmieri	University of Salerno, Italy
Roberto Pietrantuono	University of Naples Federico II, Italy
Javid Taheri	Karlstad University, Sweden
Massimo Villari	University of Messina, Italy
Stefan Wesner	Ulm University, Germany

Model-Driven Simulation for Performance Engineering of Kubernetes-Style Cloud Cluster Architectures

Federico Ghirardini, Areeg Samir, Ilenia Fronza, and Claus Pahl$^{(\boxtimes)}$

Free University of Bozen-Bolzano, Bolzano, Italy
{federico.ghirardini,areeg.samir,ilenia.fronza,claus.pahl}@unibz.it

Abstract. We propose a performance engineering technique for self-adaptive container cluster management, often used in cloud environments now. We focus here on an abstract model that can be used by simulation tools to identify an optimal configuration for such a system, capable of providing reliable performance to service consumers. The aim of the model-based tool is to identify and analyse a set of rules capable of balancing resource demands for this platform. We present an executable model for a simulation environment that allows container cluster architectures to be studied. We have selected the Kubernetes cluster management platform as the target. Our models reflect the current Kubernetes platform, but we also introduce an advanced controller model going beyond current Kubernetes capabilities. We use the Palladio Eclipse plugin as the simulation environment. The outcome is a working simulator, that applied to a concrete container-based cluster architecture could be used by developers to understand and configure self-adaptive system behavior.

Keywords: Container · Cluster · Kubernetes · Performance engineering · Simulation

1 Introduction

Container management techniques such as Docker or Kubernetes are becoming widely used in cloud and other environments. making container-based systems self-adaptive involves the continuous adjustment of their computing resources in order to provide a reliable performance under different workloads. To achieve this, a well-designed autonomous elastic system should be built considering the following three key aspects: scalability, the ability of the system to sustain workload fluctuation, cost efficiency, acquiring only the required resources by releasing initialized ones, time efficiency, acquiring and releasing resources as soon as a request is made [9]. Moreover, whenever it is possible the system should also be fault tolerant, meaning it detects and handles failures effectively.

Therefore, we focus on investigating container cluster architectures for exploring and analyzing different performance and workload patterns, capable of

© Springer Nature Switzerland AG 2020
M. Fazio and W. Zimmermann (Eds.): ESOCC 2018 Workshops, CCIS 1115, pp. 7–20, 2020.
https://doi.org/10.1007/978-3-030-63161-1_1

enhancing reliability and validity for cluster management in container-based cloud environments [6,17,20]. The main goal of our study is obtaining a reliable tool to be used as a simulation environment for autonomous elastic systems. We aim to help finding suitable settings for the management of container-based cloud resources. While various simulation tools such as CloudSim exist, we focus here on an architecture model driven approach that allows application and platform architecture settings to be modelled and changed easily. We use the container cluster management tool Kubernetes here that is now widely used in cloud environments as our platform facilitating self-adaptive systems. We use Palladio as the platform for modeling and simulation here.

An adaptive container system architecture can be abstracted, looking at the inter-collaboration of three main parts: an application (or service) provided by the system, the container platform, and a monitor for analyzing resources used and overall performance. As a consequence, the most suitable and logically applicable architectural pattern for such a system has been the MAPE-K architecture pattern (i.e., using a Monitor, Analyze, Plan, Execute and Knowledge implementation). We will provide here an abstract, but executable model for the (i) architectural aspects of platform and application and (ii) the controller for self-management. The model is essentially the configuration of a simulation environment. The first set of models (i) reflect the current Kubernetes platform, which we also use in the experimental evaluation. We also introduce an advanced controller model (ii) aiming to link observable performance anomalies to underlying workload problems that is going beyond current Kubernetes capabilities.

2   Self-adaptive Systems – Background

For our autoscaling investigation, we follow the MAPE-K control loop, i.e., monitoring the performance of the application environment used by public users and tenants (i.e. a group of users who share a common access with specific privileges to the software instance), analyzing the just planned corrective actions, using the knowledge part (i.e. the Rule base) containing the autoscaling rules of the system. Autoscaling an application involves specifying threshold-based rules to implement elasticity policies for acquiring and releasing resources [8]. To give an example, a typical autoscaling rule might look as follows: IF the workload is high (e.g., >80%) AND the response time is slow (e.g., >600 ms) THEN add/remove n instances.

In Kubernetes, a system consists of the pod and the service. The management of elastic applications in Kubernetes consists of multiple microservices, [7,23,24] which communicate with each other. Often those microservices are tightly coupled forming a group of containers that would typically, in a non-containerized setup, run together on one server. This group, the smallest unit that can be scheduled to be deployed through Kubernetes, is called a pod. These containers are co-located, hence share resources and are always scheduled together. Pods are not intended to live long. They are created, destroyed and re-created on demand, based on the state of the server and the service itself.

Since pods have a short lifetime, there is no guaranteed IP address they are served at. For that reason, Kubernetes uses the concept of a service: an abstraction on top of a number of pods, typically requiring to run a proxy for other services to communicate with it via a virtual IP address. This is used to configure load balancing for pods and expose them as a service [12].

Kubernetes is the container system for our investigation because of its autoscaling feature. Kubernetes is able to automatically scale up and down clusters. Once a cluster is running, there is the possibility of creating a Horizontal Pod Autoscaler (HPA). When defining an HPA there is the possibility to declare the exact number of pod replicas that the system should maintain (e.g., between 1 and 10). So, the autoscaler will increase and decrease the number of replicas (via deployment) to maintain an average CPU utilization of 50% (default setting) across all pods [13]. We will create simulator for this.

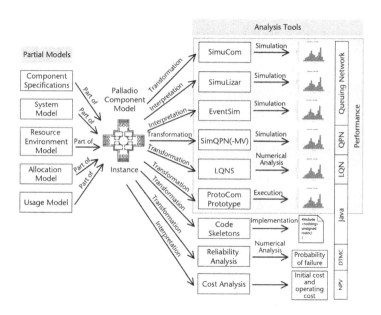

Fig. 1. Palladio simulator environment, see [21, 22].

Palladio has been chosen as the simulation platform, not only for its advanced simulation tools, but also for its architectural modeling capabilities. With Palladio we can prototype and adjust also the application and platform architecture of a system under investigation. Palladio provides several models capable of specifying the architecture and carrying out simulations, see Fig. 1. In Palladio, each model is built on top of the previous one. Palladio is Eclipse-based, thus models need to be grouped inside a single project directory.

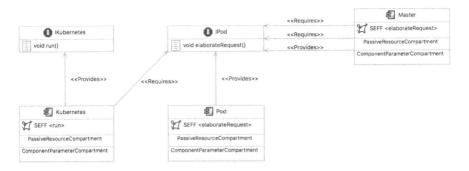

Fig. 2. Component repository model for all simulations.

3   Architecture Model

The Palladio modeling tool allows us to specify a software system architecture in order to run simulations on these systems. We discuss now how the Kubernetes containerized architecture has been abstracted and recreated inside Palladio in order create a simulation tool (called KubeSim). In the following, we introduce the different structural and behavioural models.

A **Component Repository Model** (CRM) describes interfaces, components and dependencies between elements of the system architecture. Figure 2 illustrates how the Kubernetes architecture has been abstracted and represented as a Repository model. In the model, a service is provided through Kubernetes, from pod governed databases, and accessible to a user via an internet connected device. For that reason, two interfaces are declared: one for the Kubernetes system (IKubernetes), performing a void run() action (simulate service up and running system call), and another for the pod component (IPod). Furthermore, one component has been created for the IKubernetes interface, named simply Kubernetes, and one for the IPod, named Pod. The Master component acts as the controller for load-balancing based on self-adaptive resource utilization rules.

Each component of the CRM has its own **Service Effect Specification** (SEFF), a behavioral model. Figure 3 shows the three SEFF models for the Kubernetes, Pod and Master component actions. Since the Kubernetes component requires the IPod interface to work, its behavior is reflected in an ExternalCallAction for the elaborateRequest() action. The action on the Pod component is performed internally. Moreover, in this SEFF diagram we specified actual resource demands of the system call. Resource demands are specified for the CPU (computational resource) and the HDD (storage resource) as hardware resources, in the form of stochastic expressions for work-units per second. The last SEFF models two components instead of only one: Pod1 and Pod2. This reconnects with Component Repository Model and the two arrows exiting from the Master component representing two instances of a Pod element. For simplicity, we use two sample pods.

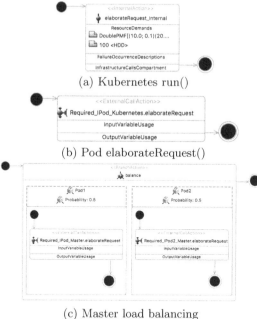

(a) Kubernetes run()

(b) Pod elaborateRequest()

(c) Master load balancing

Fig. 3. System Behaviour Models (SEFFs).

Here the execution flow is executed by a so called BranchAction, that has the task to distribute and balance the workload between the pod components. In this case, it is configured to reflect the default Kubernetes balancing rule that distributes the work evenly across all system pods. However, this setting could be varied in experiments and used like a virtual knob to tune balancing settings of the Master controller to whatever value of interest.

The **System Model** captures the composite structure of the whole Kubernetes system's architecture (not displayed as a diagram for space reasons). The system architecture for this model uses the available components declared in the Component Repository Model to constitute a complete component-based software system. This model includes dependencies between the various assembly contexts (i.e., components) of the Kubernetes architecture. The entire system provides its service over the Kubernetes platform, i.e., through the IKubernetes interface. This interface is connected to the assembly elements representing the Kubernetes component. Since Kubernetes requires pods to run the service, it is connected with a component providing the IPod interface. However, because the cluster is self-adaptive, we cannot directly connect the Kubernetes assembly to the pods, but use the Master controller node as an intermediary. The system also requires two pod interfaces. We only need to instantiate two assembly contexts for two pods and then connect the two with the Master component.

Based on the system model, we declare and allocate resources for our system environment. For that, there are the so called Deployment Models, which

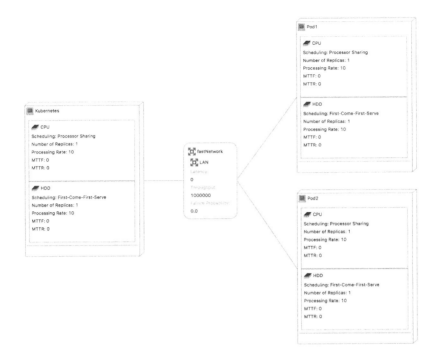

Fig. 4. Execution Environment Model configured for a Single Experiment.

include the **Execution Environment Model** and the **Component Alloca-tion Model**. We have three resource components: Kubernetes, Pod1 and Pod2. Each pod has a CPU unit with scheduling policy set to Processor Sharing (that is an approximation of a Round-Robin resource management strategy), and an HDD with scheduling policy set to First-Come-First-Serve (that is a typical behavior for hard disk drives). The Processing Rates of CPUs and HDDs can vary, therefore the values in this model are purely indicative of one single experi-ment configuration. The Execution Environment Model, see Fig. 4, also provides other settings for resources, like the Number of Replicas, Mean Time To Failure (MTTF) and Mean Time To Repair (MTTR). In order to focus on performance, these have been set to standard values, i.e., resp., 1, 0.0 and 0.0. Kubernetes con-tainers also have CPU and HDD declared resource demands (with Processing Rate set to 10 for both), with default settings for Number of Replicas, MTTF and MTTR. The three containers are connected via a LinkingResource compo-nent, that could act as a fast network, with Latency set to 0, Throughput set to 1,000,000 and Failure Probability set to 0.0.

The **Usage Model** contains a Service Effect Specification diagram specifying the system call. The Usage Model provides two different workloads for the sys-tem under study: an OpenWorkload and a ClosedWorkload. For the OpenWork-load, the user interarrival time could be specified in seconds, and the number of users coming to use the system will vary from one simulation run to the other.

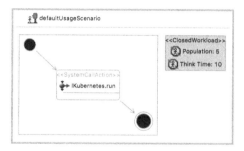

Fig. 5. Usage model for experiment.

With the ClosedWorkload we can specify the user population (i.e. the number of active users in our system), and also the single user think time (i.e. the pause the user after each run() action, in seconds) (Fig. 5).

4   Experimental Evaluation

In the experimental evaluation, we focus on simulations of the Kubernetes implementation as it is currently available, with the HPA component. Our aim was to aid specification for container cluster scaling rules. The main experimental goal for the project focused on evaluating suitable system performance. We translate this into a simple rule: keep idle time less or equal to 50% (not to waste resource power) and concurrent active job time less or equal to 25% (not to experience long overload periods that impacts on performance), for both CPU and HDD components of the pods.

As a starting point, we considered different workload patterns, distinguished in terms of three qualitative values: low, medium and high, i.e., workloads without unexpected fluctuations in relation to the three main values.

To set a desired workload inside Palladio, we use the SEFF diagram describing the core system function, and specify the resource demand in the form of a stochastic expression. In our case, the SEFF diagram to be modified is the one of elaborateRequest() action, see Fig. 3. We keep the HDD expression fixed at 100 processing unit rate for all workload types, while for the CPU component the stochastic values (expressed in a joint Probability Mass Function with double values, i.e. DoublePMF) that have been used for the different workloads are: DoublePMF [(10.0; 0.1) (20.0; 0.8) (30.0; 0.1)] for low, i.e. 10% of the time the CPU power used is being used at 10%, 80% of the time it is being used at 20% of power and in the remaining 10% of the time it is being used at 30% of power; and correspondingly DoublePMF [(40.0; 0.1) (50.0; 0.8) (60.0; 0.1)] for medium and DoublePMF [(70.0; 0.1) (80.0; 0.8) (90.0; 0.1)] for high.

The specification of a pod resource demand can been adjusted. Particularly, the CPU and HDD processing rate are the ones in which we are highly interested in, because they reflect the specification rules for assigning Kubernetes pods resource demands limits. The variable field that need to be changed for this

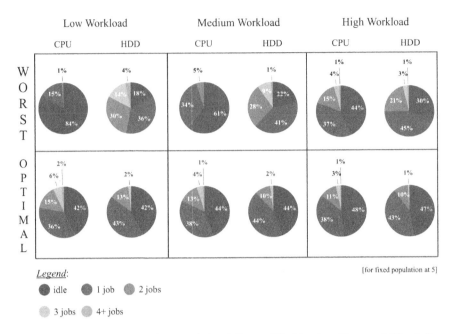

Fig. 6. Resource Utilization (idleness) for different Workloads – Best and Worst Case.

time is the Execution Environment model. Figure 6 shows the worst and best case results for CPU and HDD resources for different workload patterns and assumed processing rates. The values for CPU and HDD processing rate varied from 2 to 18 during different simulations where we followed an experimental progression based on observations obtained through the different simulating runs.

For another set of experiments, we also changed the population number, which describes the number of active users inside the system at simulation time, see Fig. 7. The aim here was to better judge the impact the number of active users could have on overall system performance. We tested the system with 1, 3 and 5 users that were equally distributed between the pods, showing an increasingly reduced idle for higher CPU loads as the population increases.

5   Discussion

Our paper has focused on creating an environment to simulate the behavior of self-adapting (scaling) container cluster architectures. We presented the models implemented in the Palladio environment, thus creating a simulation bench by defining the architecture of a systems and its resource. We have demonstrated that running simulations of applications with Kubernetes autoscaling strategies allows investigating the architectural structure of a system and its behavioural properties. This can lead to greater efficiency in implementations as the sample resource utilization experiments have shown. KubeSim tool is useful when

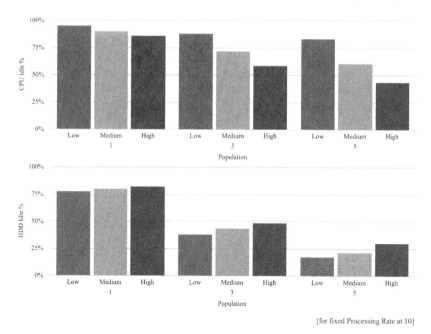

Fig. 7. Aggregated workload results for different user populations.

trying to obtain specification values to identify and configure for the controller. We were able to understand and investigate underlying functions and characteristics of self-adaption in Kubernetes – for example the case we experimentally observed that CPU and HDD performances were impacted by each other's settings. KubeSim is thus beneficial for application developers aiming to use Kubernetes.

We also look at limitations and threats to the validity of our work. We can start our the threats to validity analysis by looking to a central and potential critical aspect of our work, the experiments' sample field. While running simulations for KubeSim, we considered only a small portion of experimental values. Concretely, we restricted our sampling field as follows:

- Architecture: we took a scenario with a simplifying two pod system for illustrative purposes. We can, however, assume that our experimental results would apply also to bigger systems composed by more that two pods and used by a greater population of users as the results so far indicate linearity.
- Uncertainty: KubeSim was not exposed to unpredictable workloads and failures (as in real world platforms), thus restricting even more our sample fields and leading to more uncertainty in the validity of the results.
- Scale: applies to all KubeSim settings, for which we used small numerical values for input variables (e.g., processing and user think time in the usage model). As argued above, linearity here is possible, but not yet proven.

A final remark on restricting the sample field is in regards to the load balancer policy, for which we only tested the implemented equal balancing load rule. Our advanced controller model is a first step towards proposing an improved Kubernetes scaling strategy, which however is beyond the scope of this paper.

However, evaluating our simulation environment under all possible scenarios was beyond the scope of this paper. The overall aim was to point out a valid alternative to already present performance engineering and evaluation methods for self-adaptive container cluster systems (i.e. those who separates software engineering analysis for the architecture and the autoscaling strategies parts).

6 Towards an Advanced Controller Model

The controller implemented in Kubernetes and modelled above uses equal workload distribution as the load balancing strategy. One of our goals is to explore advanced controller settings for Kubernetes that could be implemented in an improved HPA component. Our proposal shall take into account that platform and application are not controlled by the same organisation, i.e., that some load properties of platform resources (i.e., Kubernetes core components offered by a cloud provider) are not visible for the Kubernetes user. The general situation is that in shared virtualised environments, third parties provides some resources that can be directly observed (e.g., using performance metrics such as response time) while others remain hidden from the consumer (e.g., the reason behind performance or workload anomalies, the dependency between the affected nodes and container, etc.). In order to improve the workload balancing and autoscaling capability, we can enhance the MAPE-K based controller here. We introduce a core model for anomaly detection and analysis for a cluster environment that automatically manages resource workload fluctuations. This can be implemented as an extension of the Palladio model towards dynamic auto-scaling[1, 14, 15, 25], which in the current version only considers a static load balancing strategy.

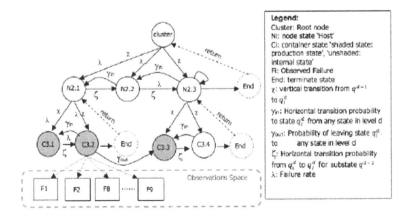

Fig. 8. HHMM for auto-scaling workload for cluster-container environments.

We differentiate two situations in which response time fluctuations occur:

- Hidden states might show anomalous behavior of the resource that might needs to be remedied by the controller (unwanted behavior such as overload, or appreciated behavior like underload).
- Emission or observation of behaviour for the user (indicating possible failure), which might result in failure if caused by a faulty hidden state.

To address this, we propose Hidden Markov Models (HMMs) to map the observed failure behaviors of a system resource to its hidden anomaly causes (e.g., overload) and to predict the occurrence of the anomaly in the future. A Hidden Markov Model (HMM) is a statistical Markov model in which the system being modeled is assumed to be a Markov process with hidden states. In simple Markov models, state transition probabilities are the only parameters, while in the hidden Markov model, there are observable emissions (e.g., in the form of response time data), dependent on the workload state.

To reflect the layered nature of application, platform and infrastructure in a Kubernetes system, we utilize a specific variant of HMM, that of Hierarchical Hidden Markov Models (HHMM) [5], see Fig. 8. HHMMs are better suited here than HMM in describing the uncertain probability distribution at node and cluster level. HHMM generate sequences by a recursive activation of one of the substates (nodes) of a state (cluster). This substate might also be hierarchically composed of substates (here pods). The HHMM decides on transition probabilities a possible (hidden) cause for an observed anomaly and then decides how to transfer load between nodes to reduce undesired performance degradations.

Each state 'hidden state' (internal 'node', production 'pod', root 'cluster') may be in an overload, underload or normal load state. Each workload is associated with response time observations that are emitted from a production state. The existence of anomalous workload in one state not only affects the current state, but possibly substates on the other level. The edge direction in the figure indicates the dependency between states. We can use vertical transitions for identifying the fault and we use horizontal transitions to show the fault that exists between states and to trace the fault/failure mapping between states at the same level.

7   Related Work

In [9,10], resource management and auto-scaling rules for self-adaptive systems was investigated, focused mainly on VM-based cloud platforms. As part of their experimental approach, a parameterized architecture model when running simulations has been used. That is, simulations were run on base of stochastic expressions, which reflected each system's component behavior. This allowed fine adjustments while setting adaptation rules for the simulation environment. We have followed these and similar approaches, but add a novel perspective in the advanced controller model here that takes the hidden/observable distinction into account for a hierarchically organised architecture.

To the best of our knowledge, there is no Kubernetes simulation environment. Models of performance concerns and resource management has been discussed [16], but a simulation tool has not been created.

In addition to work on models for self-adaptive cloud systems for performance and workload management, we also look at the simulation tool landscape. This allows us to justify our decision to choose Palladio as the model. Often, load balancing strategies can be formalised and simulated in tools like MatLab. However, this would not allow us to model the architecture in terms of applications, platform and infrastructure concerns. As we target the KubeSim tool to application developers and users of Kubernetes and similar tools, an explicit architecture model is of critical importance. The same argument also applies to other simulation tools such as CloudSim [2].

8   Conclusions

We investigated performance engineering solutions for self-adaptive container cluster systems [19], aiming to find an efficient way to determine and express autoscaling rules for such systems, in order to improve platform settings.

We created a simulation tool for Kubernetes using the Palladio platform, capable of delivering an easy to use simulation bench. KubeSim offers a developer the possibility of testing such a system by tuning different settings and metrics of the system. In fact, the novelty of KubeSim as a Kubernetes performance simulation tool is to enable reliable performance analysis with the effort of having to implement prototype implementations. With the advanced controller model [9–11], we also target a deeper investigation beyond application development.

As future work, KubeSim could include the possibility of considering faults types. Another improvement would be considering sensor noise. That is assuming and considering that the system's sensor is exposed to noise derived from hosting platform connection. Again, a last upgrade, always related to fault consideration, could be implementing a fault prediction algorithm, so that the system would be aware of an oncoming error and scale resource on its base. Another aim is to integrate the advanced controller model in KubeSim. This would allow studying alternative strategies for the Kubernetes HPA component.

Another significant area to be addressed is security and trust. In heterogeneous cluster environments, monitoring and result data should be certifiable [3,4]. Distributed ledger technologies might provide an answer here, but will have an impact on performance.

Acknowledgments. The authors are particularly grateful to the Palladio team at KIT for their support regarding the Palladio tool.

References

1. Arabnejad, H., Pahl, C., Jamshidi, P., Estrada, G.: A comparison of reinforcement learning techniques for fuzzy cloud auto-scaling. In: CCGRID (2017)

2. CloudSim: A Framework for Modeling and Simulation of Cloud Computing Infrastructures and Services (2018). http://www.cloudbus.org/cloudsim/
3. El Ioini, N., Pahl, C.: A review of distributed ledger technologies. In: Panetto, H., Debruyne, C., Proper, H.A., Ardagna, C.A., Roman, D., Meersman, R. (eds.) OTM 2018. LNCS, vol. 11230, pp. 277–288. Springer, Cham (2018). https://doi.org/10.1007/978-3-030-02671-4_16
4. El Ioini, N., Pahl, C.: Trustworthy orchestration of container based edge computing using permissioned blockchain. In: International Conference on Internet of Things: Systems, Management and Security (2018)
5. Fine, S., Singer, Y., Tishby, N.: The hierarchical hidden Markov model: analysis and applications. Mach. Learn. **32**, 41–62 (1998)
6. Fowley, F., Pahl, C., Jamshidi, P., Fang, D., Liu, X.: A classification and comparison framework for cloud service brokerage architectures. IEEE Trans. Cloud Comput. **6**(2), 358–371 (2018)
7. Heinrich, R., et al.: Performance engineering for microservices: research challenges and directions. In: International Conference on Performance Engineering Companion (2017)
8. Jamshidi, P., Pahl, C., Mendonca, N.C., Lewis, J., Tilkov, S.: Microservices: the journey so far and challenges ahead. IEEE Softw. **35**(3), 24–35 (2018)
9. Jamshidi, P., Sharifloo, A., Pahl, C., Metzger, A., Estrada, G.: Self-learning cloud controllers: fuzzy Q-learning for knowledge evolution. In: ICCAC (2015)
10. Jamshidi, P., Sharifloo, A., Pahl, C., Metzger, A., Estrada, G.: Fuzzy self-learning controllers for elasticity management in dynamic cloud architectures. QoSA (2016)
11. Jamshidi, P., Pahl, C., Mendonca, N.C.: Managing uncertainty in autonomic cloud elasticity controllers. IEEE Cloud Comput. **3**(3), 50–60 (2016)
12. Introduction to Kubernetes (2018). https://x-team.com/blog/introduction-kubernetes-architecture/
13. Autoscaling in Kubernetes (2018). http://blog.kubernetes.io/2016/07/auto scaling-in-kubernetes.html
14. Lim , H.C., et al.: Automated control in cloud computing: challenges and opportunities. In: Workshop Automated Control for Datacenters and Clouds (2009)
15. Lorido-Botran, T., Miguel-Alonso, J., Lozano, J.A.: A Review of auto-scaling techniques for elastic applications in cloud environments. J. Grid Comput. **12**(4), 559–592 (2014)
16. Medel, V., Rana, O., Banares, J.A.l., Arronategui, U.: Modelling performance & resource management in Kubernetes. In: International Conference on Utility and Cloud Computing (2016)
17. Pahl, C., El Ioini, N., Helmer, S., Lee, B.: An architecture pattern for trusted orchestration in IoT edge clouds. In: International Conference on Fog and Mobile Edge Computing (2018)
18. Pahl, C., Brogi, A., Soldani, J., Jamshidi, P.: Cloud container technologies: a state-of-the-art review. IEEE Trans. Cloud Comput. (2017)
19. Pahl, C., Jamshidi, P., Weyns, D.: Cloud architecture continuity: change models and change rules for sustainable cloud software architectures. J. Softw. Evol. Process. **29**(2), e1849 (2017)
20. Pahl, C., Jamshidi, P., Zimmermann, O.: Architectural principles for cloud software. ACM Trans. Internet Technol. (TOIT) **18**(2), 1–23 (2018)
21. Palladio Simulator (2018). http://www.palladio-simulator.com/about_palladio/
22. Reussner, R.H., et al.: Modelling and Simulating Software Architecture - The Palladio Approach. MIT Press, Cambridge (2016)

23. Taibi, D., Lenarduzzi, V., Pahl, C.: Processes, motivations, and issues for migrating to microservices architectures: an empirical investigation. Cloud Comp. 4(5), 22–32 (2017)
24. Taibi, D., Lenarduzzi, V., Pahl, C.: Architectural patterns for microservices: a systematic mapping study. In: International Conference on Cloud Computing and Services Science (2018)
25. Vaquero, L.M., Rodero-Merino, L., Buyya, R.: Dynamically scaling applications in the cloud. ACM SIGCOMM Comput. Comm. Rev. 41(51), 45–52 (2011)

On Enhancing the Orchestration of Multi-container Docker Applications

Antonio Brogi[1], Claus Pahl[2], and Jacopo Soldani[1(✉)]

[1] University of Pisa, Pisa, Italy
{brogi,soldani}@di.unipi.it
[2] Free University of Bozen-Bolzano, Bolzano, Italy
claus.pahl@unibz.it

Abstract. After introducing Docker containers in a nutshell, we discuss the benefits that can be obtained by supporting enhanced descriptions of multi-container Docker applications. We illustrate how such applications can be naturally modelled in TOSCA, and how this permits automating their management and reducing the time and cost needed to develop such applications (e.g., by facilitating the reuse of existing solutions, and by permitting to analyse and validate applications at design-time).

Keywords: Docker · TOSCA · Orchestration · Cloud applications

1 Introduction

Containers are emerging as a simple yet effective solution to manage applications in PaaS cloud platforms [19]. Containers are also an ideal solution for SOA-based architectural styles that are emerging in the PaaS community to decompose applications into suites of independently deployable, lightweight components, e.g., microservices [2,22,26]. These are natively supported by container-based virtualisation, which permits running components in independent containers, and allows containers to interact through lightweight communication mechanisms.

However, to fully exploit the potential of SOA, container-based platforms (e.g., Docker—www.docker.com) should enhance their support for selecting the containers where to run the components of an application, and for orchestrating containers to build up a multi-container application. To that end, there is a need for a modelling language to describe the features offered by a container (to satisfy the requirements of an application component), to orchestrate containers to build multi-container applications, and to deploy and manage them in clusters.

Our objective here is to highlight the need for such language, by illustrating its potential benefits on a concrete containerisation framework like Docker. In this context, the main contributions of this paper are:

© Springer Nature Switzerland AG 2020
M. Fazio and W. Zimmermann (Eds.): ESOCC 2018 Workshops, CCIS 1115, pp. 21–33, 2020.
https://doi.org/10.1007/978-3-030-63161-1_2

1. We discuss the benefits, but also the limitations of Docker, specifically with respect to composition and orchestration in multi-container applications.
2. We propose a way to represent multi-container Docker applications in TO-SCA [17], the OASIS standard for orchestrating cloud applications, as an example to discuss the advantages of enhancing their orchestration (e.g.., easing the selection and reuse of existing containers, reducing time and cost for developing multi-container applications, automating their management, etc.).

This paper is organised as follows. Section 2 provides some background on TOSCA. Sections 3 and 4 provide an introduction to Docker and discuss its current benefits and limitations, respectively. Section 5 discuss the advantages of enhancing the orchestration of multi-container Docker applications with TOSCA. Finally, Sects. 6 and 7 discuss related work and draw some concluding remarks, respectively.

2   Background: TOSCA

TOSCA [17] (*Topology and Orchestration Specification for Cloud Applications*) is an OASIS standard for specifying portable cloud applications and automating their management. TOSCA provides a modelling language to describe the structure of a cloud application as a typed topology graph, and its management tasks as plans. More precisely, each applications is represented as a *service template* (Fig. 1), consisting of a *topology template* and of optional management *plans*.

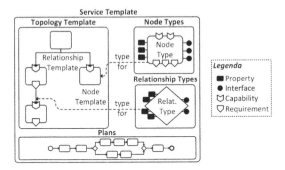

Fig. 1. TOSCA *service template.*

The topology template is a typed directed graph describing the structure of an application. Its nodes (*node templates*) model the application components, while its edges (*relationship templates*) model the relationship among those components. Both node templates and relationship templates are typed by means of *node types* and *relationship types*. A node type defines (i) the observable properties of a component, (ii) its requirements, (iii) the capabilities it offers to satisfy other components' requirements, and (iv) its management operations. Relationship types describe the properties of relationships occurring among components.

Plans permit describing the management of an application. A plan is a workflow orchestrating the management operations offered by the application components to address (part of) the management of the whole application.

3   Docker in a Nutshell

Docker is a Linux-based platform for developing, shipping, and running applications through container-based virtualisation. Container-based virtualisation exploits the kernel of the host's operating system to run multiple guest instances. Each guest instance is called a *container*, and each container is isolated from others (i.e., each container has its own root file system, processes, memory, devices and network ports).

Containers and Images. Each container packages the applications to run, along with whatever software they need (e.g., libraries, binaries, etc.). Containers are built by instantiating so-called Docker *images*.

A Docker image is a read-only template providing the instructions for creating a container. It is built by layering multiple images, with the bottom image being the *base* image, and with each image being the *parent* of the image right above it. A Docker image can be created by loading a base image, by performing the necessary updates to that image, and by *committing* the changes. Alternatively, one can write a *Dockerfile*, which is a configuration file containing the instructions for building an image[1].

It is also possible to look for existing images instead of building them from scratch. Images are stored in *registries*, like Docker Hub (hub.docker.com). Inside a registry, images are stored in *repositories*. Each repository is devoted to a software application, and it contains different versions of such software. Each image is uniquely identified by the name of the repository it comes from and by the tag assigned to the version it represents, which can be used for retrieving it.

Volumes. Docker containers are volatile. A container runs until the stop command is issued, or as long as the process from which it has been started is running. By default, the data produced by a container is lost when a container is stopped, and even if the container is restarted, there is no way to access to the data previously produced. This is why Docker introduces *volumes*.

A volume is a directory in a container, which is designed to let data persist, independently of the container's lifecycle. Docker therefore never automatically deletes volumes when a container is removed, and it never removes volumes that are no longer referenced by any container. Volumes can also be used to share data among different containers.

Docker Orchestration. The term orchestration refers to the composition, coordination and management of multiple software components, including middleware

---

[1] The latter provides a more effective way to build images, as it only involves writing some configuration instructions (like installing software or mounting volumes), instead of having to launch a container and to manually perform and commit changes.

and services [16]. In the context of container-based virtualisation, this corresponds to multi-component applications, whose components independently run in their own containers, and talk each other by exploiting lightweight communication mechanisms.

Docker supports orchestration with *swarm* and *compose*. Docker swarm permits creating a cluster of Docker containers and turning it into a single, virtual Docker container (with one or more containers acting "masters" and scheduling incoming tasks to "worker" containers). Docker compose permits creating multi-container applications, by specifying the images of the containers to run and the interconnections occurring among them. Docker compose and Docker swarm are seamlessly integrated, meaning that one can describe a multi-component application with Docker compose, and deploy it by exploiting Docker swarm.

4   Benefits and Limitations of Docker

Docker containers feature some clear benefits. Firstly, they permit *separation of concerns*. Developers only focus on building applications inside containers and system administrators only focus on running containers in deployment environments. Previously, developers were building applications in local environments, passing them to system administrators, who could discover (during deployment) that certain libraries needed by the applications were missing in the deployment environments. With Docker containers, everything an application needs to run is included within its container.

Docker containers are also *portable*. Applications can be built in one environment and easily shipped to another. The only requirement is the presence of a Docker engine installed on the target host.

Furthermore, containers are *lightweight* and fast to launch. This reduces development, testing and deployment time. They also improve the horizontal scalability of applications, as it is easy to add or remove containers whenever needed.

On the other hand, limitations do exists. Docker currently does not support *search* mechanisms other than looking for the name and tag of an image inside a registry [10]. There is currently no way to describe the internals of an image, e.g., the features offered by a container instantiated from an image, or the software it supports. A more expressive description of images would enable more powerful reuse mechanisms (e.g., adaptation of existing images), hence reducing the time needed to retrieve images and develop container-based applications.

Further limitations affect the *orchestration* of complex applications. Consider, for instance, a multi-component application made of three components, i.e., a web-based GUI, which depends on a back-end API to serve its clients, which in turn connects to a database to store application data. Currently, Docker does not provide a way to describe the runtime environment needed to run each component. A developer is hence required to manually select the image where to run each component, to extend it (by adding the component and its runtime dependencies), and to package it into a new image. The obtained images can then be composed with Docker compose to build a multi-container Docker application, which however has no explicit information about which component is hosted on which image nor on which component is interconnected on each other. Everything is hidden in a kind of "black-box" view due to the lack of information on the internals of Docker containers [11].

It is not possible to distinguish between simple dependencies determining the deployment ordering from persistent connections to set up. For instance, in the aforementioned application, Docker compose would include two interconnections, one between the containers packaging the GUI and the API, and one between those packaging the API and the database. However, the former interconnection may be unnecessary (especially in a multi-host deployment scenario), as the GUI may not require to set up a connection to the API. The GUI may indeed just require to be deployed after the API and to be configured so to forward user queries to the actual endpoint offered by the API.

Additionally, despite Docker compose and Docker swarm are seamlessly integrated, limitations do exists[2]. For instance, when a compose application is deployed with swarm, the latter may not be able to manage all interdependencies among containers, which may result in deploying all containers on the same host or in not being able to automatically deploy all containers. In the latter case, one would hence be required to manually complete the deployment.

A more expressive specification language (e.g., TOSCA [17]) would permit overcoming these limitations. By describing the environment needed to run an application component, it would be possible to specify what the component needs, and then to automatically derive the images of the underlying infrastructure (e.g., by exploiting existing reuse techniques [12,21]). It would also permit describing the management of a complex multi-component application by orchestrating the management of its components.

5   Orchestrating Multi-container Applications in TOSCA

In this section, we first show how multi-container applications can be represented in TOSCA (Sect. 5.1). We then illustrate how this permits enhancing the orchestration of multi-container Docker applications (Sect. 5.2), as well as better exploiting container-oriented design patterns (Sect. 5.3).

5.1   Multi-container Applications in TOSCA

A multi-container application essentially corresponds to a multi-component application, where each component is hosted on a container. A multi-container Docker application can be represented by a TOSCA service template, whose topology nodes represent the application components, the containers they need to run, and the volumes that must be mounted by containers. The relationships instead model the dependencies between components, containers and volumes

---

[2] A thorough discussion on this is available at docs.docker.com/compose/swarm.

(e.g., hosting a component on a container, connecting components and/or containers, or attaching a volume to a container). Plans then orchestrate the operations offered by the nodes to describe the management of a whole application.

We hence need the types to include the above mentioned nodes and relationships in a topology template. For the nodes, we can exploit the TOSCA types defined in [11], which permit distinguishing (a) *Software* components, (b) *Containers* and (c) *Volumes* (Fig. 2). For the relationships, we can instead rely on the TOSCA normative relationship types [17].

Without delving into the details on the modelling (which can be found in [11]), we show how it can be exploited to represent the multi-container Docker application mentioned in Sect. 4 (which consists of three interconnected components—i.e., a GUI, an API and a database). With the above mentioned TOSCA types, we can go beyond Docker compose (that only permits

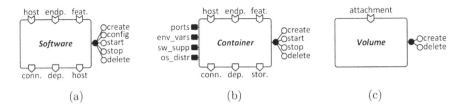

Fig. 2. TOSCA node types for multi-container Docker applications [11].

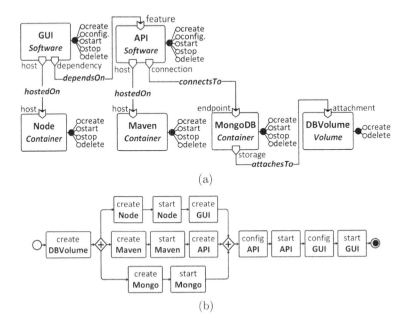

Fig. 3. Examples of (a) a topology template modelling a multi-container Docker application, and of (b) a plan orchestrating its deployment.

identifying the images of three containers, and specifying the interconnection occurring between them). As illustrated by Fig. 3(a), we can describe components and containers separately, and explicitly specify which container is hosting a component (e.g., the API is hosted on the Maven container), the dependencies among components (e.g., the API connects to the database) and the necessary volumes.

We can also program the management of the application as a whole. Each component indeed exposes the operations that permit managing its lifecycle, which can then be orchestrated to accomplish application management tasks. A concrete example is given in Fig. 3(b), which displays a BPMN-like plan orchestrating the deployment of the multi-container Docker application in Fig. 3(a).

5.2   Orchestrating Multi-container Applications with TOSCA

One may argue whether the effort of defining multi-container Docker applications in TOSCA really pays off. As we anticipated in Sect. 4, a model like that discussed in the previous section permits enhancing the orchestration of multi-container Docker applications in three main ways.

Searching for images. Docker search capabilities are currently limited, as Docker only permits looking for names and tags of images in registries [10]. TOSCA permits overcoming such limitation, as it also permits describing the internals of an image (like the features that will be offered by a container instantiated from an image, or the software distributions it will support). This enables more powerful discovery mechanisms.

For instance, in [9] we show how to automatically discover the Docker containers offering the runtime support needed by the components forming an application. The *host* requirements of GUI and API can be left pending, by only describing the runtime capabilities that must be provided by the container that can satisfy them (e.g., which software distribution they must support, which operating system they must run, etc.). Then, a concrete implementation like that in Fig. 3 can be automatically derived by reusing existing Docker containers. As we illustrated in [9], such an approach can drastically reduce the time and costs needed for developing and maintaining container-based applications.

Design-time validation. TOSCA permits explicitly indicating which are the requirements needed to run a component, which capabilities it provides to satisfy the requirements of other containers, and how requirements and capabilities are bound one another. This permits validating multi-container applications at design-time, by checking whether the requirements of a component have been properly satisfied (e.g., with the validator presented in [6]).

The same is currently not possible with Docker, which is not providing enough information to determine whether all interdependencies have been properly settled. This is because Docker compose only permits listing the images of containers to run, and the interconnections among them.

Automation of application management. We can exploit TOSCA *plans* to describe only once all the management of an application (by orchestrating the management operations of the application components). For instance, we can program how to coordinate the deployment of all the components of an application with a single *plan* (as exemplified in Fig. 3(b)).

The management of multi-container Docker applications can be further automated by exploiting management protocols [5], which permit specifying the behaviour of the nodes forming a TOSCA application, and to automatically derive the management behaviour of an application by composing the management protocols of its nodes. This permits automating various useful analyses, like determining whether management plans are valid, which are their effects (e.g., which application configuration is reached by executing a plan, or whether it generates faults), or which plans permit reaching certain application configurations or recovering faulted applications.

The above remarks highlight how Docker (and, more generally, a container-based framework) would enhance its orchestration capabilities by being integrated with expressive specification languages, such as TOSCA. This is also concretely illustrated and evaluated by the work in [9] and [11]. The latter present the components of the TOSKER open-source environment, by also empirically showing how the integration of Docker with a language like TOSCA can provide some of the aforementioned benefits.

It is also worth noting that, even if we exploited a simple application (with just three components) for illustration purposes, this is sufficient to illustrate the positive impact of an enhanced orchestration support for Docker-based frameworks. By considering complex enterprise applications [13], which can contain a much higher number of interdependent components, the potential and impact of allowing to search, reuse, orchestrate and verify multi-container applications can be even more significant. This is currently not supported by any of the frameworks that we will discuss in Sect. 6.

5.3   Container-Oriented Design Patterns in TOSCA

TOSCA templates describe the structure of (parts of) multi-component applications. This aligns with the idea of design patterns, which also describe the structure of (parts of) software applications [1], and which can be provided as templates to be directly included into TOSCA applications [4].

From an architecture perspective, multi-container Docker applications are often designed according to the microservices architectural style [14] (as Docker perfectly matches the microservices' requirement of independent deployability). Hence, microservices design patterns constitute a concrete example of design patterns that can be provided as predefined TOSCA templates, to support and ease the development of new multi-container Docker applications.

A catalogue of such design patterns is presented in [23]. Three main categories of patterns emerge, i.e., *orchestration and coordination patterns* (capturing communication and coordination from a logical perspective), *deployment patterns* (reflecting physical deployment strategies for services on hosts through Docker containers), and *data management patterns* (capturing data storage options). All patterns falling within such categories align with our discussion on how to enhance the orchestration of multi-contained Docker applications with TOSCA. They indeed provide solutions for orchestrating the management of the components and containers forming multi-container applications, and for managing the Docker volumes storing their data.

We below provide a list of the patterns falling in the above mentioned categories, which can provided as predefined templates to support the development of multi-container Docker applications in TOSCA.

Orchestration and coordination patterns. Within this category, we have design patterns for service composition and discovery.

Service Composition → API Gateway. An API Gateway is an entry point to a system. It provides a tailored API for each client to route requests to appropriate containers, aggregate the required contents, and serve them back to the clients. The API Gateway can also implement some shared logic (e.g., authentication), and it can serve as load balancer. Its main goal is to increase system performance and simplify interactions, thus reducing the number of requests per client.

Service Discovery → Client-Side Discovery, Server-Side Discovery. Multiple instances of the same service usually run in different containers. The communication among them must be dynamically defined and the clients must be able to efficiently communicate to the appropriate microservice that dynamically change instances. For this purpose, service discovery dynamically supports the resolution addresses. For the Client-Side Discovery design pattern, clients query a registry, select an available instance, and make a request directly. For the Server-Side Discovery design pattern, clients make requests via a load balancer, which queries a registry and forwards the request to an available instance. Unlike the API-Gateway pattern, this pattern allows clients and containers to talk to each other directly.

Deployment patterns. Within this category, we the most common pattern is the *Multiple Service per Host* design pattern. According to such pattern, each service in an application is deployed in a separate container, containers are distributed among a cluster of hosts, by allowing multiple containers to run on a same host. There is also a *Single Service per Host* design pattern, but it reflects a very uncommon deployment strategy.

Data management patterns. This category of patterns focuses on data storage options for applications composed by multiple services and containers.

Database-per-Service. With this design pattern, each service accesses its private database.

Database cluster. The aim of this design pattern is storing data on a database cluster. This improves scalability, allowing to move the databases to dedicated nodes.

Shared database server. The aim of this design pattern is similar to that of the Database Cluster design pattern. However, instead of using a database cluster, all services access a single shared database.

To illustrate the usefulness of the above listed patterns, we refer back to example in Sect. 4. We discussed a layered architecture with GUI, API and database components. In such scenario, the API Gateway Pattern suggests an abstraction that permits routing user requests not only to a single container, but also to different containers (e.g., for different databases). Automatic deployment using Docker compose and Swarm, as also discussed, can also be modelled by exploiting the deployment patterns we introduced.

6   Related Work

Despite Docker permits creating multi-container applications (with Docker compose) and ensuring high-availability of containers (with Docker swarm), its current orchestration capabilities are limited. Docker only permits specifying the images to run, and the interconnections occurring among the containers instantiated from such images. It is not possible to search for images other than by looking for their names and tags in registries, there is no way to validate multi-container applications at design-time, and there is a lack of support for automating the management of the components in multi-container applications.

Multi-container Docker solutions can also be created by organising containers into *clusters*. Each of these clusters consists of host nodes that hold various containers with common services, such as scheduling and load balancing. This can be done with Mesos, Kubernetes, Marathon, and Cloud Foundry's Diego.

Mesos (mesos.apache.org) is an Apache cluster management platform that natively supports LXC and Docker. It organises distributed resources into a single pool, and includes a distributed systems kernel that provides applications with resource management and scheduling. However, Mesos does not allow to structure clusters, nor to orchestrate them.

Kubernetes (kubernetes.io) is a cluster management and orchestration solution that permits structuring clusters of hosts into pods, which are in charge of running containers. Kubernetes lacks a proper support for orchestrating multi-container applications, by only permitting to specify the images to run through their names and tags. This results in limitations analogous to those we identified for Docker (see Sect. 4): It is not possible to abstractly describe the runtime environment needed to run each component (to be then automatically implemented by adopting reuse techniques), and developers are hence required to manually select the image where to run each component, to extend it, and to package the obtained runtime into a new image. The obtained images can then be composed to build a multi-container application, which however has no explicit information about which component is hosted on which image nor about dependencies occurring among components (as the only dependencies that can be modelled are the interconnections occurring among containers).

Marathon (mesosphere.github.io/marathon) and *Diego* [24] are alternative solutions for managing and orchestrating clusters of containers (on top of Mesos and Cloud Foundry, respectively). Their objectives, as well as their limitations in orchestrating multi-container applications, are similar to those of Kubernetes.

Rocket (coreos.com/rkt) is a container framework alternative to Docker, which tries to address some of the limitations of Docker, like the search and composition of container images. Images of Rocket containers can indeed be composed to form complex applications, and there is a dedicated protocol for retrieving images. However, Rocket still lacks a way of specifying topology and orchestration of multi-container applications.

To summarise, currently existing platforms lack support for the high-level specification of multi-container (Docker) applications, and this limits their capabilities for searching and reusing container images, for orchestrating them to build up multi-container applications, and for verifying designed applications.

The possibility of employing TOSCA for enhancing the orchestration of multi-container applications was suggested in [18]. In this paper, we try to concretise such by providing a discussion of its benefits.

7   Conclusions

The management of multi-component applications across multiple and heterogeneous clouds is becoming commonplace [1,15]. Additionally, with the advent of fog and edge clouds, there is an increasing need for lightweight virtualisation support [7,8,20]. In this scenario, containers can play an important role, especially to decompose complex applications into suites of lightweight containers running independent services [14,25]. However, currently available platform offer limited support for specifying and orchestrating multi-container applications.

In this paper we have illustrated how a modelling language like TOSCA would enhance the orchestration of multi-container applications, thus overcoming current limitations. While utilising TOSCA for orchestrating container-based applications requires some additional initial effort, it permits composing and automatically orchestrating them to build and manage multi-container applications [11]. TOSCA can also empower the reuse of containers, by allowing developers to search and match them based on what they feature [9].

Additionally, despite both TosKer [9,11] and Cloudify (getcloudify.org) provide a basic support for deploying multi-container Docker applications specified in a simplified profile of TOSCA, a full-fledged support for orchestrating multi-container applications is still lacking. Its development is in the scope of our future work.

It is finally worth noting that, while Docker is the de-facto standard for container-based virtualisation [19], the same does not hold for TOSCA [3] (which was exploited here just as an example). There exists promising alternatives to TOSCA that can be exploited, In the scope of our future work, we plan to comparatively assess existing topology languages to determine the most suited to our purposes, by also considering how Ansible or similar languages can be extended to develop the aforementioned full-fledged support for orchestrating multi-container applications.

References

1. Andrikopoulos, V.: Engineering cloud-based applications: towards an application lifecycle. In: Mann, Z.Á., Stolz, V. (eds.) ESOCC 2017. CCIS, vol. 824, pp. 57–72. Springer, Cham (2018). https://doi.org/10.1007/978-3-319-79090-9_4
2. Balalaie, A., Heydarnoori, A., Jamshidi, P.: Microservices architecture enables DevOps: migration to a cloud-native architecture. IEEE Softw. **33**(3), 42–52 (2016)
3. Bergmayr, A., et al.: A systematic review of cloud modeling languages. ACM Comput. Surv. **51**(1), 22:1–22:38 (2018)
4. Binz, T., Breitenbücher, U., Kopp, O., Leymann, F.: TOSCA: portable automated deployment and management of cloud applications. In: Bouguettaya, A., Sheng, Q., Daniel, F. (eds.) Advanced Web Services, pp. 527–549. Springer, New York (2014). https://doi.org/10.1007/978-1-4614-7535-4_22
5. Brogi, A., Canciani, A., Soldani, J.: Fault-aware management protocols for multi-component applications. J. Syst. Softw. **139**, 189–210 (2018)
6. Brogi, A., Di Tommaso, A., Soldani, J.: SOMMELIER: a tool for validating TOSCA application topologies. In: Pires, L.F., Hammoudi, S., Selic, B. (eds.) MODEL-SWARD 2017. CCIS, vol. 880, pp. 1–22. Springer, Cham (2018). https://doi.org/10.1007/978-3-319-94764-8_1
7. Brogi, A., Forti, S., Guerrero, C., Lera, I.: How to Place Your Apps in the Fog - State of the Art and Open Challenges. arXiv:1901.05717 [cs.DC] (2019)
8. Brogi, A., Forti, S., Ibrahim, A.: How to best deploy your fog applications, probably. In: 2017 IEEE International Conference on Fog and Edge Computing (ICFEC), pp. 105–114. IEEE (2017)
9. Brogi, A., Neri, D., Rinaldi, L., Soldani, J.: Orchestrating incomplete TOSCA applications with Docker. Sci. Comput. Program. **166**, 194–213 (2018)
10. Brogi, A., Neri, D., Soldani, J.: A microservice-based architecture for (customisable) analyses of Docker images. Softw. Pract. Exp. **48**(8), 1461–1474 (2018)
11. Brogi, A., Rinaldi, L., Soldani, J.: TosKer: a synergy between TOSCA and Docker for orchestrating multicomponent applications. Softw. Pract. Exp. **48**(11), 2061–2079 (2018)
12. Brogi, A., Soldani, J.: Finding available services in TOSCA-compliant clouds. Sci. Comput. Program. **115–116**, 177–198 (2016)
13. Fowler, M.: Patterns of Enterprise Application Architecture. Addison-Wesley Longman Publishing Co., Inc., Boston (2002)
14. Jamshidi, P., Pahl, C., Mendonca, N., Lewis, J., Tilkov, S.: Microservices: the journey so far and challenges ahead. IEEE Softw. **35**(3), 24–35 (2018)
15. Jamshidi, P., Pahl, C., Mendonca, N.: Pattern-based multi-cloud architecture migration. Softw. Pract. Exp. **47**(9), 1159–1184 (2017)
16. Liu, F., et al.: NIST cloud computing reference architecture: recommendations of the national institute of standards and technology (special publication 500–292). NIST (2012)
17. OASIS: Topology and Orchestration Specification for Cloud Applications (2013)
18. Pahl, C.: Containerization and the PaaS cloud. IEEE Cloud Comput. **2**(3), 24–31 (2015)
19. Pahl, C., Brogi, A., Soldani, J., Jamshidi, P.: Cloud container technologies: a state-of-the-art review. IEEE Trans. Cloud Comput. (2017, in press). https://doi.org/10.1109/TCC.2017.2702586
20. Pahl, C., Lee, B.: Containers and clusters for edge cloud architectures - a technology review. In: Proceedings of FiCloud 2015, pp. 379–386. IEEE (2015)

21. Soldani, J., Binz, T., Breitenbücher, U., Leymann, F., Brogi, A.: ToscaMart: a method for adapting and reusing cloud applications. J. Syst. Softw. **113**, 395–406 (2016)
22. Soldani, J., Tamburri, D.A., Van Den Heuvel, W.J.: The pains and gains of microservices: a systematic grey literature review. J. Syst. Softw. **146**, 215–232 (2018)
23. Taibi, D., Lenarduzzi, V., Pahl, C.: Architectural patterns for microservices: a systematic mapping study. In: Proceedings of the 8th International Conference on Cloud Computing and Services Science, CLOSER 2018, pp. 221–232. SciTePress (2018)
24. Winn, D.: Cloud Foundry: The Cloud-Native Platform. O'Reilly Media, Inc., Sebastopol (2016)
25. Yangui, S., Mohamed, M., Tata, S., Moalla, S.: Scalable service containers. In: Proceedings of the 2011 IEEE Third International Conference on Cloud Computing Technology and Science (CloudCom 2011), pp. 348–356. IEEE Computer Society (2011)
26. Zimmermann, O.: Microservices tenets. Comput. Sci. Res. Dev. **32**(3), 301–310 (2017)

Transactional Migration of Inhomogeneous Composite Cloud Applications

Josef Spillner$^{(\boxtimes)}$ ⓘ and Manuel Ramírez López

School of Engineering, Service Prototyping Lab (blog.zhaw.ch/splab/),
Zurich University of Applied Sciences, 8401 Winterthur, Switzerland
{josef.spillner,ramz}@zhaw.ch

Abstract. For various motives such as routing around scheduled down-times or escaping price surges, operations engineers of cloud applications are occasionally conducting zero-downtime live migrations. For mono-lithic virtual machine-based applications, this process has been stud-ied extensively. In contrast, for composite microservice applications new challenges arise due to the need for a transactional migration of all constituent microservice implementations such as platform-specific light-weight containers and volumes. This paper outlines the challenges in the general heterogeneous case and solves them partially for a specialised inhomogeneous case based on the OpenShift and Kubernetes applica-tion models. Specifically, the paper describes our contributions in terms of tangible application models, tool designs, and migration evaluation. From the results, we reason about possible solutions for the general het-erogeneous case.

1 Introduction

Cloud applications are complex software applications which require a cloud envi-ronment to operate and to become programmable and configurable through well-defined and uniform service interfaces. Typically, applications are deployed in the form of virtual machines, containers or runtime-specific archives into envi-ronments such as infrastructure or platform offered as a service (IaaS and PaaS, respectively). Recently, container platforms (CaaS) which combine infrastructure and higher-level platform elements such as on-demand volumes and schedul-ing policies have become popular especially for composite microservice-based applications [1].

The concern of continuous deployment in these environments is then to keep the applications up to date from the latest development activities [2]. Another concern is to maintain flexibility in where the applications are deployed and how quickly and easily they can be re-deployed into another environment. When a new deployment from the development environment is not desired or simply not possible due to the lack of prerequisites, a direct migration from a source to a target environment may be a solution despite hurdles to full automation [3].

ⓒ Springer Nature Switzerland AG 2020
M. Fazio and W. Zimmermann (Eds.): ESOCC 2018 Workshops, CCIS 1115, pp. 34–45, 2020.
https://doi.org/10.1007/978-3-030-63161-1_3

Cloud application migration from this viewpoint can be divided into different categories: Homogeneous and heterogeneous migrations, referring to differences in the source and target environment technologies, same-provider and cross-provider migrations, referring to the ability to migrate beyond the boundaries of a single hosting services provider, as well as offline and online/live migrations, referring to the continuity of application service provisioning while the migration goes on. On the spectrum between homogeneity and heterogeneity, inhomogeneous migrations are concerned with minor automatable differences. This paper is concerned with *live, heterogeneous/inhomogeneous, cross-provider migrations* as shown in Fig. 1.

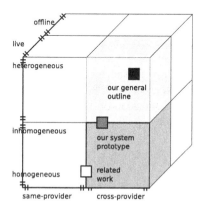

Fig. 1. Positioning within the multi-dimensional categories of cloud application migrations

An additional distinction is the representation of applications. Most of the literature covers monolithic applications which run as instances of virtual machine images where the main concern is pre-copy/post-copy main memory synchronisation [4]. Few emerging approaches exist for more lightweight compositions of stateless containers, where main memory is no longer a concern, and further platform-level components such as database services, volumes, secrets, routes and templates, some of which keep the actual state [5]. This paper is therefore concerned with migrating applications based on *container compositions* between diverse cloud platforms.

Consequently, the main contribution of the paper is a discussion of migration tool designs and prototypes for containerised Docker Compose, OpenShift and Kubernetes applications across providers. OpenShift is one of the most advanced open source PaaS stacks based on Kubernetes, a management and scheduling platform for containers, and in production use at several commercial cloud providers including RedHat's OpenShift Online, the APPUiO Swiss Container Platform, and numerous on-premise deployments [6]. Additional pure Kubernetes hosting is offered by the Google Cloud Platform, by Azure Container Services and by the overlay platform Tectonic for AWS and Azure, among other providers [7]. Both platforms orchestrate, place, schedule and scale ideally-stateless Docker containers, while simpler compositions can also be achieved with Docker Compose.

The possibility to have the same containerised application deployed and running in different cloud providers and using different container platforms or orchestration tools is useful for both researcher and for companies. It facilitates the comparison of different cloud providers or different orchestration tools. For companies, it facilitates to run the applications in the most attractive hosting options by cost or other internal constraints. Key questions to which the use of our tools gives answers typically are: Is the migration feasible? Is it lossless? How fast is it? Does the order matter?

The paper is structured as follows. First, we analyse contemporary application compositions to derive requirements for the generalised live heterogeneous migration process (Sect. 2), followed by outlining the tool design principles (Sect. 3) and architecture (Sect. 4) for a simpler subset, inhomogeneous migration. The implemented tools are furthermore described (Sect. 5) and evaluated with real application examples (Sect. 6). The paper concludes with a summary of achievements (Sect. 7) and a discussion on filling the gap to truly heterogeneous live migration.

2 Analysis

In the definition given in a ten-year review of cloud-native applications [8], such applications are designed using self-contained deployment units. In currents applications the consensus is to use containers for reasonable isolation and almost native performance. Among the container technologies, Docker containers are the most common technology, although there are alternatives including Rkt, Containerd or CRI-O, as well as research-inspired prototypical engines such as SCONE [9]. In the following, we define a well-designed cloud application as a blueprint-described application, using containers to encapsulate the logic in microservices bound to the data confined in volumes. For deploying these applications in production into the cloud, just the container technology is not enough. Generally, a proper containerised application also uses an advanced container platform or an orchestration solution to add self-healing, auto-scaling, load balancing, service discovery and other properties which make it easier and faster to develop and deploy applications in the cloud. The platform also leverages more resilience, higher availability and scalability in the application itself. Among the most popular tools and platforms used to orchestrate containers are Docker Swarm, Docker Compose, Kubernetes, OpenShift, Rancher, and similar platforms. All of these can run in different cloud providers or on-premise. Moreover, usually each cloud provider has their own container platform. In Fig. 2 a diagram about the main container platforms and container orchestrators with their different associated composition blueprints is shown. The diagram also reveals relations and classifies the approaches by licencing (open source or proprietary) and by fitness for production. This complex technological landscape leads to different blueprints for the same containerised application depending which causes practical difficulties for migrations. Despite fast ongoing consolidation, including the announced discontinuation of Docker Cloud in 2018, minor variations such as installed Kubernetes extensions continue to be a hurdle for seamless migration.

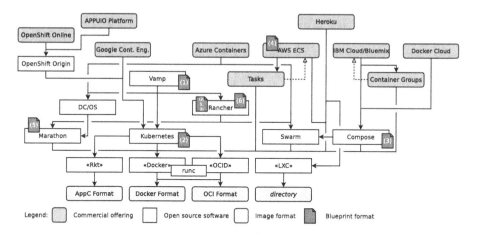

Fig. 2. Map of major container platforms and orchestration tools

The planning of the migration of a containerised application thus encompasses two key points which restrain the ability to automate the process:

– The blueprints: Even though containers encapsulate all the code in images which are meant to be portable and run everywhere, most of the real applications will need an orchestration tool to exploit all advantages that the cloud environment introduces: service discovery, definition of the number of replicas or persistence configuration. As most orchestration tools will introduce specific blueprints or deployment descriptors, the migration tool will need to convert between blueprint formats through transformation, perform minor modifications such as additions and removals of expressions, or rewrite limits and group associations (requirement R1).
– The data: Migration of the persisted data and other state information is non-trivial. In most container engines, the persistence of the data is confined to volumes. Depending of the cloud provider, the blueprints processed by the orchestration tools could reference volumes differently even for homogeneous orchestration tools, leading to slight differences and thus inhomogeneity (requirement R2).

To address these two points and increase the automation, the design of a suitable migration tool needs to account specifically for blueprint conversion and properly inlined data migration. We formalise a simplified composite application deployment as $D = \{b, c, v, \ldots\}$, respectively, where: b: blueprint; c: set of associated containers; v: set of associated volumes. For example, a simplified OpenShift application is represented as $D_{openshift} = \{b, c, v, t, is, r, \ldots\}$, where:

t: set of templates; is: set of image streams; r: set of routes. The goal of ideal heterogeneous migration m is to find migration paths from any arbitrary source deployment to any target deployment: $m = D \rightarrow D'$.

Figure 3 summarises the different realistically resulting inhomogeneous migration paths between the three possible configurations $D_{kubernetes}$, $D_{openshift}$ and $D_{compose}$. Through various modifications applied to the orchestration descriptors, sources and targets can be largely different while mostly avoiding a loss of deployment information in fulfilment of R1.

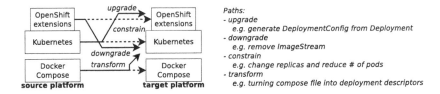

Fig. 3. Inhomogeneous application migration paths between three systems

3   General Application Migration Workflows

Requirement R1 calls for a dedicated blueprint extraction, conversion and re-deployment process. We consider four steps in this process (see Fig. 4) which shall be implemented by a migration tool:

- Step 1. Downloading the blueprints of the composite application: The tool will connect to the source platform the application is running on, will identify all the components of the application and download the blueprints to a temporary location.
- Step 2. Converting the blueprints: A conversion from source to target format takes place. Even when homogeneous technologies are in place on both sides, re-sizing and re-grouping of components can be enforced according to the constraints on the target side (fulfilling R1).
- Step 3. Deploying the application: The tool will connect to the new orchestration platform and deploy the application there.
- Step 4. Deleting the application: Once the new application instance is running in the new place, the tool can delete the old application instance from the previous place. This step is optional and only executed under move semantics as opposed to copy semantics.

A major issue is the transactional guarantee of achieving a complex running and serving application on the target platform which in all regards equals the source. To make this process successful in all cases, the tool algorithm must further fulfil the following three requirements:

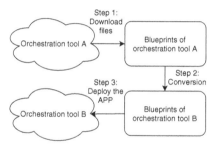

Fig. 4. Blueprints process diagram

- Connect to each of the different platforms in scope for heterogeneous migration.
- Convert between all the blueprints.
- Download and upload the application components from/to all the platforms, ensuring a re-deployment in the right order and a smooth hand-over by name service records which are typically external to both source and target platform.

With the previously described workflow, the tool can migrate stateless application or the stateless components of a stateful application. To complete the migration, the data in the containers needs to be migrated as well according to R2. In practice, this refers to volumes attached to containers, but also to databases and message queues which must be persisted in volume format beforehand. The process of the migration of a volume will be as follows:

- Step 1. Find the list of volumes linked to an application and for each one the path to the data.
- Step 2. Download the data to a temporary location. Due to the size, differential file transfer will be used.
- Step 3. Identify the same volume in the new deployment and pre-allocate the required storage space.
- Step 4. Upload the data to the new volume.

Now, we devise a fictive tool to express how the combined fulfilment of R1 and R2 in the context of heterogeneous application migration can be realised, expressed by Fig. 5 which highlights the separation into blueprints and data.

Although practicioners and researchers would benefit greatly from such a generic and all-encompassing tool, its conception and engineering would take many person months of software development work, needlessly delaying a prototype to answer the previously identified questions many companies in the field have right now. Instead, to focus on key research questions as outlined in the introduction follows a divide-and-conquer strategy. We subdivide the overall fictive tool into a set of smaller tools logically grouped into three categories, as shown in Fig. 6. Thus, we put our own prototypical work into context of a wider

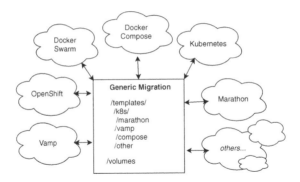

Fig. 5. Stateful application components diagram

ecosystem with some existing tools and further ongoing and future developments, making it possible to evaluate migration scenarios already now. The tools are:

- Homogeneously migrating containerised applications between multiple instances of the same orchestration tool: `os2os` (our work).
- Converting blueprints between the formats required by the platforms related to R1: Kompose (existing work).
- Rewriting Kubernetes blueprints to accomodate quotas: `descriptorrewriter` (our work).
- Migrating volumes related to R2: `volume2volume` (our work).
- Homogeneous transactional integration of volume and data migration for OpenShift as a service: `openshifter` (our early stage work).

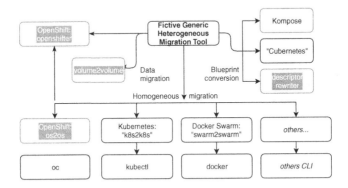

Fig. 6. Implementation strategy for fictive heterogeneous migration tool

We contribute in this paper the architectural design, implementation and combined evaluation of four tools referring to inhomogeneous OpenShift/Kubernetes/Docker Compose-to-OpenShift/Kubernetes migration. Use cases encompass intra-region replication and region switching within one provider, migration from one provider to another, and developer-centric migration of local test applications into a cloud environment. All tools are publicly available for download and experimentation[1].

4   Migration Tools Design and Architecture

The general design of all tool ensures user-friendly abstraction over existing low-level tools such as `oc` and `kubectl`, the command line interfaces to OpenShift and Kubernetes, as well as auxiliary tools such as `rsync` for differential data transfer. Common migration and copy/replication workflows are available as powerful single commands. In Openshifter, these are complemented with full transaction support so that partial migrations can be gracefully interrupted or rolled back in case of occurring issues.

As Fig. 7 shows on the left side, `os2os` uses `oc` to communicate with the source and target OpenShift clusters and temporarily stores all artefacts in local templates and volumes folders. This choice ensures that only a single provider configuration file needs to be maintained and that any features added to `oc` will be transparently available. On the right side of Fig. 7, the Openshifter tool is depicted which follows a service-oriented design. This choice ensures that the migration code itself runs as stateless, resilient and auto-scaled service. A further difference between the tools is that for Openshifter, we have explored a conceptual extension of packaged template and configuration data archives, called Helm charts, into *fat charts* which include a snapshot of the data, closing the gap to monolithic virtual machines.

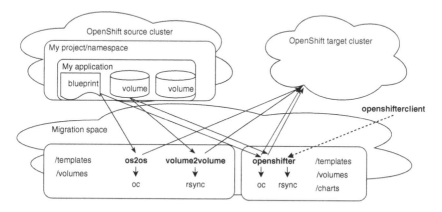

Fig. 7. OS2OS/Volume2Volume architectures (left); Openshifter architecture (right)

---

[1] Tools website: https://github.com/serviceprototypinglab/.

Exemplarily for all tools, `os2os` is composed of the following commands:

- export: Connect to one cluster and export all the components (objects) of one application in one project, saved locally in a folder called `templates`.
- up: Connect to one cluster and upload all the components of one application in one project which are saved in `templates`.
- down: Connect to one cluster and delete all the components of one application in one project.
- migrate: Combine all the commands chronologically for a full migration in a single workflow.

The tools are implemented in different ways following the different designs. Both `os2os` and `volume2volume` are inspired by Kompose. They are implemented as command-line tools using Go with Cobra as library for handling the command-line parameters. Furthermore, the command names are derived from Kompose, making it easy to learn the tool for existing Kompose users. As usual in applications using Cobra, the configuration of the tool is stored in a YAML file. It contains the credentials to connect to the clusters, the cluster endpoints, the projects and the object types to migrate, overriding the default value of all object types. The `openshifter` prototype is implemented in Python using the AIO-HTTP web library to expose RESTful methods and works without any configuration file by receiving all parameters at invocation time.

5   Evaluation

When evaluating cloud migration tools, three important questions arise on whether the migration is lossless, performing and developer-acceptable. The measurable evaluation criteria are:

- C1/Losslessness: The migration needs to avoid loss of critical application deployment information even after several roundtrips of migration between inhomogeneous systems. This is a challenge especially in the absence of features on some platforms. For instance, Kubernetes offers auto-scaling while Docker Swarm does not, leading to the question of how to preserve the information in case a migration from Kubernetes to Docker Swarm is followed by a reverse migration while the original source platform has vanished.
- C2/Performance: A quantitative metric to express which time is needed both overall and for the individual migration steps. Further, can this time be pre-calculated or predicted in order to generate automated downtime messages, or can any downtime be alleviated.
- C3/Acceptance: The migration needs to be easy to use for developers and operators as well as in modern DevOps environments.

A testbed with two local virtual machines running OpenShift 3.6 (setup S1) as well as a hosted OpenShift environment provided by the Swiss container platform APPUiO (S2) were set up to evaluate our tools experimentally according to the defined criteria C1 and C2. A synthetic scenario application consisting of three deployments and three services was prepared for that matter (A1), and the existing Snafu application (A2) was used for the comparison. The evaluation of C3 is left for future work.

5.1 Evaluation of Losslessness

For Kubernetes and OpenShift, the scenario service consists of shared Service and ConfigMap objects as well as platform-specific ones which are subject to loss; for Docker Compose, it consists of roughly equivalent directives. The deployed service was migrated from source to target and, with swapped roles between the platforms, back again from target to source. The following table reports on the loss of information depending on the system type. The Kompose tool incorrectly omits the lowercasing of object names and furthermore does not automatically complete the generated descriptors with information not already present in the Docker Compose files. To address the first issue, we have contributed a patch, whereas the second one would require a more extensive tool modification. The upgrade from Kubernetes to OpenShift works although OpenShift merely supports Deployment objects as a convenience whereas DeploymentConfig objects would be needed (Table 1).

Table 1. Losslessness of blueprint transformations

Source	Target	Loss
OpenShift	OpenShift	None (assuming equal quotas)
OpenShift	Kubernetes (manual)	ImageStream, Route, DeploymentConfig
Kubernetes	OpenShift (manual)	(Deployment)
Docker compose	Kubernetes (w/ Kompose)	None (yet incomplete & incorrect)

As a result, we have been able to automate all migrations except for the downgrade from OpenShift to Kubernetes using a combination of our tools which is invoked transparently when using Openshifter. The losslessness further refers to in-flight import and export of volume data. To avoid data corruption, applications need to perform modifications on the file level atomically, for instance by placing uploads into temporary files which are subsequently atomically renamed. Support for applications not adhering to this requirement is outside the scope of our work.

5.2 Evaluation of Performance

The synthetic scenario service A1 was exported from the source, re-deployed at the target, and torn down at the source 10 times with os2os in order to get information about the performance and its deviation in the local-to-local migration setup S1. Figure 8 shows the results of the performance experiments. An evident characteristic is that exporting objects without changing them is more stable than running the down/up commands which modify the objects and cause changes to the scheduling of the remaining objects. A second observation is that, counter-intuitively, the `down` command consumes most of the time. A plausible explanation is that instead of simple deletions, objects are rather scheduled for deletion into a queue.

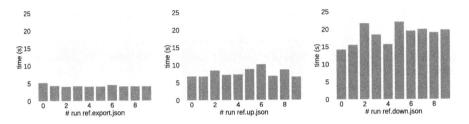

Fig. 8. Durations of the individual migration phases – export (left figure), up (middle), down (right) – between two local Kubernetes clusters

Service A2 was transformed automatically to measure the influence of the transformation logic on planned live migrations. The creation of Kubernetes descriptors with Kompose takes approximately 0.028 s. The adjustment of quotas and consolidation of pods, as performed by `descriptorrewriter`, takes approximately 0.064 s on the resulting Kubernetes descriptors. Both transformations are thus negligible which implies that apart from blueprint exports, the data transfer, which is primarily limited by the cluster connectivity, is the dominant influence on overall performance.

6   Conclusion

We have conducted a first analytical study on migrating cloud-native applications between inhomogeneous development and production platforms. The analysis was made possible through prototypical migration tools whose further development is in turn made possible by the results of the experiments. The derived findings from the experimental evaluation suggest that application portability is still an issue beyond the implementation (container) images. Future cloud platforms should include portability into the design requirements.

7   Future Work

The current prototypes only support Kubernetes-based platforms. All functionality to convert other formats has been integrated into the experiments with external and existing tools. In the future, we want to integrate them in a unified way into `openshifter`. Further, we want to work on stricter requirements concerning a production-ready migration. They encompass improved user interfaces for easier inter-region/-zone migration within one provider, automatic identification of associated state and data formats, plugins for databases and message queues which keep non-volume state, data checksumming, and pre-copy statistics about both expected timing and resource requirements of the process and the subsequent deployment.

Acknowledgement. This research has been funded by Innosuisse - Swiss Innovation Agency in project MOSAIC/19333.1.

References

1. Piraghaj, S.F., Dastjerdi, A.V., Calheiros, R.N., Buyya, R.: Efficient virtual machine sizing for hosting containers as a service (SERVICES 2015). In: 2015 IEEE World Congress on Services, pp. 31–38, June 2015
2. Rodríguez, P., et al.: Continuous deployment of software intensive products and services: a systematic mapping study. J. Syst. Softw. **123**, 263–291 (2017)
3. Ficco, M., Esposito, C., Chang, H., Choo, K.-K.R.: Live migration in emerging cloud paradigms. IEEE Cloud Comput. **3**(2), 12–19 (2016)
4. Bezerra, P., Martins, G., Gomes, R., Cavalcante, F., da Costa, A.F.B.F.: Evaluating live virtual machine migration overhead on client's application perspective. In: 2017 International Conference on Information Networking, ICOIN 2017, Da Nang, Vietnam, 11–13 January 2017, pp. 503–508 (2017)
5. Lee, J., Kang, K.: Poster: a lightweight live migration platform with container-based virtualization for system resilience. In: Proceedings of the 15th Annual International Conference on Mobile Systems, Applications, and Services, MobiSys 2017, Niagara Falls, NY, USA, 19–23 June 2017, p. 158 (2017)
6. Pahl, C.: Containerization and the PaaS Cloud. IEEE Cloud Comput. **2**(3), 24–31 (2015)
7. Burns, B., Grant, B., Oppenheimer, D., Brewer, E., Wilkes, J.: Borg, Omega, and Kubernetes. Commun. ACM **59**(5), 50–57 (2016)
8. Kratzke, N., Quint, P.-C.: Understanding cloud-native applications after 10 years of cloud computing - a systematic mapping study. J. Syst. Softw. **126**, 1–16 (2017)
9. Arnautov, S.: SCONE: secure Linux containers with Intel SGX. In: 12th USENIX Symposium on Operating Systems Design and Implementation, OSDI 2016, Savannah, GA, USA, 2–4 November 2016, pp. 689–703 (2016)

Secure Apps in the Fog: Anything to Declare?

Antonio Brogi, Gian-Luigi Ferrari, and Stefano Forti[✉]

Department of Computer Science, University of Pisa, Pisa, Italy
{antonio.brogi,gian-luigi.ferrari,stefano.forti}@di.unipi.it

Abstract. Assessing security of application deployments in the Fog is a non-trivial task, having to deal with highly heterogeneous infrastructures containing many resource-constrained devices. In this paper, we introduce: *(i)* a declarative way of specifying security capabilities of Fog infrastructures and security requirements of Fog applications, and *(ii)* a (probabilistic) reasoning strategy to determine application deployments and to quantitatively assess their security level, considering the trust degree of application operators in different Cloud/Fog providers. A life-like example is used to showcase a first proof-of-concept implementation and to illustrate how it can be used in synergy with other predictive tools to optimise the deployment of Fog applications.

Keywords: Fog computing · Application deployment · Security assessment · Executable specifications · Probabilistic programming · Trust

1 Introduction

Fog computing [11] aims at better supporting the growing processing demand of (time-sensitive and bandwidth hungry) Internet of Things (IoT) applications by selectively pushing computation closer to where data is produced and exploiting a geographically distributed multitude of heterogeneous devices (e.g., personal devices, gateways, micro-data centres, embedded servers) spanning the continuum from the Cloud to the IoT. As a complement and an extension of the Cloud, the Fog will naturally share with it many security threats and it will also add its peculiar ones. On the one hand, Fog computing will increase the number of security enforcement points by allowing local processing of private data closer to the IoT sources. On the other hand, the Fog will be exposed to brand new threats for what concerns the trust and the physical vulnerability of devices. In particular, Fog deployments will span various service providers - some of which may be not fully trustworthy - and will include accessible devices that can be easily hacked, stolen or broken by malicious users [28]. Security will, therefore, play a crucial role in the success of the Fog paradigm and it represents a concern that should be addressed *by-design* at all architectural levels [29,41]. The Fog calls for novel technologies, methodologies and models to guarantee adequate security levels to Fog deployments even when relying upon resource-constrained devices [10].

© Springer Nature Switzerland AG 2020
M. Fazio and W. Zimmermann (Eds.): ESOCC 2018 Workshops, CCIS 1115, pp. 46–61, 2020.
https://doi.org/10.1007/978-3-030-63161-1_4

Meanwhile, modern computing systems are more and more made from distributed components – such as in service-oriented and micro-service based architectures [34] – what makes it challenging to determine how they can be *best-placed* so to fulfil various application requirements [14]. In our previous work [5], we proposed a model and algorithms to determine eligible deployments of IoT applications to Fog infrastructures based on hardware, software and QoS requirements. Our prototype – FogTorchΠ – implements those algorithms and permits to estimate the QoS-assurance, the resource consumption in the Fog layer [7] and the monthly deployment cost [8] of the output eligible deployments. Various other works tackled the problem of determining "optimal" placements of application components in Fog scenarios, however, none included a quantitative security assessment to holistically predict security guarantees of the deployed applications, whilst determining eligible application deployments [6]. Therefore, there is a clear need to evaluate *a priori* whether an application will have its security requirements fulfilled by the (Cloud and Fog) nodes chosen for the deployment of its components. Furthermore, due to the mission-critical nature of many Fog applications (e.g., e-health, disaster recovery), it is important that the techniques employed to reason on security properties of deployed multi-component applications are both configurable and well-founded.

In this paper, we propose a methodology (SecFog) to (quantitatively) assess the security level of multi-component application deployments in Fog scenarios. Such quantitative assessment can be used both alone – to maximise the security level of application deployments – and synergically with other techniques so to perform multi-criteria optimisations and to determine the *best* placement of application components in Fog infrastructure. This work allows application deployers to specify security requirements both at the level of the components and at the level of the application as a whole. As per recent proposals in the field of AI [3], it exploits probabilistic reasoning to account for effectiveness against possible attacks and trust, whilst capturing the uncertainty inherent to Fog. Therefore, we propose: *(i)* a declarative methodology that enables writing an executable specification of the security policies related to an application deployment to be checked against the security offerings of a Fog infrastructure, *(ii)* a reasoning methodology that can be used to look for secure application deployments and to assess the security levels guaranteed by any input deployment, and *(iii)* a first proof-of-concept implementation of SecFog which can be used to optimise security aspects of Fog application deployments along with other metrics.

The rest of this paper is organised as follows. After reviewing some related work (Sect. 2), we offer an overview of SecFog and we introduce a motivating example (Sect. 3). Then, we present our proof-of-concept implementation of SecFog and we show how it can be used to determine application deployments whilst maximising their security level[1] (Sect. 4). Finally, we show how SecFog can be used with FogTorchΠ to identify suitable trade-offs among QoS-assurance, resource usage, monthly cost and security level of eligible deployments (Sect. 5), and we briefly conclude with some directions for future work (Sect. 6).

---

[1] Code to run the example is available at: http://pages.di.unipi.it/forti/code/secfog.pl.

2   Related Work

Among the works that studied the placement of multi-component applications to Cloud nodes, very few approaches considered security aspects when determining eligible application deployments, mainly focussing on improving performance, resource usage and deployment cost [21,24], or on performing identification of potential data integrity violations based on pre-defined risk patterns [32]. Indeed, existing research considered security mainly when treating the deployment of business processes to (federated) multi-Clouds (e.g., [15,26,40]). Similar to our work, Luna et al. [22] were among the first to propose a quantitative reasoning methodology to rank single Cloud providers based on their security SLAs, and with respect to a specific set of (user-weighted) security requirements. Recently, swarm intelligence techniques [24] have been exploited to determine eligible deployments of composite Cloud applications, considering a risk assessment score based on node vulnerabilities.

Fog computing introduces new challenges, mainly due to its pervasive geo-distribution and heterogeneity, need for QoS-awareness, dynamicity and support to interactions with the IoT, that were not thoroughly studied in previous works addressing the problem of application deployment to the Cloud [37,39]. Among the first proposals investigating these new lines, [18] proposed a from-Fog-to-Cloud search algorithm as a first way to determine an eligible deployment of (multi-component) DAG applications to tree-like Fog infrastructures. Their placement algorithm attempts the placement of components *Fog-to-Cloud* by considering hardware capacity only. An open-source simulator – iFogSim – has been released to test the proposed policy against Cloud-only deployments. Building on top of iFogSim, [23] tries to guarantee the application service delivery deadlines and to optimise Fog resource exploitation. Also [38] used iFogSim to implement an algorithm for optimal online placement of application components, with respect to load balancing. Recently, exploiting iFogSim, [17] proposed a distributed search strategy to find the best service placement in the Fog, which minimises the distance between the clients and the most requested services, based on request rates and available free resources. [20,35] proposed (linearithmic) heuristic algorithms that attempt deployments prioritising placement of applications to devices that feature with less free resources.

From an alternative viewpoint, [19] gave a Mixed-Integer Non-Linear Programming (MINLP) formulation of the problem of placing application components so to satisfy end-to-end delay constraints. The problem is then solved by linearisation into a Mixed-Integer Linear Programming (MILP), showing potential improvements in latency, energy consumption and costs for routing and storage that the Fog might bring. Also [33] adopted an ILP formulation of the problem of allocating computation to Fog nodes so to optimise time deadlines on application execution. A simple linear model for the Cloud costs is also taken into account. Finally, dynamic programming (e.g., [30]), genetic algorithms (e.g., [33]) and deep learning (e.g., [36]) were exploited promisingly in some recent works.

Overall, to the best of our knowledge, no previous work included a quantitative assessment of the security level of candidate Fog application deployments.

3 Methodology Overview

The OpenFog Consortium [1] highlighted the need for Fog computing platforms to guarantee privacy, anonymity, integrity, trust, attestation, verification and measurement. Whilst security control frameworks exist for the Cloud (e.g., the EU Cloud SLA Standardisation Guidelines [2] or the ISO/IEC 19086), to the best of our knowledge, no standard exists yet that defines security objectives for Fog application deployments. Based on recent surveys about security aspects in Fog computing (i.e., [24,25,28]), we devised a simple example of taxonomy[2] (Fig. 1) of security capabilities that can be offered by Cloud and Fog nodes and therefore used for reasoning on the security levels of given Fog application deployments.

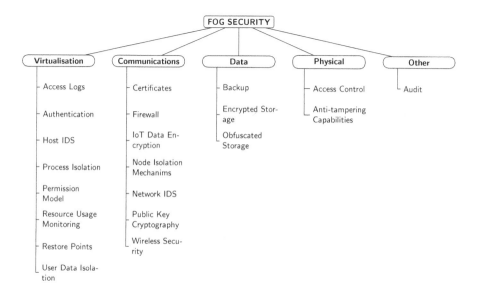

Fig. 1. An example of taxonomy of security capabilities in Fog computing.

Security features that are common with the Cloud might assume renewed importance in Fog scenarios, due to the limited capabilities of the available devices. For instance, guaranteeing physical integrity of end-user data isolation at an access point with Fog capabilities might be very difficult. Apropos, the possibility to encrypt or obfuscate data at Fog nodes, along with encrypted IoT communication and physical anti-tampering machinery, will be key to protect those application deployments that need data privacy assurance.

Figure 2 shows the ingredients needed to perform the security assessment by means of the SecFog methodology.

---

[2] The proposed taxonomy can be easily modified, extended and refined so as to include new security categories and third-level security features as soon as normative security frameworks will get established for the Fog.

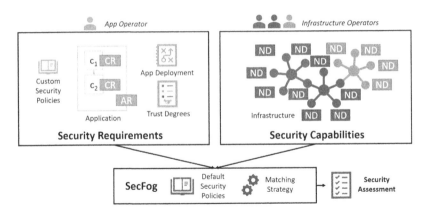

Fig. 2. Bird's-eye view of SecFog.

On the one hand, we assume that infrastructure operators declare the *security capabilities* featured by their nodes[3]. Namely, for each node she is managing, the operator publishes a Node Descriptor (ND) featuring a list of the node security capabilities along with a declared measure of their effectiveness against potential attacks (in the range $[0,1]$), as shown in Fig. 4. On the other hand, based on the same common vocabulary, application operators can define (non-trivial) *custom security policies*. Such properties can complete or override a set of *default security policies* available in SecFog implementation.

For instance, one can derive that application components deployed to nodes featuring Public Key Cryptography capabilities can communicate through End-to-End Secure channel. A different stakeholder might also require the availability of Certificates at both end-points to consider a channel End-to-End Secure. Similarly, one can decide to infer that a node offering Backup capabilities together with Encrypted Storage or Obfuscated Storage can be considered a Secure Storage provider. Custom and default properties are used, along with ground facts, to specify the *security requirements* of a given application as Component Requirements (CR) or Application Requirements (AR), or both. For instance, application operators can specify that a certain component c is securely deployed to node n when n features Secure Storage and when the communication with component c' happens over an End-to-End Secure channel.

Finally, the security level of an *application deployment* can be assessed by matching the security requirements of the application with the security capabilities featured by the infrastructure and by multiplying the effectiveness of all exploited security capabilities, weighting them as per *trust degrees*, which may be assigned by application deployers to each infrastructure operator. This last step can be used both to assess the security level of a single (possibly partial)

---

[3] For the sake of simplicity, in this paper, we assume that operators exploit the vocabulary of the example taxonomy in Fig. 1. In reality, different operators can employ different vocabulary and then rely on mediation mechanisms [31].

input application deployment and to generate and test all eligible deployments according to the declared security requirements. We now go through a motivating example that we will retake later on by exploiting the SecFog prototype.

3.1 Motivating Example

We retake the application example of [8]. Consider a simple Fog application (Fig. 3) that manages fire alarm, heating and A/C systems, interior lighting, and security cameras of a smart building. The application consists of three microservices:

- IoTController, interacting with the connected cyber-physical systems,
- DataStorage, storing all sensed information for future use and employing machine learning techniques to update sense-act rules at the IoTController so to optimise heating and lighting management based on previous experience and/or on people behaviour, and
- Dashboard, aggregating and visualising collected data and videos, as well as allowing users to interact with the system.

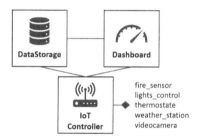

Fig. 3. Fog application.

Each microservice represents an independently deployable component of the application [27] and has hardware and software requirements[4] in order to function properly. Application components must cooperate so that well-defined levels of service are met at runtime. Hence, communication links supporting component-component and component-thing interactions should provide suitable end-to-end latency and bandwidth.

Figure 4 shows the infrastructure – two Cloud data centres, three Fog nodes – to which the smart building application is deployed. For each node, the available security capabilities and their effectiveness against possible attacks (as declared by the infrastructure operator) are listed in terms of the taxonomy of Fig. 1.

---

[4] For the sake of readability, we omit the application requirements. The interested reader can find all the details in [8].

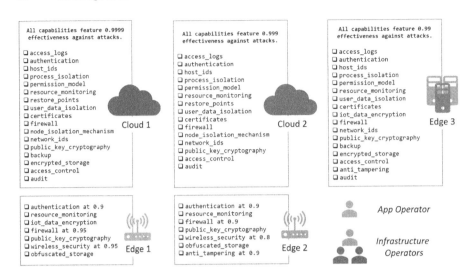

Fig. 4. Fog infrastructure description.

Table 1 lists all the deployments of the given application to the considered infrastructure which meet all set software, hardware and network QoS requirements, as they are found by FogTorchΠ in [8]. For each deployment, FogTorchΠ outputs the QoS-assurance (i.e., the likelihood it will meet network QoS requirements), an aggregate measure of Fog resource consumption, and an estimate of the monthly cost for keeping the deployment up and running. Deployments annotated with * are only available when Fog 2 features a 4G connection which costs, however, 20 € a month in addition to the costs reported in Table 1.

In [8], the deployments Δ2 and Δ16 are selected as the best candidates depending on the type of mobile connection (i.e., 3G vs 4G) available at Fog 2.

As the majority of the existing approaches for application placement, [8] focuses on finding deployments that guarantee application functionality and end-user preferences, but ignoring security aspects in the featured analysis.

Nevertheless, the application operators can define the following Component Requirements:

- IoTController requires Physical Security guarantees (i.e., Access Control ∨ Anti-tampering Capabilities) so to avoid that temporarily stored data can be physically stolen from the deployment node,
- DataStorage requires Secure Storage (viz., Backup ∧ (Obfuscated Storage ∨ Encrypted Storage)), the availability of Access Logs, a Network IDS in place to prevent distributed Denial of Service (dDoS) attacks, and
- Dashboard requires a Host IDS installed at the deployment node (e.g., an antivirus software) along with a Resource Usage Monitoring to prevent interactions with malicious software and to detect anomalous component behaviour.

Table 1. Eligible deployments of the example application.

Dep. ID	IoTController	DataStorage	Dashboard	QoS	Resources	Cost
$\Delta 1$	Fog 2	Fog 3	Cloud 2	98.6%	48.4%	€ 856.7
$\Delta 2$	Fog 2	Fog 3	Cloud 1	98.6%	48.4%	€ 798.7
$\Delta 3$	Fog 3	Fog 3	Cloud 1	100%	48.4%	€ 829.7
$\Delta 4$	Fog 2	Fog 3	Fog 1	100%	59.2%	€ 844.7
$\Delta 5$	Fog 1	Fog 3	Cloud 1	96%	48.4%	€ 837.7
$\Delta 6$	Fog 3	Fog 3	Cloud 2	100%	48.4%	€ 887.7
$\Delta 7$	Fog 3	Fog 3	Fog 2	100%	59.2%	€ 801.7
$\Delta 8$	Fog 3	Fog 3	Fog 1	100%	59.2%	€ 875.7
$\Delta 9$	Fog 1	Fog 3	Cloud 2	96%	48.4%	€ 895.7
$\Delta 10$	Fog 1	Fog 3	Fog 2	100%	59.2%	€ 809.7
$\Delta 11$	Fog 1	Fog 3	Fog 1	100%	59.2%	€ 883.7
$\Delta 12^*$	Fog 2	Cloud 2	Fog 1	94.7%	16.1%	€ 870.7
$\Delta 13^*$	Fog 2	Cloud 2	Cloud 1	97.2%	5.4%	€ 824.7
$\Delta 14^*$	Fog 2	Cloud 2	Cloud 2	98.6%	5.4%	€ 882.7
$\Delta 15^*$	Fog 2	Cloud 1	Cloud 2	97.2%	5.4%	€ 785.7
$\Delta 16^*$	Fog 2	Cloud 1	Cloud 1	98.6%	5.4%	€ 727.7
$\Delta 17^*$	Fog 2	Cloud 1	Fog 1	94.7%	16.1%	€ 773.7

Furthermore, the Application Requirements require guaranteed end-to-end encryption among all components (viz., all deployment nodes should feature Public Key Cryptography) and that deployment nodes should feature an Authentication mechanism. Finally, application operators assign a trust degree of 80% to the infrastructure providers of Cloud 1 and Cloud 2, and of 90% to the infrastructure providers of Fog 3 and Fog 2. Naturally, they consider their management of Fog 1 completely trustworthy.

4 Proof-of-Concept

Being SecFog a declarative methodology based on probabilistic reasoning about declared infrastructure capabilities and security requirements, it was natural to prototype it relying on probabilistic logic programming. To implement both the model and the matching strategy we used a language called *ProbLog* [12]. ProbLog is a Python package that permits writing logic programs that encode complex interactions between large sets of heterogeneous components, capturing the inherent uncertainties that are present in real-life situations. ProbLog programs are composed of *facts* and *rules*. The facts, such as

```
p::f.
```

represent a statement f which is true with probability p^5. The rules, like

```
r :- c1, ... , cn.
```

represent a property r inferred when $c1 \wedge \cdots \wedge cn$ hold[6]. ProbLog programs are logic programs in which some of the facts are annotated with (their) probabilities. Each program defines a probability distribution over logic programs where a fact p::f. is considered true with probability p and false with probability $1 - p$. The ProbLog engine [13] determines the success probability of a query q as the probability that q has *a* proof, given the distribution over logic programs.

Our proof-of-concept of SecFog is listed in Fig. 5. It offers a secureApp(A,D) predicate that, given an app A and the list of its components L, looks for deployments of the application (line 3) and checks whether they can be considered secure (line 4). The deployment(L,D) predicate generates possible deployments of an application by recurring on the list of its components (line 5–8). Then, for any generated deployment, the predicate secureDeployment(D) recursively checks whether each component can be securely deployed according to its Component Requirements (line 11) and that the deployment node N is managed by a trustworthy operator Op (lines 12–13). Finally, it checks if the Application Requirements can be also satisfied (line 14).

```
secureApp(A,D) :-                        (1)
    app(A,L),                            (2)
    deployment(L, D),                    (3)
    secureDeployment(D).                 (4)

deployment([],[]).                       (5)
deployment([C|Cs],[d(C,N)|D]) :-         (6)
    node(N, _),                          (7)
    deployment(Cs,D).                    (8)

secureDeployment([]).                    (9)
secureDeployment([d(C,N)|D]) :-          (10)
    secureComponent(C,N),                (11)
    node(N, Op),                         (12)
    trustworthy(Op),                     (13)
    extras(N),                           (14)
    secureDeployment(D).                 (15)
```

Fig. 5. SecFog proof-of-concept.

The application operator is therefore asked to define a secureComponent(C, N) clause, specifying the Component Requirements for each of the application components, and a (possibly empty) extras(N) specifying the Application

---

[5] A fact declared simply as f. is assumed to be true with probability 1.

[6] f, r and {ci} can include variable (upper-case) or constant (lower-case) terms. The OR operator $\vee$ is denoted by a semicolon like in c1; c2.

Requirements that are required by all application components. It is worth noting that the predicate `secureApp(A,D)` can be queried to determine secure application deployments as well as to verify whether a given candidate deployment is actually secure.

4.1 Motivating Example Continued

In this section, we retake the example of Sect. 3.1 and we show how ProbLog permits to naturally express both security capabilities of an infrastructure and security requirements of an application. Node Descriptors can be expressed by listing ground facts, possibly featuring a probability that represents their effectiveness against attacks according to the infrastructure provider. For instance, `fog1` directly operated by the application operator `appOp` is described as

```
node(fog1,appOp).
0.9::authentication(fog1).
resource_monitoring(fog1).
iot_data_encryption(fog1).
0.95::firewall(fog1).
public_key_cryptography(fog1).
0.95::wireless_security(fog1).
obfuscated_storage(fog1).
```

All the Node Descriptors made following this template form a description of the *security capabilities* available in the infrastructure.

Application operators can define the topology of an application by specifying an identifier and the list of its components. For instance, the application of Fig. 3 can be simply denoted by the fact

```
app(smartbuilding, [iot_controller, data_storage, dashboard]).
```

Then, they can define the *security requirements* of the application both as Component Requirements and Application Requirements. In our example, the Component Requirements can be simply declared as

```
secureComponent(iot_controller, N) :-
    physical_security(N).

secureComponent(data_storage, N) :-
    secure_storage(N),
    access_logs(N),
    network_ids(N).

secureComponent(dashboard, N) :-
    host_ids(N),
    resource_monitoring(N).
```

where the custom security policies `physical_security(N)` and `secure_storage(N)` are defined as

```
secure_storage(N) :-
    backup(N),
    (encrypted_storage(N); obfuscated_storage(N)).

physical_security(N) :- anti_tampering(N); access_control(N).
```

Analogously, the Application Requirements that concern the application as a whole can be specified by specifying the extras(N) predicate as follows

```
extras(N) :- public_key_cryptography(N), authentication(N).
```

Finally, application operators can express their *trust degrees* towards each infrastructure operator as the probability of trusting it (i.e., $t \in [0, 1]$). In our example, we have

```
0.8::trustworthy(cloudOp1).
0.8::trustworthy(cloudOp2).
0.9::trustworthy(fogOp).
trustworthy(appOp).
```

Our prototype can be used to find (via a *generate & test* approach) all deployments that satisfy the security requirements of the example application to a given infrastructure, by simply issuing the query:

```
query(mySecureApp(smartbuilding,D)).
```

As shown in Fig. 6, relying on ProbLog out-of-the-box algorithms, SecFog prototype returns answers to the query along with a value in $[0, 1]$ that represents the aggregate *security level* of the inferred facts, i.e. the probability that a

```
secureApp(smartbuilding,[d(iot_controller,cloud1), d(data_storage,cloud1), d(dashboard,cloud1)]):    0.79928029
secureApp(smartbuilding,[d(iot_controller,cloud1), d(data_storage,cloud1), d(dashboard,cloud2)]):    0.63699776
secureApp(smartbuilding,[d(iot_controller,cloud1), d(data_storage,cloud1), d(dashboard,fog3)]):    0.69114513
secureApp(smartbuilding,[d(iot_controller,cloud1), d(data_storage,fog3), d(dashboard,cloud1)]):    0.67752684
secureApp(smartbuilding,[d(iot_controller,cloud1), d(data_storage,fog3), d(dashboard,cloud2)]):    0.53996463
secureApp(smartbuilding,[d(iot_controller,cloud1), d(data_storage,fog3), d(dashboard,fog3)]):    0.66417689
secureApp(smartbuilding,[d(iot_controller,cloud2), d(data_storage,cloud1), d(dashboard,cloud1)]):    0.63757163
secureApp(smartbuilding,[d(iot_controller,cloud2), d(data_storage,cloud1), d(dashboard,cloud2)]):    0.63642441
secureApp(smartbuilding,[d(iot_controller,cloud2), d(data_storage,cloud1), d(dashboard,fog3)]):    0.55131415
secureApp(smartbuilding,[d(iot_controller,cloud2), d(data_storage,fog3), d(dashboard,cloud1)]):    0.54045108
secureApp(smartbuilding,[d(iot_controller,cloud2), d(data_storage,fog3), d(dashboard,cloud1)]):    0.67448315
secureApp(smartbuilding,[d(iot_controller,cloud2), d(data_storage,fog3), d(dashboard,fog3)]):    0.66238504
secureApp(smartbuilding,[d(iot_controller,fog2), d(data_storage,cloud1), d(dashboard,cloud1)]):    0.5827336
secureApp(smartbuilding,[d(iot_controller,fog2), d(data_storage,cloud1), d(dashboard,cloud2)]):    0.46441781
secureApp(smartbuilding,[d(iot_controller,fog2), d(data_storage,cloud1), d(dashboard,fog3)]):    0.55988355
secureApp(smartbuilding,[d(iot_controller,fog2), d(data_storage,fog3), d(dashboard,cloud1)]):    0.54885163
secureApp(smartbuilding,[d(iot_controller,fog2), d(data_storage,fog3), d(dashboard,cloud2)]):    0.54687823
secureApp(smartbuilding,[d(iot_controller,fog2), d(data_storage,fog3), d(dashboard,fog3)]):    0.67268088
secureApp(smartbuilding,[d(iot_controller,fog3), d(data_storage,cloud1), d(dashboard,cloud1)]):    0.70503715
secureApp(smartbuilding,[d(iot_controller,fog3), d(data_storage,cloud1), d(dashboard,cloud2)]):    0.56188935
secureApp(smartbuilding,[d(iot_controller,fog3), d(data_storage,cloud1), d(dashboard,fog3)]):    0.69114513
secureApp(smartbuilding,[d(iot_controller,fog3), d(data_storage,fog3), d(dashboard,cloud1)]):    0.67752684
secureApp(smartbuilding,[d(iot_controller,fog3), d(data_storage,fog3), d(dashboard,cloud2)]):    0.67509079
secureApp(smartbuilding,[d(iot_controller,fog3), d(data_storage,fog3), d(dashboard,fog3)]):    0.83038718
```

Fig. 6. Results of the motivating example.

deployment can be considered secure both according to the declared effectiveness against attacks of the infrastructure capabilities and to the trust degree of the application operator in each exploited infrastructure provider.

If the application operator is only considering security as a parameter to lead her search, she would try to maximise the obtained metric and, most probably, deploy all three components to **Fog 3**. However, security might need to be considered together with other parameters so to find a suitable trade-off among them. In the next section, we propose a simple multi-objective optimisation and we apply it to our motivating example.

5 Multi-objective Optimisation

Naturally, the quantitative results obtained with ProbLog can be used to optimise the security level of any application deployment, by simply taking the maximum value for our query. As we will show over an example in the next section, it is possible to exploit the SecFog methodology to optimise the security level together with other metrics. In this work, as in [16], given a deployment Δ, we will try to optimise the objective function

$$r(\Delta) = \sum_{m \in M} \omega_m \cdot \widehat{m(\Delta)}$$

where M is the set of metrics to be optimised, ω_m is the weight[7] assigned to each metrics (so that $\sum_{m \in M} \omega_m = 1$) and $\widehat{m(\Delta)}$ is the normalised value of metric m for deployment Δ, which – given the set D of candidate deployments – is computed as:

– $\widehat{m(\Delta)} = \frac{m(\Delta) - \min_{d \in D} \{m(d)\}}{\max_{d \in D} \{m(d)\} - \min_{d \in D} \{m(d)\}}$ when the $m(\Delta)$ is to be maximised, and

– $\widehat{m(\Delta)} = \frac{\max_{d \in D} \{m(d)\} - m(\Delta)}{\max_{d \in D} \{m(d)\} - \min_{d \in D} \{m(d)\}}$ when $m(\Delta)$ is to be minimised.

Therefore, since we assumed that the higher the value of $r(\Delta)$ the better is deployment Δ, we will choose $\overline{\Delta}$ such that $r(\overline{\Delta}) = \max_{\Delta \in D} \{r(\Delta)\}$. In what follows, we solve the motivating example by employing this optimisation technique on all attributes of Table 1 along with the security levels computed in Sect. 4.

5.1 Motivating Example Continued

In our motivating example, we will attempt to maximise QoS-assurance and security, whilst minimising cost (in which we include the cost for the 4G connection at **Fog 2** when needed). However, different application operators may want to either maximise or minimise the Fog resource consumption of their

---

[7] For the sake of simplicity, we assume here $\omega_m = \frac{1}{|M|}$, which can be tuned differently depending on the needs of the application operator.

deployment, i.e. they may look for a Fog-ward or for a Cloud-ward deployment. Hence, concerning this parameter, we will consider both situations. Table 2 shows the values of the Fog-ward (i.e., $r_F(\Delta)$) and of the Cloud-ward (i.e., $r_C(\Delta)$) objective functions.

In the Fog-ward case, when looking for the best trade-off among QoS-assurance, resource consumption, cost and security level, the most promising deployment is not $\Delta 2$ anymore (as it was in [7]). Indeed, $\Delta 3$ scores a much better ranking when compared to $\Delta 2$. Furthermore, in the Fog-ward case, the 4G upgrade at Fog 2, which makes it possible to enact $\Delta 15$ and $\Delta 16$, is not worth the investment due to the low score of both deployments. Conversely, in the Cloud-ward case (even though $\Delta 3$ would still be preferable), $\Delta 16$ features a good ranking value, despite requiring to upgrade the connection available at Fog 2.

Table 2. Ranking of eligible deployments.

Dep. ID	IoTController	DataStorage	Dashboard	$r_F(\Delta)$	$r_C(\Delta)$
$\Delta 1$	Fog 2	Fog 3	Cloud 2	0.53	0.28
$\Delta 2$	Fog 2	Fog 3	Cloud 1	0.63	0.38
$\Delta 3$	Fog 3	Fog 3	Cloud 1	0.85	0.60
$\Delta 6$	Fog 3	Fog 3	Cloud 2	0.75	0.50
$\Delta 15^*$	Fog 2	Cloud 1	Cloud 2	0.15	0.40
$\Delta 16^*$	Fog 2	Cloud 1	Cloud 1	0.51	0.76

6   Concluding Remarks

In this paper, we proposed a declarative methodology, SecFog, which can be used to assess the security level of multi-component application deployments to Fog computing infrastructures. With a proof-of-concept implementation, we have shown how SecFog helps application operators in determining secure deployments based on specific application requirements, available infrastructure capabilities, and trust degrees in different Fog and Cloud providers. We have also shown how SecFog can be used synergically with other predictive methodologies to perform multi-objective optimisation of security along with other metrics (viz., deployment cost, QoS-assurance, resource usage). In our future work we plan to:

- enhance SecFog by including a more expressive trust model, capable of describing indirect trust relations among involved stakeholders like in [4],
- evaluate the possibility to use SecFog with meta-heuristic optimisation techniques (e.g., genetic or swarm intelligence algorithms), also taming the time complexity of the generate & test approach we prototyped, and
- further engineer our ProbLog proof-of-concept implementation and show its applicability to actual use cases (e.g., based on the Fog application of [9]).

Acknowledgments. This work has been partly supported by the project *"DECLWARE: Declarative methodologies of application design and deployment"* (PRA_2018_66) funded by the University of Pisa, Italy.

References

1. OpenFog Consortium. http://www.openfogconsortium.org/
2. EU Cloud SLA Standardisation Guidelines (2014). https://ec.europa.eu/digital-single-market/en/news/cloud-service-level-agreement-standardisation-guidelines
3. Belle, V.: Logic meets probability: towards explainable AI systems for uncertain worlds. In: Proceedings of the Twenty-Sixth International Joint Conference on Artificial Intelligence, IJCAI, pp. 19–25 (2017)
4. Bistarelli, S., Martinelli, F., Santini, F.: Weighted datalog and levels of trust. In: 3rd International Conference on Availability, Reliability and Security, pp. 1128–1134 (2008)
5. Brogi, A., Forti, S.: QoS-aware deployment of IoT applications through the fog. IEEE Internet Things J. **4**(5), 1185–1192 (2017)
6. Brogi, A., Forti, S., Guerrero, C., Lera, I.: How to Place Your Apps in the Fog - State of the Art and Open Challenges. arXiv:1901.05717 [cs.DC] (2019)
7. Brogi, A., Forti, S., Ibrahim, A.: How to best deploy your Fog applications, probably. In: Rana, O., Buyya, R., Anjum, A. (eds.) Proceedings of 1st IEEE International Conference on Fog and Edge Computing (2017)
8. Brogi, A., Forti, S., Ibrahim, A.: Deploying fog applications: how much does it cost, by the way? In: Proceedings of the 8th International Conference on Cloud Computing and Services Science, pp. 68–77. SciTePress (2018)
9. Brogi, A., Forti, S., Ibrahim, A., Rinaldi, L.: Bonsai in the fog: an active learning lab with fog computing. In: 2018 Third International Conference on Fog and Mobile Edge Computing (FMEC), pp. 79–86. IEEE (2018)
10. Choo, K.K.R., Lu, R., Chen, L., Yi, X.: A foggy research future: advances and future opportunities in fog computing research (2018)
11. Dastjerdi, A.V., Buyya, R.: Fog computing: helping the internet of things realize its potential. Computer **49**(8), 112–116 (2016)
12. De Raedt, L., Kimmig, A.: Probabilistic (logic) programming concepts. Mach. Learn. **100**(1), 5–47 (2015). https://doi.org/10.1007/s10994-015-5494-z
13. De Raedt, L., Kimmig, A., Toivonen, H.: ProbLog: a probabilistic prolog and its application in link discovery. In: Proceedings of the 20th International Joint Conference on Artificial Intelligence, pp. 2468–2473 (2007)
14. Forti, S.: Supporting application deployment and management in fog computing. Papers From the 12th Advanced Summer School on Service-Oriented Computing (SummerSOC 2018), pp. 64–75 (2018)
15. Goettelmann, E., Dahman, K., Gateau, B., Dubois, E., Godart, C.: A security risk assessment model for business process deployment in the cloud. In: 2014 IEEE International Conference on Services Computing, pp. 307–314. IEEE (2014)
16. Guerrero, C., Lera, I., Juiz, C.: Resource optimization of container orchestration: a case study in multi-cloud microservices-based applications. J. Supercomput. **74**(7), 2956–2983 (2018)
17. Guerrero, C., Lera, I., Juiz, C.: A lightweight decentralized service placement policy for performance optimization in fog computing. J. Ambient. Intell. Hum. Comput. (2018)

18. Gupta, H., Vahid Dastjerdi, A., Ghosh, S.K., Buyya, R.: iFogSim: a toolkit for modeling and simulation of resource management techniques in the Internet of Things, edge and fog computing environments. Softw. Pract. Exp. **47**(9), 1275–1296 (2017)
19. Arkian, H.R., Diyanat, A., Pourkhalili, A.: MIST: fog-based data analytics scheme with cost-efficient resource provisioning for IoT crowdsensing applications. J. Netw. Comput. Appl. **82**, 152–165 (2017)
20. Hong, H.J., Tsai, P.H., Hsu, C.H.: Dynamic module deployment in a fog computing platform. In: 2016 18th Asia-Pacific Network Operations and Management Symposium (APNOMS), pp. 1–6 (2016)
21. Kaur, A., Singh, M., Singh, P., et al.: A taxonomy, survey on placement of virtual machines in cloud. In: 2017 International Conference on Energy, Communication, Data Analytics and Soft Computing (ICECDS), pp. 2054–2058. IEEE (2017)
22. Luna, J., Taha, A., Trapero, R., Suri, N.: Quantitative reasoning about cloud security using service level agreements. IEEE Trans. Cloud Comput. **5**(3), 457–471 (2017)
23. Mahmud, R., Ramamohanarao, K., Buyya, R.: Latency-aware application module management for fog computing environments. Trans. Internet Technol. **19**, 1–21 (2018)
24. Mezni, H., Sellami, M., Kouki, J.: Security-aware SaaS placement using swarm intelligence. J. Softw. Evol. Process. **30**(8), e1932 (2018)
25. Mukherjee, M., et al.: Security and privacy in fog computing: challenges. IEEE Access **5**, 19293–19304 (2017)
26. Nacer, A.A., Goettelmann, E., Youcef, S., Tari, A., Godart, C.: Obfuscating a business process by splitting its logic with fake fragments for securing a multi-cloud deployment. In: 2016 IEEE World Congress on Services (SERVICES), pp. 18–25. IEEE (2016)
27. Newman, S.: Building microservices: designing fine-grained systems. O'Reilly Media Inc., Sebastopol (2015)
28. Ni, J., Zhang, K., Lin, X., Shen, X.: Securing fog computing for internet of things applications: challenges and solutions. IEEE Comm. Surv. Tutor. **20**, 601–628 (2017)
29. OpenFog: OpenFog Reference Architecture (2016)
30. Rahbari, D., Nickray, M.: Scheduling of fog networks with optimized knapsack by symbiotic organisms search. In: 2017 21st Conference of Open Innovations Association (FRUCT), pp. 278–283 (2017)
31. Rodríguez, M.A., Egenhofer, M.J.: Determining semantic similarity among entity classes from different ontologies. Trans. Knowl. Data Eng. **15**(2), 442–456 (2003)
32. Schoenen, S., Mann, Z.Á., Metzger, A.: Using risk patterns to identify violations of data protection policies in cloud systems. In: Braubach, L., Murillo, J.M., Kaviani, N., Lama, M., Burgueño, L., Moha, N., Oriol, M. (eds.) ICSOC 2017. LNCS, vol. 10797, pp. 296–307. Springer, Cham (2018). https://doi.org/10.1007/978-3-319-91764-1_24
33. Skarlat, O., Nardelli, M., Schulte, S., Dustdar, S.: Towards QoS-aware fog service placement. In: 2017 IEEE 1st International Conference on Fog and Edge Computing (ICFEC), pp. 89–96 (2017)
34. Soldani, J., Tamburri, D.A., Van Den Heuvel, W.J.: The pains and gains of microservices: a systematic grey literature review. J. Syst. Softw. **146**, 215–232 (2018)

35. Taneja, M., Davy, A.: Resource aware placement of IoT application modules in fog-cloud computing paradigm. In: 2017 IFIP/IEEE Symposium on Integrated Network and Service Management (IM), pp. 1222–1228 (2017)
36. Tang, Z., Zhou, X., Zhang, F., Jia, W., Zhao, W.: Migration modeling and learning algorithms for containers in fog computing. Trans. Serv. Comput. **12**, 712–725 (2018)
37. Varshney, P., Simmhan, Y.: Demystifying fog computing: characterizing architectures, applications and abstractions. In: 2017 IEEE 1st International Conference on Fog and Edge Computing (ICFEC), pp. 115–124 (2017)
38. Wang, S., Zafer, M., Leung, K.K.: Online placement of multi-component applications in edge computing environments. IEEE Access **5**, 2514–2533 (2017)
39. Wen, Z., Yang, R., Garraghan, P., Lin, T., Xu, J., Rovatsos, M.: Fog orchestration for Internet of Things services. IEEE Internet Comput. **21**(2), 16–24 (2017)
40. Wen, Z., Cała, J., Watson, P., Romanovsky, A.: Cost effective, reliable and secure workflow deployment over federated clouds. Trans. Serv. Comput. **10**(6), 929–941 (2017)
41. Zhang, P., Zhou, M., Fortino, G.: Security and trust issues in fog computing: a survey. Futur. Gener. Comput. Syst. **88**, 16–27 (2018)

14th International Workshop on Engineering Service-Oriented Applications and Cloud Services

WESOACS 2018 Preface

The International Workshop on Engineering Services-Oriented Applications and Cloud Services (WESOACS) is a long-established forum (formerly known as WESOA) for innovative ideas from research and practice in the field of software engineering for modern service-oriented application systems. This year, the 14th meeting took place on September 12 in Como, Italy.

Service-oriented applications play an important role in many diverse areas, from cloud/edge computing to Web/enterprise applications. While there is agreement on the main principles for designing, developing, and deploying applications based on distributed software services, methods, and tools that support the development of such applications are still the subject of intense research. These research topics include lifecycle management, development methodologies, enterprise architectures, analysis and design, and in particular service engineering technologies for cloud computing environments in general, and more specifically for edge/fog-based applications and intelligent cyber-physical systems. Additionally, the DevOps approach that inextricably links software service development and operations and involves agile processes, microservices, continuous delivery, containers, and cloud technologies is an important part of the current transformation of IT.

The WESOACS technical program included five research papers and one invited presentation, organized in three sessions. Professor Elisabetta Di Nitto opened the workshop with her invited presentation titled "An Overview on DevOps and Infrastructure-as-Code." The first paper in the technical program ("Towards a Generalizable Comparison of the Maintainability of Object-Oriented and Service-Oriented Applications") discusses the differences between object and service orientation, notes the lack of empirical research on this topic, and details the results of a study conducted by the authors.

The second paper ("Implementation of a Cloud Services Management Framework") describes the implementation of a Service Consumer Framework (SCF) for the management of design-time and runtime activities of enterprise applications that use externally provided cloud services. The third paper ("Decentralized Billing and Subcontracting of Application Services for Cloud Environment Providers") proposes a decentralized billing and subcontracting system for regional cloud service providers, based on blockchain technology that allows to collectively offer services in a distributed environment and to bill each user of the service individually without a central service.

The fourth paper ("May Contain Nuts: The Case for API Labels") addresses the challenge of managing and describing APIs. The paper presents the vision of standardized API labels, which summarize and represent critical aspects of APIs, as a means to ease API management. Finally, the fifth paper ("On Limitations of Abstraction-Based Deadlock-Analysis of Service-Oriented Systems") proposes an approach based on Mayr's Process Rewrite Systems to model both concurrent and stack behaviors of concurrent service-oriented systems and keep the deadlock problem decidable.

The participants had ample opportunity for professional exchange and networking, so that the 14th edition of the event can once again be regarded as a success.

We wish to thank all authors for their contributions, the Program Committee members for their hard work, and the ESOCC 2018 workshop chairs for their help makethings work.

March 2020

Andreas S. Andreou
Luciano Baresi
George Feuerlicht
Winfried Lamersdorf
Guadalupe Ortiz
Willem-Jan van den Heuvel
Christian Zirpins

WESOACS 2018 Organization

Workshop Organizers

Andreas S. Andreou	Cyprus University of Technology, Cyprus
Luciano Baresi	Politecnico di Milano, Italy
George Feuerlicht	Prague University of Economics and Business, Czech Republic
Winfried Lamersdorf	University of Hamburg, Germany
Guadalupe Ortiz	University of Cádiz, Spain
Willem-Jan van den Heuvel	Tilburg University, The Netherlands
Christian Zirpins	Karlsruhe University of Applied Sciences, Germany

Program Committee

Mike Papazoglou	University of Tilburg, The Netherlands
Ioannis Stamelos	Aristotle University of Thessaloniki, Greece
Elisabetta di Nitto	Politecnico di Milano, Italy
Danilo Ardagna	Politecnico di Milano, Italy
Sam Jesus Guinea	Politecnico di Milano, Italy
George Pallis	University of Cyprus, Cyprus
Patricia Lago	University of Amsterdam, The Netherlands
Herodotos Herodotou	Cyprus University of Technology, Cyprus
Sotirios P. Chatzis	Cyprus University of Technology, Cyprus
Efi Papatheocharous	SICS, Sweden
Spyros Likothanassis	University of Patras, Greece
Efstratios Georgopoulos	TEI of Kalamata, Greece
Georgios J. Fakas	Uppsala University, Sweden
Chi-Hung Chi	CSIRO, Australia
Frank Leymann	University of Stuttgart, Germany

Implementation of a Cloud Services Management Framework

Hong Thai Tran[1] and George Feuerlicht[1,2,3(✉)]

[1] Faculty of Engineering and Information Technology, University of Technology Sydney,
Sydney, Australia
{HongThai.Tran,George.Feuerlicht}@uts.edu.au
[2] Unicorn College, V Kapslovně 2767/2, 130 00 Prague 3, Czech Republic
[3] Prague University of Economics, W. Churchill Square. 4, 130 67 Prague 3, Czech Republic

Abstract. Rapid growth of various types of cloud services is creating new opportunities for innovative enterprise applications. As a result, enterprise applications are increasingly reliant on externally provided cloud services. It can be argued that traditional systems development methods and tools are not adequate in the context of cloud services and that new methods and frameworks that support these methods are needed for management of lifecycle of cloud services. In this paper, we describe the implementation of a Service Consumer Framework (SCF) – a framework for the management of design-time and runtime activities throughout the lifecycle of enterprise applications that use externally provided cloud services. The SCF framework has been evaluated during the implementation of a large-scale project and is being continuously improved to incorporate additional types of cloud services.

Keywords: Cloud computing · Service management · Frameworks

1 Introduction

Most enterprise applications today use third party cloud services to implement a significant part of their functionality. This results in hybrid environments that require the integration of on-premises services with public cloud services made available on a pay-per-use basis by external cloud providers. The use of third party cloud services (e.g. payment services, storage services, etc.) in enterprise applications has many benefits, but at the same time presents challenges as both the functional and non-functional characteristics of cloud services are controlled by autonomous cloud service providers. Service consumers are primarily responsible for the selection of services, integration of cloud services into on-premises enterprise applications and managing continuity of operation during runtime. With the increasing use of cloud services, it is important that cloud service consumers use suitable methods and tools to manage the entire lifecycle of enterprise applications [1]. A comprehensive framework is needed to support all phases of service consumer lifecycle including the selection of cloud services, integration of services with enterprise applications and runtime monitoring and management of services.

© Springer Nature Switzerland AG 2020
M. Fazio and W. Zimmermann (Eds.): ESOCC 2018 Workshops, CCIS 1115, pp. 67–78, 2020.
https://doi.org/10.1007/978-3-030-63161-1_5

Cloud services management has been an active area of research with numerous publications addressing different cloud service lifecycle phases, in particular cloud service selection [2–7] and service integration and monitoring [8–11]. However, most of these research efforts take service provider perspective and do not address the issues that arise when on-premises enterprise applications consume externally provided cloud services. A typical scenario illustrating this situation involves an on-premises application that consumes a range of cloud services (e.g. payment services: PayPal and eWay, storage services: DropBox, Google Drive and AWS S3, mapping services: Google Maps, etc.) via published APIs (Application Programming Interfaces) [12]. Management of such heterogeneous environments requires both design-time and run-time support to minimize the software maintenance effort and to ensure continuity of operation.

The main motivation for our research is to provide a detail description of the service development lifecycle as it applies to cloud service consumers (as distinct from cloud service providers) and to implement a prototype framework that supports this lifecycle. In our previous work we have proposed a Service Consumer Framework (SCF) [13] and described a cloud Service Consumer System Development Lifecycle (SC-SDLC) [14] for managing cloud services from a service consumer perspective. In this paper, we describe how the SCF supports design-time and run-time activities throughout the SC-SDLC (Sect. 3), and detail the implementation of this framework (Sect. 4). In the next section (Sect. 2), we review related work on the methods and frameworks for the management of cloud services. Section 5 are our conclusions and directions for future work.

2   Related Work

While the management of cloud services in enterprise applications is still a subject of extensive investigation, there is a general agreement in the literature about the individual lifecycle phases. A method for managing integrated lifecycle of cloud services was proposed by Joshi et al. [15]. The authors have identified performance metrics associated with each lifecycle phase that include data quality, cost, and security metrics based on SLA (Service Level Agreement) and consumer satisfaction, and they have proposed a service repository with a discovery capability for managing cloud services lifecycle [16]. The authors divide cloud services lifecycle into five phases: requirements specification, discovery, negotiation, composition, and consumption. During the service discovery phase, service consumers search for services using service description and provider policies in a simple services database. Service information is stored as a Request for Service (RFS) that contains functional specifications, technical specifications, human agent policy, security policy and data quality policy. Field et al. [17] present a European Middleware Initiative (EMI) Registry that uses a decentralized architecture to support service discovery for both hierarchical and peering topologies. The objective of the EMI Registry is to provide robust and scalable service discovery that contains two components: Domain Service Registry (DSR) and Global Service Registry (GSR). Service discovery is based on service information stored in service records that contain mandatory attributes such as service name, type of service, service endpoint, service interface, and service expiry date.

Cloud-based application development frameworks and architectures have been the subject of intense recent interest in the context of microservices and DevOps [18, 19]. According to Rimal et al. [20] the most important current challenge is the lack of a standard architectural approach for cloud computing. The authors explore and classify architectural characteristics of cloud computing and identify several architectural features that play a major role in the adoption of cloud computing. The paper provides guidelines for software architects for developing cloud architectures. Another notable effort in this area is the Seaclouds project [21, 22] that aims to develop a new open source framework for Seamless Adaptive Multi-Cloud management of service-based applications. The authors argue that lack of standardization results in vendor lock-in that affects all stages of the cloud applications' lifecycle, forcing application developers to have a deep knowledge of the providers' APIs. Seaclouds is a software platform and a reference architecture designed to address the heterogeneity of cloud service APIs at IaaS (Infrastructure as a Service) and SaaS (service as a Service) levels. The Seaclouds platform supports Discovery and Matchmaking, Cloud Service Optimization, Application Management, Monitoring and SLA Enforcement, and Application Migration. The authors of the Nucleous project [23] have investigated the practicability of abstracting the differences of vendor specific deployment and management APIs and creating an intermediary abstraction layer based on four selected PaaS platforms (cloudControl, Cloud Foundry, Heroku, and OpenShift), and concluded that the diversities among the platforms can be successfully harmonized. Using the Nucleous platform the effort involved in switching providers can be minimized, increasing the portability and interoperability of PaaS applications, helping to avoid critical vendor lock-in.

Unlike the above-mentioned initiatives, we do not aim to implement a framework for multi-cloud deployment, monitoring and orchestration of cloud services across multiple cloud platforms. Our focus is on designing a framework that improves the manageability and reliability of enterprise applications that consume cloud services from different providers with varied QoS (Quality of Service) characteristics.

3 Service Consumer Framework and SC-SDLC

Service Consumer Framework is a research prototype designed for the purpose of evaluating the functionality required for supporting the SC-SDLC. SCF constitutes a layer between on-premises enterprise applications and external cloud services and consists of four main components: Service Repository, Service Adaptors, Workflow Engine and Monitoring Centre. The service repository records information about enterprise applications and related cloud services throughout the entire service lifecycle. The service adaptor module contains adaptors for various categories of services. The function of a service adaptor is to present a unified API for services from different cloud providers for the same type of service (e.g. a payment service), transforming outgoing application requests into the format supported by the current version of the corresponding external service, and incoming responses into format compatible with on-premises applications. The main function of the workflow engine is to provide failover capability in the event of a cloud service not being available by routing application requests to an alternative cloud service. The monitoring centre uses log data collected from service adaptors and the workflow engine to monitor cloud services and to analyze their runtime performance.

We have described the SC-SDLC in previous publications [24, 25]; in this section we briefly describe the main SC-SDLC lifecycle phases and discuss how the Service Consumer Framework supports activities during these phases. We have identified the following five phases of SC-SDLC: Requirements Specification, Service Identification, Service Integration, Service Monitoring and Service Optimization. We classify these phases into design-time activities: requirements specification, service identification and service integration, and run-time activities: service monitoring and service optimization. Typically, business analysts are involved with the requirements specification phase, while service identification, integration and optimization phases are the domain of application developers. Service monitoring phase is the responsibility of system administrators.

The SC-SDLC is closely interrelated with the Service Consumer Framework that provides support for lifecycle phases and activities. Figure 1 illustrates how the Service Consumer SDLC is supported by the Service Consumer Framework.

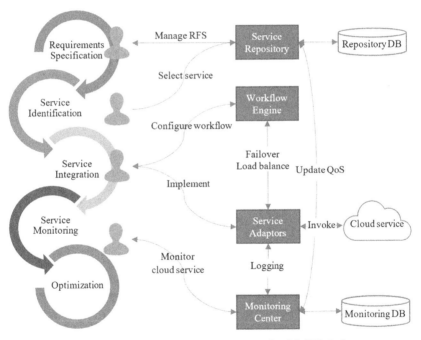

Fig. 1. Service consumer framework support for SC-SDLC phases

During the service requirements specification phase, business analysts record functional and non-functional requirements of the services in the service repository. Functional specification of the service describes what functions the service should provide and its characteristics may vary according to the type of service (i.e. application service, infrastructure service, etc.). The QoS (Quality of Service) non-functional attributes include service availability, response time, security requirements, and may also include requirements such as data location and the maximum cost of the service. Once the service is fully described and classified, the service consumer creates a Request for Service

(RFS) and records this information in the service repository. Services are categorized according to service type (e.g. payment, storage, mapping, etc.) and this information is used during the service identification phase to search the service repository.

The service identification phase involves searching the service repository for services that match the RFS attempting to identify an existing service that is already certified for use (e.g. payment service with availability of 99.99 and sub-second response time). The SCF incorporates an API that supports a repository query function (described in Sect. 4.1) that searches the service repository database for suitable candidate services. Service repository database stores detail information that includes service features available in different versions (i.e. functional description of the service) as well as non-functional parameters, including service reliability information recorded during runtime. Service repository can be searched based on various parameters to identify candidate services that are then checked for compatibility with the service specifications. If no suitable certified service is found, the service consumer will attempt to identify the service from the services available from external cloud providers. Following verification of the functionality and performance, the service is certified and recorded in the service repository. Certification involves extensive testing of the functionality and performance of the service. If no suitable cloud service is found, the service may have to be developed internally (i.e. as an on-premises service).

The service integration phase involves the integration of cloud services with on-premises enterprise applications. This activity varies depending on the type of cloud service and may involve the development of a service adaptor and design of specialized workflows to improve the reliability of applications by incorporating failover capability. The SCF repository records the relationships between services (service versions) and corresponding enterprise applications. The final activity of the cloud service integration phase comprises integration testing, provisioning, and deployment, similar to activities during the implementation of on-premises application.

The service monitoring phase involves measuring runtime QoS attributes and comparing their values with those specified in the corresponding SLA. System administrators use the monitoring centre to identify performance issues. Local monitoring is required as QoS values measured at the consumer site may differ from the values published by cloud service providers. Data generated during the monitoring phase is stored in the monitoring database.

The final SC-SDLC phase is concerned with service optimization and continuous service improvement. Service optimization may involve replacing existing services with new versions as these become available, or by identifying alternative cloud services from a different provider with improved QoS characteristics.

4   SCF Implementation

This section describes the implementation details of the components of the SCF framework. Additional implementation details are available in [26] and the SCF source code has been published on GitHub (https://github.com/tranhongthai/SCF). The SCF prototype is developed using .Net technologies: Microsoft SQL Server [27] was used to implement the service repository and monitoring center databases, ASP.Net MVC 5

[28] was used to build the service repository and the service monitoring center tools, and Windows Communication Foundation (WCF) [29] was used to implement service repository and monitoring centre APIs. The SCF is deployed on an AWS (Amazon Web Services) EC2 server and the databases are implemented as AWS RDS (Relational Database System) services. The workflow engine and service adaptors are implemented as Class Libraries (DLL) in C# programming language and released using NuGet - Microsoft package manager for .NET (https://www.nuget.org/packages). Table 1 lists the main SCF modules, technologies used for their implementation and deployment platforms.

Table 1. SCF implementation technologies and deployment platforms

SCF modules	Implementation technology	Deployment platform
Service repository	ASP.NET MVC Microsoft SQL Server	AWS EC2 AWS RDS
Service adaptors	Class Library (.DDL)	Nuget
Workflow engine	Class Library (.DDL)	Nuget
Monitoring center	Windows service application Microsoft SQL Server Window foundation communication	AWS EC2 AWS RDS

4.1 Service Repository

Service repository is a key component of SCF framework that maintains information about cloud services throughout the entire service lifecycle. A simplified data model (Entity-Relationship Diagram) of the service repository is shown in Fig. 2. *Service* is a central entity of the service repository with attributes that describe services and include service requirements as captured by the SLA. In order to manage service evolution and keep track of changes in service functionality, information about service versions is stored in the repository. The *ServiceVersion* entity includes functional and non-functional descriptors of the service that are further described by the information in the related *QoS* and *ServiceFeature* entities. This allows service versions to have different QoS values and features. *ServiceCategory* is used to categorize services according to their type (e.g. payment, storage, etc.); the self-referencing relationship produces a service type hierarchy, so that for example, a storage service constitutes a subtype of an infrastructure service. *ServiceProvider* entity represents service providers and contains service provider attributes including provider description and provider ranking (indication of provider reputation). The *Application* entity represents on-premises applications that are associated with requirements specifications (*Specification*) that are matched with services (ServiceVersion) based on the compatibility of functional and non-functional attribute values. Results of service invocations are logged at runtime, and are represented by the *Log* entity. Service log records include response time, results of service invocations, and other non-functional attributes collected at run-time and used for analysis of service performance. Responsibility for managing services is assigned to system administrators and represented by the *Administrators* entity.

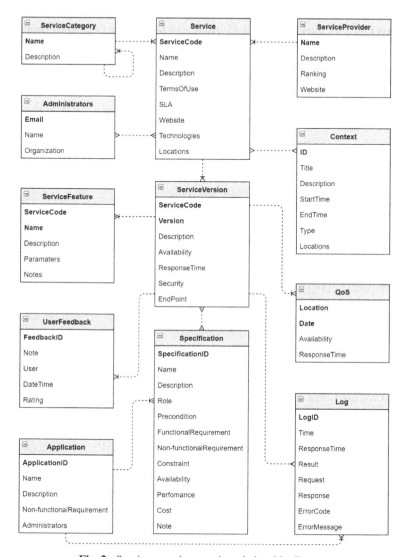

Fig. 2. Service repository entity relationship diagram

Service Repository Interface
Service repository APIs are implemented using WCF and provide access to repository information. The following methods have been implemented:

- **Search:** this method is used to query the service repository database and to retrieve services based on the specified values of QoS parameters (e.g. service type, availability, response time, etc.)
- **GetInfo:** this method retrieves information about a specific cloud service, including basic service description and QoS information
- **UpdateQoS:** this method is used to insert and update the QoS information for a specified cloud service

4.2 Service Adaptors

Service adaptors implement generic interfaces for different types of services (e.g. a payment service) that support common service functions (e.g. payment, refund, etc.). This allows runtime substitution of cloud services and can improve the overall reliability of enterprise applications. At design time, cloud services can be replaced by alternative services with improved QoS characteristics, as these become available. The main function of a service adaptor is to transform application requests into the format supported by the current version of the corresponding external service, and to ensure that incoming responses maintain compatibility with internal applications. Generic messages and methods that support common service functions are defined for each service type and mapped into the corresponding messages and methods of specific cloud provider services. So that for example, the Dropbox adaptor transforms the generic *Download* request into the Dropbox *DownloadAsync* request, and the Google Drive Adaptor transforms this request into *GetByteArrayAsync* request. The use of service adaptors across all enterprise applications alleviates the need to modify individual applications when a new version of the cloud service API is released. Another function of service adaptors is to perform runtime logging of performance parameters that are used to calculate QoS attributes.

Service Adaptor Library

The Service Adaptor Library contains generic APIs that include methods for various types of services. For example, a generic payment service interface contains three common methods: Pay, Refund, and CheckBalance that use generic messages (PaymentRequest, PaymentResponse, RefundRequest, RefundResponse, etc.). Service adaptors inherit the generic interface and implement the body of the methods. The Service Adaptor Library currently contains adaptors for PayPal, eWay, Stripe payment services, and Dropbox and GoogleDrive storage services. We intent to expand the range of adaptors, but at the same time we recognize that this may not be a workable solution in situations where the functionality of services from different cloud providers is significantly different.

4.3 Workflow Engine

The purpose of the workflow engine is to implement simple workflows using a combination of adaptors and pre-defined sub-workflows (i.e. workflow fragments that implement a specific function, e.g. the Retry Fault Tolerance reliability strategy). The SCF workflow engine it is not intended to replicate a fully-functional orchestration engine (e.g.

BPEL engine). The workflow engine determines the sequence of service invocations for a given application requirement, and is typically used to configure adaptors to provide failover function using various fault tolerance strategies. We have demonstrated, using payment services PayPal and eWay, that relatively simple fault tolerance strategies such as Retry Fault Tolerance, Recovery Block Fault Tolerance or Dynamic Sequential Fault Tolerance strategy can lead to significant improvements in application availability [30]. Figure 3 shows an example of a workflow that uses Dropbox and Google Drive as alternative storage systems. During normal operation, the data is replicated across both storage systems. The workflow engine switches between the storage systems to maintain continuity of operation in the event of a single storage system failure; on recovery, the storage systems are re-synchronized.

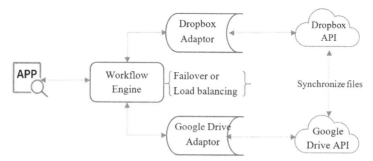

Fig. 3. Example of a fault tolerant cloud storage workflow

Workflow Engine Library

Workflow Engine is a class library developed using the C# programming language. A workflow can contain a sequence of service adaptors and sub-workflows (pre-configured workflows, e.g. Retry Fault Tolerance strategy for payment services). When executing a workflow, adaptors and sub-workflows invoke individual cloud services in a pre-defined sequence.

4.4 Monitoring Center

The function of the monitoring centre is to monitor the runtime performance of cloud services and to calculate QoS values that are used for optimizing applications. The Monitoring Centre provides three basic functions:

- **Recording log data:** This function collects service log data from enterprise applications. The *Log Collector* is invoked by service adaptors or by enterprise applications and records log data in the monitoring database. At the same time, alerts are generated that indicate fault conditions and departures from the expected QoS values.
- **QoS calculation:** This function calculates the response time and availability of cloud services using recorded log data. The resulting QoS values can be used for cloud service selection during the service identification phase.

- **Cloud service monitoring:** The availability and runtime performance of cloud services is compared to the expected QoS values as specified in the RFS.

The monitoring centre consists of *Monitoring Centre Database, Log Collector, QoS Analysis* and *Service Monitor* modules. The monitoring centre database is implemented using Microsoft SQL server and stores log records generated by service invocations. The log records include the service identifier (ServiceCode) and the application identifier (ApplicationID) of the enterprise application that executed the API call, service execution start (StartTime) and end times (EndTime), result of the call (i.e. success/failure) and error codes generated by the adaptor. Service adaptors record the runtime logs in the monitoring database using the log collector module. Whenever the log collector detects a service failure, the monitoring centre sends a notification to the relevant system administrators. The log data is used to generate hourly, daily and monthly reports of average availability and response time for individual cloud services. The QoS analysis module developed using C# programming language is deployed on a AWS EC2 server and configured to execute as a Window Service. The service monitor module is developed using ASP.Net MVC 5 and is deployed as a client tool for monitoring the cloud services. The service monitor module displays the runtime QoS information for individual cloud services and compares these values with the QoS values defined in the requirements specification.

5   Conclusions

We have argued that traditional systems development methods and tools are not adequate in the context of cloud services, and that a new approach that supports cloud service consumer lifecycle activities is required. In our earlier work, we have proposed a Service Consumer System Development Lifecycle (SC-SDLC) that focuses on the activities of cloud service consumers. In this paper, we describe implementation of the Service Consumer Framework (SCF) that supports design and runtime activities throughout the SC-SDLC phases. SCF is a research prototype intended to evaluate the feasibility of a relatively *light-weight* solution suitable for SMEs (Small and Medium size Enterprises) that are in the process of developing enterprise applications that consume externally provided cloud services. We have evaluated the implementation of several fault tolerant strategies (RFT, RBFT and DSFT) and found that the experimental results obtained using the SCF are consistent with theoretical predictions, indicating significant improvements in service availability when compared to invoking cloud services directly [30]. Both the SC-SDLC and SCF have been evaluated during the development of a Hospital Management application for Family Medical Practice (https://www.vietnammedicalpractice.com/), a leading international primary health care provider in Vietnam [26]. We have received positive feedback indicating that the SC-SDLC method guided developers throughout the project and SCF framework provided a suitable tool for recording information about cloud services and the various SC-SDLC phases, leading to an improvement in overall productivity. Additionally, the cross-provider failover capability implemented using the workflow engine, and monitoring center features were regarded as having potential to significantly reduce outages and improve application availability. Areas of potential future improvement include the definition of guiding principles and documentation of best practices for each SC-SDLC phase.

References

1. Rehman, Z.-U., Hussain, O.K., Hussain, F.K.: User-side cloud service management: state-of-the-art and future directions. J. Netw. Comput. Appl. **55**, 108–122 (2015)
2. Arun, S., Chandrasekaran, A., Prakash, P.: CSIS: cloud service identification system. Int. J. Electr. Comput. Eng. (IJECE) **7**(1), 513–520 (2017)
3. Ghamry, A.M., Alkalbani, A.M., Tran, V., Tsai, Y.-C., Hoang, M.L., Hussain, F.K.: Towards a public cloud services registry. In: Bouguettaya, A., et al. (eds.) WISE 2017. LNCS, vol. 10569, pp. 290–295. Springer, Cham (2017). https://doi.org/10.1007/978-3-319-68783-4_20
4. Hajlaoui, J.E., et al.: QoS based framework for configurable IaaS cloud services discovery. In: 2017 IEEE International Conference on Web Services (ICWS). IEEE (2017)
5. Rotem, R., Zelovich, A., Friedrich, G.: Cloud services discovery and monitoring. Google Patents (2016)
6. Yang, K., et al.: Model-based service discovery—prototyping experience of an OSS scenario. BT Technol. J. **24**(2), 145–150 (2006)
7. Zisman, A., et al.: Proactive and reactive runtime service discovery: a framework and its evaluation. IEEE Trans. Softw. Eng. **39**(7), 954–974 (2013)
8. Ciuffoletti, A.: Application level interface for a cloud monitoring service. Comput. Stand. Interfaces **46**, 15–22 (2016)
9. Qu, L., et al.: Context-aware cloud service selection based on comparison and aggregation of user subjective assessment and objective performance assessment. In: 2014 IEEE International Conference on Web Services (ICWS). IEEE (2014)
10. Qu, L., Wang, Y., Orgun, M.A.: Cloud service selection based on the aggregation of user feedback and quantitative performance assessment. In: 2013 IEEE International Conference on Services Computing (SCC). IEEE (2013)
11. Montes, J., et al.: GMonE: a complete approach to cloud monitoring. Futur. Gener. Comput. Syst. **29**(8), 2026–2040 (2013)
12. ProgrammableWeb. ProgrammableWeb - API Directory (2018). https://www.programmable web.com/. Accessed 20 July 2018
13. Feuerlicht, G., Tran, H.T.: Service consumer framework. In: Proceedings of the 16th International Conference on Enterprise Information Systems-Volume 2 (2014). SCITEPRESS-Science and Technology Publications, Lda
14. Tran, H.T., Feuerlicht, G.: Service development life cycle for hybrid cloud environments. J. Softw. (2016)
15. Joshi, K., et. al.: Integrated lifecycle of IT services in a cloud environment. In: Proceedings of The Third International Conference on the Virtual Computing Initiative (ICVCI 2009), Research Triangle Park, NC (2009)
16. Joshi, K.P., Yesha, Y., Finin, T.: Automating cloud services life cycle through semantic technologies. IEEE Trans. Serv. Comput. **7**(1), 109–122 (2014)
17. Field, L., et al.: The EMI registry: discovering services in a federated world. J. Grid Comput. **12**(1), 29–40 (2014)
18. Mahmood, Z., Saeed, S.: Software Engineering Frameworks for the Cloud Computing Paradigm. Springer, London (2013). https://doi.org/10.1007/978-1-4471-5031-2
19. Thönes, J.: Microservices. IEEE Softw. **32**(1), 116–116 (2015)
20. Rimal, B.P., et al.: Architectural requirements for cloud computing systems: an enterprise cloud approach. J. Grid Comput. **9**(1), 3–26 (2011)
21. Brogi, A., et al.: SeaClouds: a European project on seamless management of multi-cloud applications. ACM SIGSOFT Softw. Eng. Notes **39**(1), 1–4 (2014)
22. Brogi, A., et al.: SeaClouds: an open reference architecture for multi-cloud governance. In: Tekinerdogan, B., Zdun, U., Babar, A. (eds.) ECSA 2016. LNCS, vol. 9839, pp. 334–338. Springer, Cham (2016). https://doi.org/10.1007/978-3-319-48992-6_25

23. Kolb, S., Röck, C.: Nucleus-unified deployment and management for platform as a service (2016)
24. Feuerlicht, G., Thai Tran, H.: Adapting service development life-cycle for cloud. In: Proceedings of the 17th International Conference on Enterprise Information Systems-Volume 3 (2015). SCITEPRESS-Science and Technology Publications, Lda
25. Tran, H.T., Feuerlicht, G.: Service development life cycle for hybrid cloud environments. JSW 11(7), 704–711 (2016)
26. Tran, H.T.: A framework for management of cloud services (2017). University of Technology Sydney
27. SQL Server 2017 on Windows and Linux | Microsoft. https://www.microsoft.com/en-au/sql-server/sql-server-2017. Accessed 20 July 2018
28. Anderson, R.: ASP.NET MVC 5 (2018). https://docs.microsoft.com/en-us/aspnet/mvc/mvc5. Accessed 20 July 2018
29. Windows Communication Foundation (2018). https://docs.microsoft.com/en-us/dotnet/framework/wcf/. Accessed 20 July 2018
30. Tran, H.T., Feuerlicht, G.: Improving reliability of cloud-based applications. In: Aiello, M., Johnsen, E.B., Dustdar, S., Georgievski, I. (eds.) ESOCC 2016. LNCS, vol. 9846, pp. 235–247. Springer, Cham (2016). https://doi.org/10.1007/978-3-319-44482-6_15

On Limitations of Abstraction-Based Deadlock-Analysis of Service-Oriented Systems

Mandy Weißbach$^{(\boxtimes)}$ and Wolf Zimmermann

Institute of Computer Science, Martin Luther University Halle-Wittenberg,
Von-Seckendorff-Platz 1, 06120 Halle, Germany
{mandy.weissbach,wolf.zimmermann}@informatik.uni-halle.de

Abstract. Deadlock-analysis of concurrent service-oriented systems is often done by P/T-net-based approaches. We show that there is a concurrent service-oriented system with synchronous (stack behavior) and asynchronous procedure (concurrent behavior) calls with a deadlock that is not discovered by classical P/T-net-based approaches. Hence, P/T-net-based approaches lead to false statements on absence of deadlocks. We propose an approach based on Mayr's Process Rewrite Systems to model both, concurrent and stack behavior while the deadlock problem remains decidable.

Keywords: Deadlock-analysis · Concurrency · Petri Net abstraction · Service-oriented system

1 Introduction

Van der Aalst's workflow nets is a P/T (place/transition)-net-based approach for checking soundness properties, i.e., the absence of deadlocks or livelocks of business process workflows and their (de)composition [10]. This approach is refinement-based, i.e., the workflow nets are refined to an implementation. The approach might be well-suited for an initial implementation but it is well-known that maintaining the consistency of the model and the corresponding implementation requires disciplined programmers. Hence, it is not uncommon that the model for a service and its implementation becomes more and more inconsistent. Furthermore, there exists certainly many services that are not implemented as a refinement of workflow nets. This does not mean that the approach using workflow nets as a tool for checking soundness property is superfluous, if it is used in the other direction: abstract an implementation to P/T-net and check the abstracted P/T-net for absence of deadlocks.

Since P/T-nets are unable to model stack behavior, any P/T-net-based abstraction of an implementation including stack behavior (recursive procedure calls) can not capture this behavior. In [13] it was shown that finite-state approaches for protocol conformance checking may lead to false positives if recursion is allowed, i.e., the approach reports the absence of protocol conformance

© Springer Nature Switzerland AG 2020
M. Fazio and W. Zimmermann (Eds.): ESOCC 2018 Workshops, CCIS 1115, pp. 79–90, 2020.
https://doi.org/10.1007/978-3-030-63161-1_6

violations while the real behavior produces one. In [5] we have shown that using Mayr's Process Rewrite Systems (PRSs), the concurrent and recursive behavior can be modeled adequately, i.e., false positives can not occur. [1] shows that this PRS-based abstraction can also be made compositional and is therefore as appropriate for service compositions as P/T-nets. In this paper, we answer the question whether a similar situation occurs for deadlock analysis using workflow nets (and composing them to P/T-nets).

It turns out that we have a similar phenomenon as for protocol conformance checking:

> There is a service-oriented system S with a deadlock where the abstraction of its services to workflow nets and their composition leads to a deadlock-free P/T-net.

Thus, if van der Aalst's workflow nets are used to model the behavior of services, it may lead to false statements on the absence of deadlocks.

Section 2 introduces P/T-nets, the Abstraction and Composition Process, and the Programming Model of our service-oriented system. In Sect. 3 we explain the main results on limitations of deadlock analysis with the help of an example presented in Sect. 2. Related Work is discussed in Sect. 4. Section 5 concludes our work.

2 Foundations

P/T-Nets. A *place/transition net* (short P/T-net) is a tuple $\Pi \triangleq (P, T, E, \lambda, \mu_0)$ where

- P is a finite set of *places*
- T is a finite set of *transitions*, $P \cap T = \emptyset$.
- $E \subseteq P \times T \cup T \times P$
- $\lambda : E \to \mathbb{N}$ is a labeling function
- $\mu_0 : P \to \mathbb{N}$ is the initial marking

A state in Π is a function $\mu : P \to \mathbb{N}$. Informally, $\mu(p)$ is the number of *tokens* in place p.

Note that $(P \cup T, E)$ is a bipartite directed graph. The set of *pre-places* of a transition t is defined as $Pre(t) \triangleq \{p : (p, t) \in E\}$. Analogously, the set of *post-places* of t is defined as $Post(t) \triangleq \{p : (t, p) \in E\}$.

A transition t of Π is *enabled* in state μ if $\mu(p) \geq \lambda((p, t))$ for all $p \in Pre(t)$, i.e., p contains at least as many tokens as the edge label of (p, t).

If an enabled transition t *fires* in state μ, then the next state μ' is computed as follows:

$$\mu'(p) \triangleq \begin{cases} \mu(p) + \lambda(t, p) & \text{if } p \in Post(t) \setminus Pre(t) \\ \mu(p) - \lambda(p, t) & \text{if } p \in Pre(t) \setminus Post(t) \\ \mu(p) - \lambda(p, t) + \lambda(t, p) & \text{if } p \in Pre(t) \cap Post(t) \\ \mu(p) & \text{otherwise} \end{cases}$$

In this paper, a P/T-net Π may also have a *final state* μ_f. A state δ $(\neq \mu_f)$ is called a *deadlock* if no transition is enabled in δ. The absence of deadlocks is decidable for P/T-nets. It is furthermore decidable if the final state μ_f is always reachable from the initial state μ_0.

Figure 3 shows an example. As usual, places are depicted as circles, transitions are depicted as squares, and tokens are depicted as bullets in places. Here $\mu_0(q_0) = 1$, and $\mu_0(q) = 0$ for all $q \in P \setminus \{q_0\}$. There is no label at the edges. By default, this means $\lambda(e) = 1$ for all $e \in E$. For example, transition t_0 is enabled in μ_0. If t_0 fires, then for the next state it holds $\mu_1(q_1) = 1$, $\mu_1(i_b) = 1$, and $\mu_1(q) = 0$ for each $q \in P \setminus \{q_1, i_b\}$.

A workflow net is a triple $WF \triangleq (\Pi, I, O)$ where $\Pi = (P, T, E, \lambda, \mu_0)$ is a P/T-net, $I \subseteq P$ is a set of *input places*, $O \subseteq P$ is a set of *output places*, and $I \cap O = \emptyset$. Figure 2 shows four workflow nets. The input and output places are the places on the border of the box.

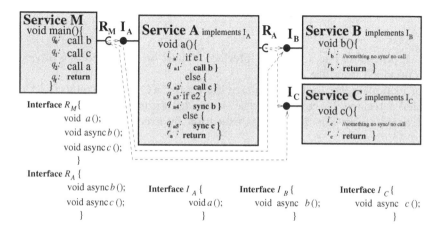

Fig. 1. A service-oriented system with services M, A, B and C. Service M acts as a client. Procedure a is a synchronous procedure while procedures b and c are asynchronous procedures.

Programming Model and Abstraction Process. Figure 1 shows a service-oriented system with a client service M and services A, B and C. Furthermore, Fig. 1 defines the interfaces R_M, R_A, I_A, I_B, and I_C. An *interface* is a finite set of procedure signatures (denoted in C-style).

A service X may provide an interface I_X (*provided interface*), i.e., the procedures in this interface I_X have to be implemented by X. This implementation may call procedures of other services. The set of signatures of these called procedures is the *required interface* R_X of X.

In Fig. 1, service M has no provided interface and services A, B, and C have the provided interfaces I_A, I_B, and I_C, respectively. Furthermore service M has a required interface R_M and service A has a required interface R_A. Services B and C have no required interfaces.

Table 1. Control-flow abstractions to P/T-nets

Each procedure p in a required interface R must be connected to a procedure p in a provided interface I.

For example, R_M contains the signature **void a()** and is connected to the provided interface I_A containing the same signature **void a()**. The service-oriented system in Fig. 1 starts its execution by executing **main** in the client service M.

Procedures can be synchronous or asynchronous. If a synchronous procedure is being called, the caller waits until the callee has been completed. Therefore synchronous procedure calls behave like classical procedures. In case of recursion, their semantics behaves as stacks. If an asynchronous procedure is being called, the caller and the callee are concurrently be executed. For example, in Fig. 1 procedure a is synchronous and procedures b and c are asynchronous, indicated by the keyword **async**. It is not possible to connect synchronous procedures to asynchronous procedures and vice versa.

There are two possibilities of synchronization for asynchronous procedure calls: First, the caller reaches a **sync**-statement. In this case, the caller waits until the callee returns. Second, the caller reaches a **return**-statement. Then, the caller waits until the callee returns. For example, the statement q_{a4} waits until the call of the asynchronous procedure b in q_{a1} has been completed. The other control structures are the classical ones with the classical semantics.

Table 1 shows different control structures and their abstraction to P/T-nets. The main principle is that each program point corresponds to a place. Each procedure p has a unique entry place i_p and a unique return place r_p.

A token in a place means that the control is at the corresponding program point in the state of program execution. Important control structures are atomic statements, e.g., assignments, conditionals, synchronous procedure calls and returns, asynchronous procedure calls and returns, and synchronizations. Loops and case statements are abstracted similarly to conditionals.

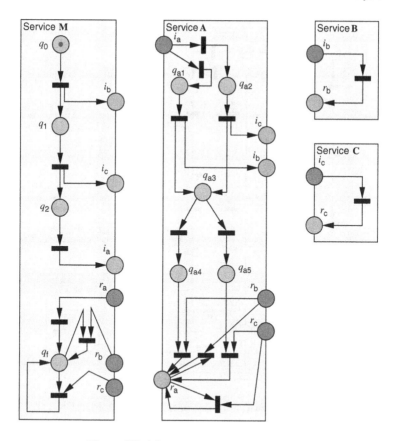

Fig. 2. Workflow net abstraction of Fig. 1

Note that for each procedure p in a provided interface I_X of a service X, i_p is an input place and r_p is an output place of the workflow net WF_X for X. Similarly, for each procedure q of a required interface R_X of a service X, i_q is an output place and r_q an input place of WF_X. We further assume that a service containing only required interfaces is a client and has an initial marking μ_0 such that $\mu_0(q_0) = 1$ if q_0 is the first program point of *main* and $\mu_0(q_0) = 0$ otherwise. For all non-client services, there is no token in the initial marking.

Figure 2 shows the workflow nets of the abstractions obtained from the service-oriented system in Fig. 1.

Composition. A service-oriented system is implemented by connecting the required interfaces of a service (external call to another service) to a corresponding provided interface of another service. Following the ideas of [7], the *composition of workflow nets* $WF_1, \ldots, WF_n$ is a P/T-net

$$P_c \triangleq (P_1 \cup \cdots \cdots P_n, T_1 \cup \cdots \cup T_n, E_1 \cup \cdots \cup E_n, \lambda_1 \cup \cdots \lambda_n, \mu_0^{(1)} \cup \cdots \cup \mu_0^{(n)})$$

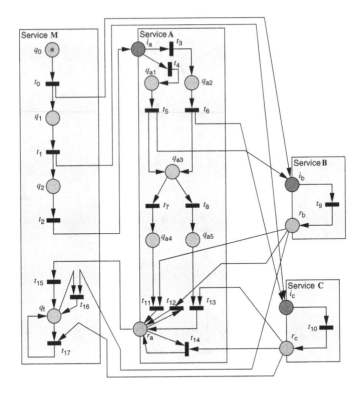

Fig. 3. Composition of the workflow nets in Fig. 2

under the assumption that all places in the workflow nets $WF_i = (\Pi_i, I_i, O_i)$ with $\Pi_i = (P_i, T_i, E_i, \lambda_i, \mu_0^{(i)})$, $i = 1, \ldots, n$ are pairwise disjoint except for input and output places.

Figure 3 shows the composition of the workflow nets in Fig. 2.

Remark 1. Suppose service X calls a procedure p of a service Y. Then output place i_p of the workflow net WF_X is identified with input place i_p of the workflow net WF_Y. Similarly, the output place r_p of WF_Y is identified with the input place r_p of WF_X.

Note that the output places i_b of services M and A of our example in Fig. 1 are both identified with the input place i_b of service B. Similarly, output place r_b of service B is identified with the input places r_b of services M and A, respectively.

In a certain sense, the treatment of procedures is similar to the treatment in context-insensitive interprocedural program analysis. We therefore call this kind of composition *context-insensitive composition*. In contrast, in *context-sensitive compositions* the workflow net for a procedure p is copied for each call. However, this is impossible if recursion is allowed.

Remark 2. Our approach is similar to [7]. There, the workflow nets are called modules and in addition, each module has a unique starting place α and a unique final place ω. Hence, the abstractions to workflow nets as discussed in our work are modules in the sense of [7]. Our notion of composition corresponds to the notion of syntactic composition of modules.

Remark 3. For Mayr's process rewrite systems (PRS), P/T-nets are equivalent to the class of (P,P)-PRS [8]. The abstraction mechanism leads to a set of PRS rules for each service [5]. The composition is called *combined abstraction* [1]. For the special class of (P,P)-PRS, this corresponds to the composition of workflow nets as described above.

3   Limitations of Deadlock Analysis

Claim 1. *The P/T-net abstraction (cf. Fig. 3) of the service-oriented system in Fig. 1 is deadlock-free.*

Proof. It must be shown that the final state μ_f (i.e. $\mu_f(q_f) = 1$ and $\mu_f(q) = 0$ for all places $q \neq q_f$ is always reached from the initial state μ_0. For simplicity, for all places q not mentioned in the definition of a state μ, we assume $\mu(q) = 0$.

Step 1: Each state $\mu_1 \in M_1 \triangleq \{\mu : \mu(r_a) = 1, \mu(i_b) + \mu(r_b) + \mu(i_c) + \mu(r_c) = 2\}$
  always reaches μ_f
Step 2: Each state $\mu_2 \in M_2 \triangleq \{\mu : \mu(q_{a3}) = 1, \mu(i_b) + \mu(i_b) \geq 1, \mu(i_c) + \mu(i_c) \geq 1, \mu(i_b) + \mu(i_b) + \mu(i_c) + \mu(i_c) = 3\}$ always reaches a state $\mu_1 \in M_1$
Step 3: μ_0 always reaches a state $\mu_2 \in M_2$.

If we have proven this, then the initial state q_0 always reaches q_f.

Remark 4. M_1 contains all states where r_a has one token and services B and C together have two tokens. M_2 describes all states where q_{a3} has one token, services B and C have at least one token and both service, B and C have together three tokens.

Step 1: It is sufficient to consider only situations where service B and C has tokens in r_b and r_c since tokens in i_b and i_c mean that transitions t_9 are t_{10} enabled and i_b and i_c do not have othter successors. We consider the following two cases:

(i) r_a, r_b, and r_c have one token, i.e. only transitions t_{12}, t_{14} and t_{15} are enabled.
(ii) r_a has one token and r_b has two tokens, i.e., only transitions t_{12} and t_{15} are enabled.

The case where r_a has one token and r_c has two tokens is analogous to (ii). The following tables show all possible firing sequences of (i) and (ii). Each of this firing sequences end in the final state μ_f:

(i) : t_{12}, t_{14}, t_{15} (ii) : t_{12}, t_{12}, t_{15}
     t_{12}, t_{15}, t_{17} t_{12}, t_{15}, t_{16}
     t_{14}, t_{12}, t_{15} t_{15}, t_{16}, t_{16}
     t_{14}, t_{15}, t_{16}

Step 2: Analogously to Step 1, it is sufficient to consider only situations where service B and C have their tokens in r_b and r_c, respectively. We consider the case where r_b has two tokens and r_c has one token. The other case (r_b has one token and r_c has two tokens) is proven analogously. In this state, t_7 and t_8 are the only two transitions being enabled. The following firing sequence all lead to a state $\mu_1 \in M_1$:

$$t_7, t_{11} \text{ reaches state } \mu(r_a) = \mu(r_b) = \mu(r_c) = 1$$
$$t_8, t_{13} \text{ reaches state } \mu(r_a) = 1, \mu(r_b) = 2, \mu(r_c) = 0$$

Step 3: According to the discussions of Steps 1 and 2, it is sufficient to consider only situations where i_b and i_c have at least one token, respectivly, and $\mu(i_b) + \mu(i_c) = 3$. We show that a state $\mu_2 \in M_2$ is alywas be reached from the initial state. Under the above circumstances, the simulation of the P/T-net always starts with the firing sequence t_0, t_1, t_2 reaches a state where i_a, i_b and i_c contain one token, respectively. Now, the transitions t_3 and t_4 are the only enabled transitions (except the inner transitions t_9 and t_{10}). If t_3 fires, then only t_6 is enabled, leading to one token in q_{a3}, one token in i_b, and two tokens in i_c. If t_4 fires, then only t_5 is enabled leading to one token in q_{a3}, two tokens in i_b, and one tokens in i_c. Both states are in M_2.

Table 2. Execution Semantics with Cactus Stacks (program points)

Control Structure	Cactus Stack	Control Structure	Cactus Stack
assignment	q_1 → q_2	asynchronous procedure call	q_1 → q_2 q_3
synchronous procedure call	q_1 → q_2 q_3	return asynchronous procedure call	q_1 q_2 → q_2
return synchronous procedure call	q_1 q_2 → q_2	synchronization	q_1 q_2 → q_3

Now we look at the execution of the service-oriented system in Fig. 1. The runtime system is based on cactus stacks. Cactus stacks were introduced as tree of stacks by [3]. Our execution model includes states of unbounded recursion and unbounded concurrency. These states can be represented by cactus stacks. Thus, the execution transforms cactus stacks into cactus stacks. Table 2 shows these transisitions. If a synchronous procedure is called, there is transisition to the next program point and a stack frame with the initial state of the called procedure is pushed onto a stack. If an asynchronous procedure is called, a new stack frame is created that forks from the caller. The top stack frame of the caller and the bottom element of the new stack are linked together (like a saguaro cactus). Thus, synchronization is only possible with two elements that are forked from a top-of-stack frame.

Claim 2. *The service-oriented system in Fig. 1 may end in a deadlock.*

Proof. Table 3 shows an execution trace of the service-oriented system in Fig. 1. In the first step q_0 forks to q_1 and i_b. Then, the control moves from i_b to r_b which waits for synchronization or the return from **main**. Hence, the only possible step is the asynchronous call of **c**. In the next step the control moves to r_c. Now, the only possibility is the (synchronous) call of **a**. This means that the next state q_f and the initial state i_a are pushed on the stack. After this call it is not possible to synchronize with r_b and r_c forked from q_f since q_f is not a top element of a stack. The final cactus stack is a deadlock since q_{a5} waits for synchronization with r_c but there is no r_c for synchronization.

Table 3. Derivation from the initial state to a deadlock

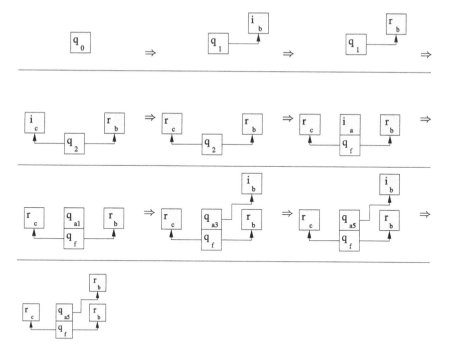

Remark 5. [5] discusses the abstraction to general PRS and shows a $1-1$ correspondence betweem cactus stacks (of program points) and process-alegebraic expressions. Hence, the deadlock can be found by using general PRS.

Remark 6. The deadlock in Table 3 means that the control reached r_c, q_{a_5} and twice r_b. This means that the P/T-net in Fig. 3 reaches a state that contains two tokens in r_b, one token in r_c, and one token in q_{a5}. Thus t_{13} is enabled and it is the only transition being enabled. Hence, the deadlock in the execution of the service-oriented system does not correspond to a deadlock in the P/T-net abstraction (based on workflow nets).

4   Related Work

Woflan [11] is a Petri Net-based analysis tool which verifies parallel business process worklflows. Recursion of processes are not considered. It is not clear whether their composition is context-sensitive or context-insensitive.

In [9] recursive Petri Nets (rPNs) are used to model the planning of autonomous agents which transport goods from location A to location B and their coordinating problem. The model of rPNs is used to model dynamic processes (e.g., agent's request). Deadlocks can only arise when interactions between agents (e.g., shared attributes) invalidates preconditions. For that reason a coordinating algorithm is introduced to prevent these interactions between agents.

A refinement-based approach is described in [6]. Hicheur models healthcare processes based on algebraic and recursive Petri Nets [4], a high level algebraic Petri Net. Hicheur et al. use recursive Petri Net to model subprocesses that are called by a process (e.g., the main process), i.e. a context-sensitive composition. However, to the best of our knowledge, we are not aware of any work on deadlock analysis for recursive Petri Nets.

Bouajjani et al. [2] propose an abstraction-based approach to model control structures of recursively parallel programs (e.g., Cilk, X10, Multilisp). Their approach is based on recursive vector addition systems. They explore the decidability and complexity of state-reachability. It seems that their model is slightly more general than ours as there are situations where the reachability problem becomes undecidable.

Our approach is similar to [7], cf. Remark 2. However, it seems that exactly one call to a module is being considered. Hence, context-sensitivity does not play a role in the notion of composition.

We are not aware of any work stating out the drawback of deadlock analysis of systems with synchronous and asynchronous procedure calls and also synchronization concepts.

5   Conclusion

We presented an example of a service-oriented system with synchronous procedures, asynchronous procedures and a barrier-based synchronization mechanism. We have discussed a straightforward abstraction mechanism to workflow nets and their context-insensitive composition to P/T-nets. Furthermore, we have also shown a runtime based on cactus stacks (which was already be defined as a runtime system of Simula67 [3]). Our main result is an example that the work-flow net approach doesn't satisfy its goals for deadlock analysis: the resulting P/T-net is free of deadlocks (Claim 1) while the execution of the service-oriented system leads to a deadlock (Claim 1). Note, that our example is not a spurious counterexample. A spurious counterexample would be a deadlock in the P/T-net while the service-oriented system is deadlock-free. In our previous work [12], we showed another phenomenon using workflow nets abstractions: the approach only has spurious counterexamples while the real one is not discovered.

Our result shows that in general, deadlock checking based on straightforward P/T-net abstraction with context-insensitive composition should not be used to prove deadlock-freeness. In contrast, PRS-abstractions are able to model the stack behavior of synchronous procedure calls as well. On the other hand, it might be that context-sensitive composition might solve the problem for bound recursion depth. Unbound recursion would require an infinite expansion of the procedure calls.

In future work it remains to investigate the concurrent and recursive concept and also the synchronization concept of other languages (e.g., Java Threads, Simula and so on). Another open issue is the occurence of deadlocks in a cer-tain recursion depth. We conjecture that if a deadlock associated with recursive behavior (recursion or recursive callbacks) in a service-oriented system occurs, in its PRS-abstraction it always occurs in recursion depth one. If the conjecture would be true, it should be possible to use a P/T-net-based abstraction for dead-lock checking (possibly with a special class of context-sensitive compositions of workflow nets).

References

1. Both, A., Zimmermann, W.: Automatic protocol conformance checking of recur-sive and parallel component-based systems. In: Chaudron, M.R.V., Szyperski, C., Reussner, R. (eds.) CBSE 2008. LNCS, vol. 5282, pp. 163–179. Springer, Heidelberg (2008). https://doi.org/10.1007/978-3-540-87891-9_11
2. Bouajjani, A., Emmi, M.: Analysis of recursively parallel programs. In: ACM SIG-PLAN Notices, vol. 47, pp. 203–214. ACM (2012)
3. Dahl, O.J., Nygaard, K.: Simula: an algol-based simulation language. Commun. ACM **9**, 671–678 (1966)
4. Haddad, S., Poitrenaud, D.: Modelling and analyzing systems with recursive Petri Nets. In: Boel, R., Stremersch, G. (eds.) Discrete Event Systems. The Springer International Series in Engineering and Computer Science, vol. 569. Springer, Boston (2000). https://doi.org/10.1007/978-1-4615-4493-7_48
5. Heike, C., Zimmermann, W., Both, A.: On expanding protocol conformance check-ing to exception handling. SOCA **8**(4), 299–322 (2014). https://doi.org/10.1007/s11761-013-0146-2
6. Hicheur, A., Ben Dhieb, A., Barkaoui, K.: Modelling and analysis of flexible health-care processes based on algebraic and recursive Petri Nets. In: Weber, J., Perseil, I. (eds.) FHIES 2012. LNCS, vol. 7789, pp. 1–18. Springer, Heidelberg (2013). https://doi.org/10.1007/978-3-642-39088-3_1

7. Martens, A.: Analyzing web service based business processes. In: Cerioli, M. (ed.) FASE 2005. LNCS, vol. 3442, pp. 19–33. Springer, Heidelberg (2005). https://doi.org/10.1007/978-3-540-31984-9_3

8. Mayr, R.: Process rewrite systems. Inf. Comput. **156**(1–2), 264–286 (2000)

9. Seghrouchni, A.E.F., Haddad, S.: A recursive model for distributed planning. In: Proceedings of the 2nd International Conference on Multi-Agent Systems (ICMAS 1996), pp. 307–314 (1996)

10. Aalst, W.M.P.: Workflow verification: finding control-flow errors using Petri-Net-based techniques. In: van der Aalst, W., Desel, J., Oberweis, A. (eds.) Business Process Management. LNCS, vol. 1806, pp. 161–183. Springer, Heidelberg (2000). https://doi.org/10.1007/3-540-45594-9_11

11. Verbeek, E., van der Aalst, W.M.P.: Woflan 2.0 a Petri-Net-based workflow diagnosis tool. In: Nielsen, M., Simpson, D. (eds.) ICATPN 2000. LNCS, vol. 1825, pp. 475–484. Springer, Heidelberg (2000). https://doi.org/10.1007/3-540-44988-4_28

12. Weißbach, M., Zimmermann, W.: on abstraction-based deadlock-analysis in service-oriented systems with recursion. In: De Paoli, F., Schulte, S., Broch Johnsen, E. (eds.) ESOCC 2017. LNCS, vol. 10465, pp. 168–176. Springer, Cham (2017). https://doi.org/10.1007/978-3-319-67262-5_13

13. Zimmermann, W., Schaarschmidt, M.: Automatic checking of component protocols in component-based systems. In: Löwe, W., Südholt, M. (eds.) SC 2006. LNCS, vol. 4089, pp. 1–17. Springer, Heidelberg (2006). https://doi.org/10.1007/11821946_1

Decentralized Billing and Subcontracting of Application Services for Cloud Environment Providers

Wolf Posdorfer$^{(\boxtimes)}$, Julian Kalinowski, Heiko Bornholdt,
and Winfried Lamersdorf

Department of Informatics, University of Hamburg,
Vogt-Kölln-Straße 30, 22527 Hamburg, Germany
`posdorfer@informatik.uni-hamburg.de`

Abstract. This paper proposes a decentralized billing and subcontracting system for regional cloud service providers. Based on blockchain technology, this system allows, on the one hand side, to collectively offer services in a distributed environment in a strict or ad-hoc federation and, on the other, to bill each user of such a services individually without a respective central service. In order to do so, it uses a blockchain-based transaction process which uses specialized tokens in order to enable a fair and secure distribution of requested cloud services. It maintains the ability to achieve consensus by validating the respective blockchain (part). In result, the proposed system is not bound to a specific technology, but rather open to any blockchain that allows arbitrary data or modeling of custom transactions.

Keywords: Blockchain · Cloud computing · Cloud environment provider · Consensus · Decentralized ledgers

1 Introduction

Enabled by the increasing need to offload work intensive or space hungry applications into cloud environments, a few major players have emerged to dominate the market. This oligarchy is not only dangerous for the end consumer but also greatly hinders a fair and competitive market for smaller regional providers [7]. A study shows that in 2017 four companies dominate the cloud market with a combined share of over 50% [16].

By imposing secret migration hindrances through inflexible APIs these major players are enforcing a vendor lock-in which negatively affects smaller providers, as a complete stack migration to their service becomes either unfeasible or simply impossible. Due to their higher market power they can essentially also dictate the service prices by which smaller providers have to abide to stay somewhat competitive.

The introduction of Bitcoin in 2008 triggered a new movement in decentralization. Blockchains enable consensus-based replication of data in an untrustworthy environment. Every participating node has the same identical view of all the

© Springer Nature Switzerland AG 2020
M. Fazio and W. Zimmermann (Eds.): ESOCC 2018 Workshops, CCIS 1115, pp. 91–101, 2020.
https://doi.org/10.1007/978-3-030-63161-1_7

transactions and their respective order. The underlying database is fully replicated and provides a high reliability. Even though the blockchain was initially created to serve the single purpose of being a "cryptocurrency" the technology can be used for many other applications and business processes.

We propose a scenario in which a multitude of smaller cloud environment providers can form a federation. Allowing them to bundle their resources into one virtual cloud provider. By utilizing the blockchain technology we can achieve a verifiable billing and subcontracting system. This enables all providers to act as equals and provides fair distribution and payment for the requested cloud services. The proposed process is generalizable to other use cases whenever they have a similar system composition and the process can be divided into sub-steps. The following use case will outline the process in the billing and subcontracting of cloud services.

Our approach differs from [14] in that it is not locked into Ethereum-VM compatible blockchains relying solely on smart contracts for application logic. By defining standard transaction types, which can be run on any blockchain, we do not impose technological restrictions. This also mitigates the requirements of Proof-of-Work, allowing for shorter block times and less energy consumption. Also in contrast to [18] our approach does not require a registry of current provider prices. Computing hours are not distributed in an auction style system where cheaper services are always favored, thus no price war is created between smaller providers.

2   Use Case

This section will provide a use case for a decentralized billing platform to illustrate the benefits it can provide. With a decentralized subcontracting and billing platform of application services in cloud environments multiple smaller cloud computing providers can form a federation to act as a single provider, thus allowing them to be more competitive in todays market. Instead of offering their services as single entities they can offer a combined service that is transparent for the end user.

Figure 1 shows an exemplary composition of a customer requesting 90 h of service and three providers (Provider 1–3), with two subcontractors (Sub3a & Sub3b).

2.1   Cloud Service Billing

One of the necessities of a decentralized platform where multiple providers share an incoming workload is the correct billing of the performed computation hours by each participant. In this scenario we assume that a customer has paid for a service in advance and that the service will run as long as its being paid for. Depending on the configuration the fiat money will be evenly distributed between all the providers connected to the federation. In Fig. 1 the customer requests 90 h, which is evenly distributed as 30 h for each provider.

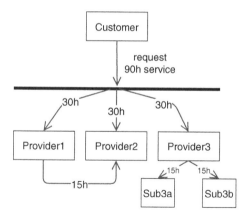

Fig. 1. Service billing and subcontracting

2.2   Cloud Service Subcontracting

On the assumption that all connected cloud service providers have limited resources it is quite possible that an even distribution of workload between them will lead to bottlenecks. By allowing providers to offload a complete or partial workload to another provider these bottlenecks can be overcome. It even allows a single provider to act as a proxy to subcontractors, e.g., regional providers. Figure 1 shows how Provider3 subcontracts to two additional providers Sub3a and Sub3b.

3   Blockchain

A blockchain is a decentralized data structure, whose internal consistency is being maintained by reaching consensus over an application state in a network. The data itself is fully replicated and kept in synchrony over every participating node [2].

To change the state of the blockchain a transaction has to be submitted. Each transaction is bundled into a block, which will be chained together by calculating a hash over the transactions and a hash pointing to the previous block. Thus effectively chaining each block to its predecessor and creating a definite order. Figure 2 depicts an exemplary blockchain datastructure showing three blocks, their linking via the predecessors hash (Prev_Hash) and the root hash of a merkle-tree (Tx_Root) containing transactions (Tx0 - Tx3).

3.1   Transaction

The fundamental data structures of the blockchain are transactions and blocks. The transaction is the smallest data unit being processed and capable of changing the overall state of the blockchain. Network participants can create them and

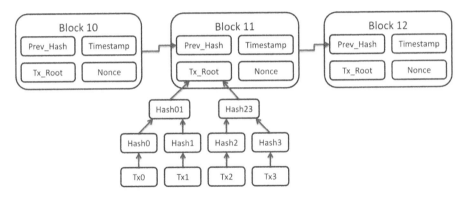

Fig. 2. Simplified blockchain datastructure

propagate them to other nodes through a peer-to-peer network. Depending on the blockchain technology used transactions can contain different arbitrary data. In Bitcoin [13] and other cryptocurrencies they contain info about the sender, receiver and quantity of currency (simplified). Even function calls are possible, by using smart contracts or chain code as used in Ethereum [19]. But blockchains are not limited to the usage of currency or smart contracts. They can also be used for several other applications like supply chain management, voting or ballots, crowd funding or to store data in general.

3.2 Block

After a transaction has been published and propagated through the network it will be bundled into a block. The transactions will be stored and hashed with a suited algorithm and data structure, usually variants of the SHA-algorithm and Merkle-Trees. Every block consist of a header containing the predecessors blocks hash, its own transactions hash (root hash) and depending on the used technology other information like timestamps, version, block height, target, nonce or others.

By using the preceding block hash they are effectively chained together all the way back to the genesis block. The chaining of blocks creates a traceability over all transactions and thus also the overall state and state changes of the blockchain.

3.3 Consensus

The key element behind every blockchain is its consensus algorithm. Through it the blockchain ensures that the majority of nodes has the same valid shared state in the long-term. Depending on the used algorithm the majority of nodes necessary for a valid block typically lies at 51% in chain-based algorithms or $+\frac{2}{3}$ in Byzantine Fault Tolerant (BFT)-based algorithms.

Chain-Based/Append-Based Algorithms. In Bitcoin and similar technologies the consensus algorithm is referred to as *Proof-of-Work* (PoW) [4,13,19]. Its goal is to provide trust through a cryptographic challenge. The challenge consists of finding a *Nonce* so that the resulting hash of Nonce and Root-Hash meets a certain target or difficulty in the form of amount of leading zeros. Every node interested in solving the challenge by brute-forcing nonces is called a *Miner*, while the process itself is referred to as *Mining*. Its rather simple to verify the validity of the produced block by other nodes. The difficulty ensures that very rarely two different blocks are propagated through the network at the same time. Also it ensures that it becomes harder and harder to forge previous blocks by recalculating hashes with different nonces.

To create a block a miner selects a set of transactions calculates the root hash and starts brute-forcing nonces until he finds one that meets the current difficulty. The difficulty is automatically adjusted by the network in order to keep the median time between two blocks in roughly the same timespan. With the increased participation in the cryptographic challenge the amount of computing power also increases as a direct result of the PoW algorithm and self-adjusting difficulty.

In contrast to PoW the *Proof-of-Stake* (PoS) algorithms try to mitigate the waste of resources [6,9,10]. In PoS miners can stake their own coins (or other values) in order to create blocks more easily. Owning and staking a higher amount of coins results in a higher likelihood of creating a block. Other algorithms impose additional requirements on the coins, like the coin-age, to limit the usage of massive amount of coins.

BFT-Based/Propose-Based Algorithms. BFT-based algorithms try to solve the consensus problem by using algorithms that solve the byzantine generals problem [17]. Usually they are loosely based on the PBFT-algorithm [5] and 2-Phase-Commit-algorithms [12]. In BFT-based PoS algorithms there is a certain set of nodes called Validators, who are responsible for consensus. Validators each take turns in proposing new blocks. This ensures that only one block for a given height is valid. Unlike in chain-based algorithms where more than one block can compete to be the next block. This also means that there can be no forks in the chain. While in chain-based algorithms any number of nodes can choose to not partake in the block-finding process, in BFT style algorithms a minimum set of more than $\frac{2}{3}$ (or $+\frac{2}{3}$) of validators need to be online at any given time. If there are less than $+\frac{2}{3}$ the proposed block will not reach consensus.

3.4 Process

Every blockchain independent of its underlying consensus algorithm follows the same sequence of steps until a new block which is accepted by other nodes is appended. Every blockchain participant is running the same client, which either contains the application layer (like Bitcoin) or an API for a custom application (like Hyperledger [1]). Every node is linked to a certain amount of other nodes via a peer-to-peer network which allows the distribution of messages.

Once the application layer has created a transaction, which contains data depending on the use-case/technology, it will be passed to the validation component. The transaction validation depends highly on the use case, e.g., checking if an account balance is sufficient. If it is valid the transaction will be placed into the *mempool* and broadcasted to other peers, who repeat this process. Ideally this ensures that every network participant has the same valid transactions in its mempool.

Once a node has qualified for creating a block (or proposing) it will select a number of transactions from the mempool and bundle them into a block. Depending on certain criteria like transaction age or transaction fees the node can choose which transactions to include. After forming the block the node will distribute it to its peers. Upon receiving a block the node has to perform its own validity checks on the block and transactions within the block, as to not append an incorrect state to its own blockchain.

4   Problem Definition

A classic approach for managing cross-company payments, costs and distribution of revenue would be to establish and make use of a trusted third party. This trusted third party keeps track of everything that is relevant to the system, such as commissions, orders, computing hours and billable hours. This implies that the third party will get to know details about business relationships between the companies and, of course, the account balances.

Instead of trusting a third party with this data, it is desirable to keep as much of the data private as possible and to instead distribute the trust amongst all parties.

Since in the sketc.hed scenarios, we will have multiple participants, potentially distrusting each other (dishonesty can lead to personal advantage), a blockchain solution seems appropriate [20]. It provides data integrity with multiple untrusted writers without a trusted third party. Additionally, blockchain transactions can be designed in a way that they support required business processes in a network of equal partners, where nobody is in control, and yet everybody can verify the correctness of a process.

The concept of blockchain was created with transparency in mind, which is why all stored data is available for everyone to validate [13]. The validation in turn provides the necessary security for a distributed database with multiple participants who potentially distrust each other. Each participant is given the opportunity to vote for his own sense of correctness of a given transaction in the blockchain and to do so, he must have access to the data. This is why validation is a critical part of a blockchain and it is tightly coupled with transparency.

In the given scenario however, full transparency might not be a valid option as data are trade secrets and should not be made publicly available. While a blockchain can be private, not offering public access for anyone who is interested, transparency of sensible information remains a problem: At least all authorized participants would be able to read all data, which is bad by itself, especially when direct competitors are involved in the same system. On the other hand transparency is highly necessary to ensure a working validation and checking for transaction correctness to guarantee reaching consensus.

5   Approach

The general idea is that, instead of transferring fiat money, trading happens on the blockchain using tokens. This enables a fast, reliable and secure way for exchanging a value representation without having to pay fees, enabling participants to reflect every single transfer of value in the blockchain. Additionally, the blockchain will provide a decentralized way of clearing, such that the tokens can be exchanged for fiat money after a given period. This period may be inspired by the underlying business process and common for all participants. It may also depend on individual preferences and should not be restricted, however.

5.1   Billing and Subcontracting Scenario

In this scenario, there are two groups of participants, service *providers* and *customers*. Each provider may maintain business relationships with other providers, although there will not always be a direct connection between any two of them in this graph of relationships. Instead, multiple smaller strongly connected subgraphs corresponding to individual groups of co-operation are possible.

Figure 3 shows a sample graph of this scenario, where C_i are customers and P_i are providers. The edges are labeled with the amount of tokens that are being sent. Dotted edges represent distribution of a previous token, performed by a provider. Marked in *red* for each provider is the sum of tokens after all the transactions are performed, e.g., the net sum for each provider.

The customers (or a central proxy) are the only entities that may issue new *tokens*, just like a mint would do with fiat money. Tokens (representing money or computing hours) are then given to one or more providers, who can in turn split them and pass them on to other providers.

In this scenario, tokens, once issued, can be distributed and passed from provider to provider. However, they can never vanish and a provider can only pass on a token he owns and hasn't already spent otherwise.

Now, after all tokens have been transferred according to the underlying business process, each provider knows his token balance at any time, which corresponds e.g., to computing hours.

In order to exchange his tokens for fiat money, he must be able to generate a proof showing anyone with access to the blockchain data that he is the rightful owner of his tokens.

5.2   Transaction Types

Based on the previously introduced use case at least the following three transaction types are necessary to model the business processes. Every Transaction can

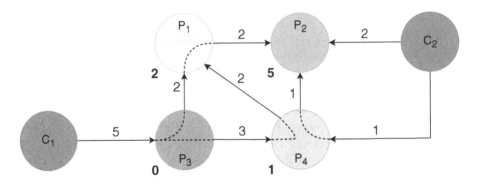

Fig. 3. Billing scenario

contain multiple input tokens and multiple output tokens. Input tokens must be owned by the same participant, while outputs can be assigned to different parties. The following transaction types are not unique to a special blockchain, but can be implemented on any technology that allows custom transactions, like: Corda [3], Ethereum [19], Hyperledger [1], Tendermint [11] and others. Bitcoin and its descendants are unsuited because of their strict transaction formats and limited transaction payload size.

Initialization (INIT) is used to publish newly created tokens into the system. Only customers can create new tokens, backing them against fiat currency. This transaction type does not require any input tokens as the customer is actively *minting* them and also contains only one output.

Distribution (DIST) allows a single party to transfer or split their tokens as required by the business process. It can be used to sell parts of their computing hours to others.

Payout (POUT) transaction is used to exchange tokens for fiat money with a customer. It contains multiple input tokens from the same owner and a single output token towards the customer.

Figure 4 shows an exemplary transaction flow. The customer deposits fiat money and converts it to 100 Tokens (T). The *100T* are then issued to Provider1 using the *INIT* transaction type. After this transactions has been validated and finalized in a block, every participant can now confirm that Provider1 owns *100T*. When Provider1 is unable to provide the 100T worth of computing hours he can offload it to another provider. Provider1 distributes his tokens using the *DIST* transaction to split his balance between himself and Provider2. Again after validation and finalization in a block, everyone can confirm that Provider1 and Provider2 both own *50T*. Once Provider2 wants to convert his tokens back into fiat money he issues a *POUT* transaction, reassigning his *50T* back to the customer. Upon receiving the tokens the customer will issue the respective amount of fiat money to Provider2 off-chain.

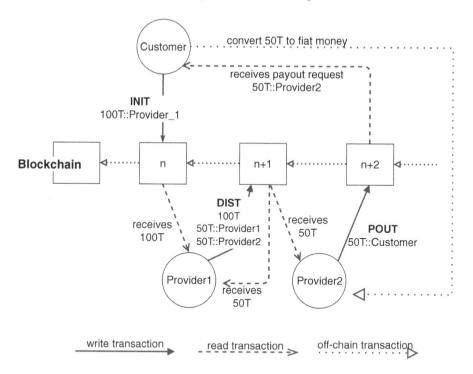

Fig. 4. Example transaction flow

A minor impracticality in this scenario is the huge reliance on trust. In order to mitigate wrongdoings by customers a proxy-service will have to be placed in between to deposit the fiat money and issue the corresponding tokens respectively. This ensures that the customer has actually deposited fiat money and the providers can later retrieve it.

5.3 Validation and Transparency

As stated in Sect. 4, validation of transactions is performed by any active participant. This requires full access to the transaction data, which, in our scenario, means every participant can see any tokens being sent between customers (or proxy) and service providers. But as previously stated full transparency is not desired for at least the following three aspects:

– Amount of tokens in possession by a single provider should not be revealed.
– Offloading relations should be hidden from other providers not participating in the corresponding customer's job.
– General anonymity is also not ensured as every token assignment must be directed to a specific provider.

A reasonable validation rule, executed by every participant of the system, would be: *"For any tokens that are distributed and payed-out, is there a valid incoming token transaction for this provider?"* In a fully transparent blockchain system, this would be trivial to check as everyone has access to the balances and can take a look at past transactions. However, in a system with private balances and transaction data, there may be no validation possible at all (thus rendering the blockchain approach pointless). This implies that designing a privacy-protective solution may come with a trade-off between privacy and validation.

The natural approach in favor of privacy would be full encryption of the transaction data. All data would be private and visible for the sender and recipient only. Obviously, nobody may validate this data except for the sender and receiver, respectively.

6   Future Work and Conclusion

The proposed blockchain based solution shows a generalizable method to provide a decentralized billing and subcontracting process for cloud environment providers. It can be adapted to a multitude of other business processes that share the same characteristics. Whenever a process is started from a single entity and can be divided into measurable subparts the proposed solution is a suitable candidate.

Another exemplary use case can be the execution of distributed workflows. Where an orchestrator (customer) distributes actions of the workflow to services (provider), which in turn can divide the actions into subactions and redistribute them to other services all in a traceable and verifiable manner on the blockchain.

As transaction transparency and transaction validation are closely reliant on each other new methods for privacy protection must be established. As full data encryption is not feasible, because it breaks validation, other steps must be taken when specific use cases highly require data protection.

One of the measures to take to ensure validation is the usage of homomorphic encryption [8]. Homomorphic encryption allows for token values to be encrypted while still maintaining the ability to construct sums and verify input and output values.

When introducing encryption the encrypted values or token sums must also remain unforgeable. Thus a binding value must be chosen in the form of a verifiable secret. A commitment solves these issues as it firstly hides the input value and secondly is also binding [15].

References

1. Androulaki, E., et al.: Hyperledger fabric: a distributed operating system for permissioned blockchains. In: Proceedings of the Thirteenth EuroSys Conference, p. 30. ACM (2018)
2. Antonopoulos, A.M.: Mastering Bitcoin: Unlocking Digital Cryptocurrencies. O'Reilly Media Inc., Newton (2014)
3. Brown, R.G., Carlyle, J., Grigg, I., Hearn, M.: Corda: An introduction. R3 CEV, August 2016

4. Buterin, V., et al.: A next-generation smart contract and decentralized application platform. White paper (2014)
5. Castro, M., Liskov, B., et al.: Practical byzantine fault tolerance. In: OSDI, vol. 99, pp. 173–186 (1999)
6. David, B.M., Gazi, P., Kiayias, A., Russell, A.: Ouroboros praos: An adaptively-secure, semi-synchronous proof-of-stake protocol. IACR Cryptol. ePrint Arch. **2017**, 573 (2017)
7. Feng, Y., Li, B., Li, B.: Price competition in an oligopoly market with multiple IaaS cloud providers. IEEE Trans. Comput. **63**(1), 59–73 (2014)
8. Gentry, C., Boneh, D.: A Fully Homomorphic Encryption Scheme, vol. 20. Stanford University Stanford, Stanford (2009)
9. Jain, A., Arora, S., Shukla, Y., Patil, T., Sawant-Patil, S.: Proof of stake with casper the friendly finality gadget protocol for fair validation consensus in ethereum (2018)
10. King, S., Nadal, S.: Ppcoin: Peer-to-peer crypto-currency with proof-of-stake. self-published paper, 19 August 2012
11. Kwon, J.: Tendermint: Consensus without mining. Draft v. 0.6, fall (2014)
12. Lampson, B., Sturgis, H.E.: Crash recovery in a distributed data storage system (1979)
13. Nakamoto, S.: Bitcoin: A peer-to-peer electronic cash system (2008)
14. Neidhardt, N., Köhler, C., Nüttgens, M.: Cloud service billing and service level agreement monitoring based on blockchain. In: EMISA, pp. 65–69 (2018)
15. Pedersen, T.P.: Non-interactive and information-theoretic secure verifiable secret sharing. In: Feigenbaum, J. (ed.) CRYPTO 1991. LNCS, vol. 576, pp. 129–140. Springer, Heidelberg (1992). https://doi.org/10.1007/3-540-46766-1_9
16. Synergy Research Group: The leading cloud providers continue to run away with the market (2017). https://www.srgresearch.com/articles/leading-cloud-providers-continue-run-away-market
17. Vukolić, M.: The quest for scalable blockchain fabric: proof-of-work vs. BFT replication. In: Camenisch, J., Kesdoğan, D. (eds.) iNetSec 2015. LNCS, vol. 9591, pp. 112–125. Springer, Cham (2016). https://doi.org/10.1007/978-3-319-39028-4_9
18. Wang, H., Shi, P., Zhang, Y.: Jointcloud: A cross-cloud cooperation architecture for integrated internet service customization. In: 2017 IEEE 37th International Conference on Distributed Computing Systems (ICDCS), pp. 1846–1855. IEEE (2017)
19. Wood, G.: Ethereum: a secure decentralised generalised transaction ledger. Ethereum Project Yellow Paper **151**, 1–39 (2018)
20. Wüst, K., Gervais, A.: Do you need a blockchain? Cryptology ePrint Archive, Report 2017/375 (2017). https://eprint.iacr.org/2017/375

May Contain Nuts: The Case
for API Labels

Cesare Pautasso[1(✉)] and Erik Wilde[2]

[1] Software Institute, Faculty of Informatics, USI, Lugano, Switzerland
`c.pautasso@ieee.org`
[2] CA Technologies, Zürich, Switzerland

Abstract. As APIs proliferate, managing the constantly growing and evolving API landscapes inside and across organizations becomes a challenge. Part of the management challenge is for APIs to be able to describe themselves, so that users and tooling can use descriptions for finding and filtering APIs. A standardized labeling scheme can help to cover some of the cases where API self-description allows API landscapes to become more usable and scalable. In this paper we present the vision for standardized API labels, which summarize and represent critical aspects of APIs. These aspect allow consumers to more easily become aware of the kind of dependency they are going to establish with the service provider when choosing to use them. API labels not only summarize critical coupling factors, but also can include claims that require to be validated by trusted third parties.

1 Introduction

APIs are the only visible parts of services in API-based service landscapes. The technical interface aspect of APIs has been widely discussed with description languages such as WSDL, RAML, and Swagger/OpenAPI. The non-functional aspects are harder to formalize (e.g., see the survey by García et al. [8]) but can also benefit from a framework in which information can be represented and used.

The idea of "API Labels" is equivalent to that of standardized labeling systems in other product spaces, for example for food, for device energy consumption, or for movie/games audience ratings. In these scenarios, labels enable consumers to understand a few key (and often safety-critical) aspects of the product. This framework is not intended to be a complete and exhaustive description of the product. Instead, it focuses on areas that are important and helpful to make an initial product selection. The assumption is that the information found on the label can be trusted, so that consumers can make decisions based on labels which are correct and do not contain fraudulent information.

In the API space, numerous standards and best practices have evolved how APIs can be formally described for machine processing and/or documented for human consumption [14] (e.g., WSDL [4], WADL [9], RESTdesc [24], hRESTS [12], RADL [19], RAML, Swagger/OpenAPI [22], SLA★ [10],

© Springer Nature Switzerland AG 2020
M. Fazio and W. Zimmermann (Eds.): ESOCC 2018 Workshops, CCIS 1115, pp. 102–113, 2020.
https://doi.org/10.1007/978-3-030-63161-1_8

RSLA [21], SLAC [23] just to mention a few). However, there still is some uncertainty how to best combine and summarize these, and how to use them so that API description, documentation, and labeling can be combined. This paper proposes the API Labels Framework (AFL) to introduce API labels as a synthesis of existing API descriptions combined with additional metadata which can help customers assess several practical qualities of APIs and their providers and thus be useful to reduce the effort required to determine whether an API can be worthy of consideration.

The main motivation for labeling APIs is probably not so much about a way to enable providers to put marketing labels on their APIs nor is it a way to summarize information that is already present in existing formal API descriptions. Instead, it is about providing assurances for API consumers about crucial characteristics of the service behind the API that may not be visible on its surface.

The rest of this paper is structured as follows. In Sect. 2 we present general background on labeling and related work which has inspired the current paper. In Sect. 3 we apply the concept of labeling to APIs and discuss how to use OpenAPI Link Objects and Home Documents to make API labels easy to find. We discuss the issue of how to establish trust for API labels in Sect. 4 and then introduce different label types in Sect. 5. The following Sect. 6 provides a non-exhaustive set of label type examples. The problem of discovering labels and ensuring that they can evolve over time are identified in Sect. 7.2. Finally we draw some conclusions in Sect. 8 and outline possible directions for future work in Sect. 9.

2   Background and Related Work

Labeling helps to identify, describe, assess and promote products [13]. Branding and labeling contribute to differentiate competing products by assuring the consumer of a guaranteed level of quality or by restoring consumer's confidence after some negative publicity leading to a loss of reputation. More specifically, food labeling has also been used to educate consumers on diet and health issues [5]. Labeling can thus be used as a marketing tool [1] by providers or as a provider selection tool by consumers [2].

This work is inspired by previous work on designing simplified privacy labels of Web sites [11] based on the now discontinued P3P standard [7]. It shares similar goals to provide a combined overview over a number of "API Facts". However, one important difference is that P3P was a single-purpose specification intended to standardize everything required for embedding privacy labels. It thus had fixed methods to locate privacy policies (four variations of discovering the policy resource), fixed ways how those were represented (using an XML-based vocabulary), and a fixed set of acceptable values (also encoded into the XML vocabulary) to be used in these policies.

The work presented in this paper is bigger in scope, and on the framework level. As such, we do not authoritatively prescribe any of the aspects that P3P was defining. Instead, we are assuming that with organizations and user groups using API labels, certain patterns will emerge, and will be used inside these communities. We can easily envision a future where our framework is used as a foundation to define a more concrete set of requirements, but this is out of scope for this paper, and most likely would benefit substantially from initial usage and feedback of the API label framework presented here.

3   Labeling APIs

The idea of API labels is that they apply not just to individual resources, but to a *complete API*. Many APIs will provide access to a large set of resources. It depends on the API style how APIs and individual resources relate [18]. In the most popular styles for APIs today, which are HTTP-based, the API is established as a set of resources with distinct URI identities, meaning that the API is a set of (potentially many) resources. One exception to this are RPC-oriented API styles (such as the ones using SOAP, grpc or GraphQL) which "tunnel" all API interactions through a single "API endpoint". In that latter case, there is no such thing as a "set of HTTP-oriented resources establishing the API", but since we are mostly concerned with today's popular HTTP-based styles, the question of the scope of API labels remains relevant.

Applications consuming APIs are coupled to them, and the choice of API to be consumed introduces critical dependencies for consumers [17]. Consumers need to be made aware about non-functional aspects, concerning the short-term availability and long-term evolution of API resources [15]. Likewise, when a resource is made available by a different API, different terms of service may apply to its usage.

From the consumer point of view, the concept of an "API boundary" can seem arbitrary or irrelevant, or both. API consumers most importantly want to implement applications. To do so, they need to discover, select and invoke one or more APIs. However, even when from the strict application logic point of view the "boundary" between APIs may not matter (applications will simply traverse resources either driven by application logic or by hypermedia links), it still may be relevant for non-functional aspects, such as when each API resource is made available by a different provider and therefore different terms of service apply to its usage.

Generally speaking, the Web model is that applications use various resources to accomplish their goals, and these resources often will be provided by more than one API. In this case the question is how it is possible to get the API labels for every resource, if applications want to do so. What is the scope of API labels, and how is it possible, starting from *any* resource of an API, to find its API labels? And how can an application know when traversing resources that it traverses an "API boundary"? The Web (and HTTP-based URIs) has no built-in notion to indicate "API boundaries", so the question is how to establish such a model.

It seems wasteful to always include all API label information in all resources, given that in many cases, applications will not need this information and thus it would make API responses unnecessarily large. However, there are approaches how this can be done in more efficient ways, and currently there are two solutions available (OpenAPI Link Objects and Home Documents). It is important to keep in mind that it is up to an API designer to decide if and how they will use these techniques to make labels easy to find.

3.1 OpenAPI Link Objects

The API description language *OpenAPI* (formerly known as *Swagger*) has added the concept of a *link object* with its first major release under the new name, version 3.0. Essentially, link objects are links that are defined in the OpenAPI description, and then can be considered to be applicable to specific resources of the API. In essence, this creates a shortcut mechanism where these links are factored out from actual API responses, and instead become part of the API description.

It is important to keep in mind that because of this design, the actual links in the OpenAPI link object never show up in the API itself; instead they are only part of the OpenAPI description. This design allows OpenAPI consumers to use these links without producing any runtime overhead, but it makes these links "invisible" for anybody not using the OpenAPI description and interpreting its link objects.

This design of OpenAPI thus can be seen as effective optimization, because it creates no runtime overhead. On the other hand, it limits self-descriptiveness and introduces substantial coupling by making the links in link objects exclusively visible to clients knowing and using the OpenAPI description.

For this reason, we believe that in environments where this coupling has been introduced already, OpenAPI link objects may be a good solution. This can be any environment where the assumption is that API consumers always know the OpenAPI descriptions of the APIs they are consuming. This may be a decision that is made in certain organizations or communities, but cannot be considered a design that is used in unconstrained API landscape.

In unconstrained API landscapes, it seems that the coupling introduced by making the knowledge and usage of all OpenAPI descriptions mandatory is substantial, and may be counterproductive to the self-describing and loosely coupled consumption of APIs. If the design goal is to focus on self-description and loose coupling, then OpenAPI link objects probably are not the best choice, and instead the approach of *home documents* may be the better one.

3.2 Home Documents

An alternative model to that of OpenAPI is established by the mechanism of *home documents* [16]. The idea of home documents is that there is a "general starting point" for an API. This starting point can provide a variety of information about the API, including information about its API labels. The home document then can be linked to from API resources, and there is a specific home link relation that is established as part of the home document model.

Using this model, all resources of an API can provide *one* additional link, which is to the API home document. The home document then becomes the starting point for accessing any information about the API, including an API's labels. This model means that there is an overhead of one link per resource. However, given modern mechanisms such as HTTP/2.0 header compression, it seems that this overhead is acceptable in the majority of cases, even if that link is not so much a functional part of the API itself, but instead provides access to metadata about the API.

One of the advantages of the idea of home documents and providing `home` links for resources is that this makes the API (or rather its resources) truly self-describing: Consumers do not need any additional information to find and use the information about an API's home document.

One downside to this model is that home documents are not yet a stable standard used across many APIs. The draft has been around for a while and has evolved over time, but it is not guaranteed that it will become a stable standard. One other hand, since this work is rooted in general Web architecture, even without the specification being a stable standard already using it is acceptable, and in fact this is how many IETF standards are conceived: drafts are proposed, already adopted by some, and the eventual standard then is informed by gathering feedback from those who already have gained experience with it.

4   Trusting API Descriptions and Documentations

API labels provide a human-readable format to summarize API descriptions including hyperlinks to relevant documentation and specifications. API labels are also meant to be machine processable to provide the basis for automated support for API landscape visualization and filtering capabilities.

One example for this are the link relation types for Web services [26]. These could be readily used as API labels (if they are made discoverable through the general API label mechanism). Some of the resources are likely just human-readable (for example API documentation provided as PDF), while other resources might be machine-readable and to some extent even machine-understandable (for example API description provided as OpenAPI which can be used by testing and documentation generation tools).

API labels are not meant to provide a complete specification of APIs and replace existing languages and service discovery tools. Instead, they are designed to include information that is currently not found in API descriptions as written by service providers, because this information may include claims that need to be verified by trusted third parties. Additionally, the summary described in the label can lead to more detailed original sources that can be used to confirm the validity of the summarized information.

While it is in a provider's best interest to provide a correct representation of its APIs functional characteristics (operation structure, data representation formats, suggested interaction conversations) so that clients may easily consume the API appropriately, questionable providers may be tempted to misrepresent some of the Quality of Service levels they may be capable of guaranteeing. Hence labeling APIs could provide the necessary means to certify and validate the provided API metadata information complementing other means to establish and assess the reputation of the API provider [3]. This is a rather challenging task that would require to deal with a number of non-trivial issues.

For example, how would consumers establish trust with a given API label certification authority? Is one centralized authority enough or should there be multiple ones taking into advantage the decentralized nature of the Web [6]? If multiple parties can certify the same API, how should consumers deal with conflicting labels? How to ensure labels can be certified in an economically sustainable way (are consumers willing to pay to get verified labels?) without leading to corruption (providers are willing to pay to get positive labels)? How would the authority actually verify the QoS claims of the provider? How to avoid that a provider obtains good results when undergoing a certification benchmark but poor performance during normal operations when servicing ordinary customer requests? How to ensure API labels are not tampered with? Should labels be signed by reference or by value?

While it is out of scope of this paper to deal with all of these issues, we believe some form of delegation where APIs reference labels via links to label resources hosted by third parties will be one of the key mechanisms to enable trust into certified API labels. This way, even if the label value itself is not provided by the API, but by using the delegation mechanism, we could still make it discoverable through the API.

5 Label Types

In order to be understandable, labels must follow a framework of well-defined types that can be "read" as API labels. Some of these may already exist as evolving or existing standards. The link relations for Web services discussed in the previous section can be considered potential API labels that are defined in an evolving standard. An example for an existing standard is the `license` link relation defined in RFC 4946 [20], which is meant to convey the license attached to resources made available through a service.

A label type identifies the kind of label information that is represented by attaching a label of this type. In principle, there are three different ways of how label types can communicate label information to consumers:

– By Value: If the label is simply an identifier, then the meaning of the label is communicated by the label value itself. The question then is what the permissible value space is (i.e., which values can be used to safely communicate a well-defined meaning between label creators and label readers). The value space can be fixed and defined by enumerating the values associated with the label type, or it can be defined in a way so that it can evolve. This second style of managing an evolving value space often is implementing through registries [27], which effectively decouples the definition of the label type and the definition of its value space.

- By Format: If the label is intended to communicate its meaning by reference, then it will link to a resource that represents the label's meaning. It is possible for label types to require that the format is always the same, and must be used when using that label. This is what P3P (the example mentioned earlier) did, by defining and requiring that P3P policies always must be represented by the defined format. This approach allows to build automation that can validate and interpret labels, by depending on the fact that there is one format that must be used for a given label type.
- By Link: It is also possible to not require the format being used. This is the most webby and open-ended approach, where a label links to a resource representing the label's value, but the link does not pre-determine the format of the linked resource. This approach has the advantage that label value representations can evolve and new ones can be added when required, but it has the disadvantage that there is no a priori interoperability of label producers and label consumers.

Returning to the examples given above, it becomes obvious that the existing mechanisms discussed so far that could be considered to be used as API labels already use different approaches from this spectrum. The link relation for licenses [20] is based on the assumption that a license is identified by value, thus requiring licenses to be identified by shared URI identifiers. P3P [7] defines its own format that has to be used for representing P3P labels. The link relations for Web services [26] identify information by link, and do not constrain the format that has to be used with those link relations.

6   API Label Examples

In this section we collect a preliminary list of API label types and values, characterizing several technical and non-technical concepts [25] which are meant to assist consumers during their API selection process. We have compiled this list based on the relevant literature, our experience, including feedback from our industry contacts.

- *Invocation Style:* This label defines on a technical level which kind style is required for clients to invoke the API. We distinguish between Synchronous RPC, Synchronous Callbacks, Asynchronous Events/Messages, REST, and Streaming.
- *Protocol Interoperability:* Which are the interaction protocols supported by the API? Which versions of the protocols? Examples values: SOAP, HTTP, GraphQL
- *Privacy:* Where is the data managed by the API stored? While clients do not care whether their data is stored in SQL or XML, they do worry whether their data is located in a different country and thus subject to different regulations.
- *Service Level Agreement:* Does an SLA explicitly exist? If it does: how is it enforced? are there penalties for violations? can it be negotiated? This helps to

roughly distinguish between APIs without SLAs from APIs having an explicitly (formally or informally) defined SLA, which can be further annotated to highlight whether service providers make serious efforts to stand behind their promises and whether they are willing to adapt to client needs by negotiating the terms of the agreement with them as opposed to offering a number of predefined usage plans.

– *Pricing:* Also related to SLA, clients want to know: whether there a free price plan? Can the API paid price plans be considered as cheap, reasonable, or expensive? This label needs to be computed based on the client expectations or by comparing with similar APIs.

– *Availability Track Record:* Does the API provider explicitly promises high availability? How well does the promise (e.g., "five nines" or 99.999%) matches the reality? Is the API provider's availability improving or getting worse? Additionally, clients need to know how to set their timeouts before giving up and determining that the API is no longer available. The Availability Track Record should label APIs for which such information is explicitly found in the corresponding SLA.

– *Maturity/Stability:* The Maturity label should provide a metric to determine whether the API has reached flying altitude and can be considered as mature enough, i.e., it is likely to be feature complete and stable during the entire lifecycle of clients consuming it. This can be inferred from versioning metadata, or some kind of metric summarizing the API version history (e.g., the number of changes over time, or how many alternative versions of the same API are supported in parallel by the provider). Conversely, if APIs are not yet mature and unstable, clients would benefit from knowing how much time they have to react to breaking API changes. Different providers may allow different amounts of time between announcing changes and carrying them out. In a similar way, as APIs eventually disappear, does the provider support some notion of *sunset* metadata? Are API features first deprecated and eventually retired, or does the API provider simply remove features without any warning?

– *Popularity:* How many clients are using the API? Is this the mostly used API within the ecosystem/architecture? is it in the top 10 APIs based on daily traffic? or only very few clients rarely invoke it?

– *Alternative Providers:* Are there alternative and competing providers for the API? or there exists only one monopolistic provider? How easy is it to replace the service provider of the API? How easy is it to find a replacement API within minimal differences from the current one?

Additional label types describing energy consumption, sustainability, quality management (e.g. ISO 9001 compliance) or trust certificates are possible.

7 A Recipe for API Labels

As mentioned already, the exact way of how to implement labels is not yet standardized. In this paper, we discuss the parts that need to be in place to use API labels, but we do not prescribe one single correct way. In order to summarize these parts, and to give organizations looking at using API labels a useful starting point, we are summarizing the required parts in an "API label landscape". We also recommend specific ways of solving these individual issues. In particular, Sect. 7.1 provides methods to make labels findable, and Sect. 7.2 provides methods to manage the types and the values of those findable labels so that the set of labels used in an API landscape can organically grow over time.

7.1   Findable Labels

In order for API labels to be usable and useful, they must be findable. One possibility is to manage them separate from APIs themselves, but this approach is likely to let APIs and their labels go out of sync easily. A more robust approach is to make API labels parts of APIs themselves, which allows labels to be managed and updated by the APIs themselves, and also allows labels to be found and accessed by those that have access to these APIs.

Using such an approach, making API labels findable amounts to allowing them to be accessed through the API. For this to be consistent across APIs, there need to be conventions that are used across APIs to find and access labels. What these conventions look like, depends on the style and technology of APIs. For HTTP APIs that are based on the resource-oriented or the hypermedia style of APIs this amount to providing resources that represent label information.

In terms of currently available practices, using home documents as described in Sect. 3.2 works well, if it is acceptable as a general API guideline to require APIs to provide home documents. If it is, labels still need to be made discoverable from that home document. We are suggesting to represent labels in a way that represents a set of labels, and that has the ability to "delegate" label representation to third parties, so that scenarios like the ones discussed in Sect. 4 can be implemented.

7.2   Extensible Label Sets

Once there is a defined way how labels can be found for APIs and, as suggested above, through the APIs themselves, then the next question is what types of labels can be found (Sect. 6 suggests a starting set of label types). It is likely that the set of label types is going to evolve over time, so the question is not only which types of labels to support, but also how to manage the continuous evolution of that set of types.

A flexible way to manage label sets is to use registries [27], as mentioned in Sect. 5. Once the necessary registry infrastructure is in place, registries need to be combined with policies so that values in the registry have a well-defined way how they evolve. For API label types and their corresponding values, a rather standard set of policies for registry management would most likely work well:

– Initial Set Any API label landscape will start with a set of initial label types. This set should be the "minimal viable product", meaning that it is more important to get API label use off the ground, than to have the perfectly curated set of label types. Likewise, the initial values of each label type will be chosen among values with a fixed and well-understood meaning.

- Additions after community review and consensus: The label landscape will continually grow, with new label types and values being added as required. Additional label types should have some motivation documented, and that motivation should be the starting point for a community review. If there is sufficient consensus to add the type, it is added to the set of existing label types. In a similar way, new values should undergo some review so that they broadly follow the general idea of the label type, and ideally do not created overlaps or conflicts with existing entries.
- Semantics of registered label types and values do not change: API labels should always mean the same, so the meaning of an API label type should never be changed. Once it has been registered, users will start using it and will depend on its registered meaning, so changing its meaning would be a breaking change for all uses of the API label. One exception to this rule is that it is possible to clarify and correct the meaning of a registered label value, but this should be used very carefully because any change being made to a label value's meaning should retroactively invalidate or change the way how a label value has been used before.
- Registered label types and values cannot be removed, but can be retired: Label types should never change meaning, but their usage may not be supported or required anymore. If that is the case, there should be a mechanism how a label type or value can be marked as *deprecated* in the registry, so that it becomes clear that this label may appear, but that it should not be actively used anymore. As opposed to removing it from the registry, the semantics of the deprecated value remain registered and available, allowing everybody to still look up what an assigned label type or value means. However, the status also makes it clear that this value should not be used for new labels.

While this recipe for managing label types and values is not the only possible way, it ensures that label management can evolve, and does not suffer from breaking changes along the way. This is thanks to the combination of stable semantics, and the policies on how to evolve them. Because this is a general pattern how to achieve robust extensibility, a very similar recipe can be used to manage the evolution of the value space of individual labels.

8   Conclusion

In this position paper we have made the case for API Labels. Labeling APIs is driven by the real world needs of consumers to quickly assess the main quality attributes of an API and its provider, which are likely to affect the consumer application built using the API in the long term. We have proposed the *API Label Framework (ALF)*: a framework based on the "API the APIs" principle to make API self-descriptive by attaching API labels as metadata to API resources. We also included an initial proposal for a number of possible label types. Some of these can be automatically derived by summarizing information found in

API descriptions written by the providers. Other require some external input by a third-party authority. For API Labels to become a trusted mechanism for API annotation, comparison and selection, there needs to be a verification and validation process which guarantees that consumers can trust the "facts" mentioned in the label.

9   Future Work

As part of future work we plan to make labels self-describing by creating identifiers for each label type you want to support and make label values self-describing by clearly defining the value space for each label. Tooling will be required to automatically extract labels and validate the consistency of labels with the corresponding detailed API descriptions so that API owners can easily test their labels and see how they are working. Once a number of machine-readable API labels become available, tooling to crawl labels will make it easier for developers to explore the "label graph" of the labels that one or more API providers define.

Also policies around label changes will need to be established so that it is well-defined when and how to expect label updates and how these are communicated by tracking the history of a given API. Given that label types and values themselves will likely evolve, it will be important to determine how the set of possible known values is defined and where can the identified label types can be reused from. Registries [27] for API labels and possibly their value spaces are like to play a key role for addressing this challenge.

References

1. Atkinson, L., Rosenthal, S.: Signaling the green sell: the influence of eco-label source, argument specificity, and product involvement on consumer trust. J. Advert. **43**(1), 33–45 (2014)
2. Becker, T.: To what extent are consumer requirements met by public quality policy? In: Quality Policy and Consumer Behaviour in the European Union, pp. 247–266. Wissenschaftsverlag Vauk Kiel KG (2000)
3. Bidgoly, A.J., Ladani, B.T.: Benchmarking reputation systems: a quantitative verification approach. Comput. Human Behav. **57**, 274–291 (2016). https://doi.org/10.1016/j.chb.2015.12.024
4. Booth, D., Liu, C.K.: Web Services Description Language (WSDL) Version 2.0 Part 0: Primer. World Wide Web Consortium, Recommendation REC-wsdl20-primer-20070626, June 2007
5. Caswell, J.A., Mojduszka, E.M.: Using informational labeling to influence the market for quality in food products. Am. J. Agric. Econ. **78**(5), 1248–1253 (1996)
6. Chu, Y.H., Feigenbaum, J., LaMacchia, B., Resnick, P., Strauss, M.: REFEREE: trust management for web applications. Comput. Netw. ISDN Syst. **29**(8–13), 953–964 (1997)
7. Cranor, L.F.: Web Privacy with P3P. O'Reilly & Associates, Sebastopol (2002)
8. García, J.M., Fernandez, P., Pedrinaci, C., Resinas, M., Cardoso, J.S., Cortés, A.R.: Modeling service level agreements with linked USDL agreement. IEEE Trans. Serv. Comput. **10**(1), 52–65 (2017). https://doi.org/10.1109/TSC.2016.2593925

9. Hadley, M.: Web application description language (WADL). Technical report. TR-2006-153, Sun Microsystems, April 2006
10. Kearney, K.T., Torelli, F., Kotsokalis, C.: SLA⋆: an abstract syntax for service level agreements. In: Proceedings of the 11th IEEE/ACM International Conference on Grid Computing (GRID), pp. 217–224 (2010)
11. Kelley, P.G., Bresee, J., Cranor, L.F., Reeder, R.W.: A nutrition label for privacy. In: Proceedings of the 5th Symposium on Usable Privacy and Security, p. 4. ACM (2009)
12. Kopecký, J., Gomadam, K., Vitvar, T.: hRESTS: an HTML microformat for describing RESTful web services. In: IEEE/WIC/ACM International Conference on Web Intelligence, Sydney, Australia, pp. 619–625, December 2008. https://doi.org/10.1109/WIIAT.2008.469
13. Kotler, P.: Marketing Management: Analysis, Planning, Implementation and Control. Prentice Hall, Upper Saddle River (1997)
14. Lethbridge, T.C., Singer, J., Forward, A.: How software engineers use documentation: the state of the practice. IEEE Software **20**(6), 35–39 (2003). https://doi.org/10.1109/MS.2003.1241364
15. Li, J., Xiong, Y., Liu, X., Zhang, L.: How does web service API evolution affect clients? In: IEEE 20th International Conference on Web Services (ICWS), pp. 300–307, June 2013
16. Nottingham, M.: Home Documents for HTTP APIs. Internet Draft draft-nottingham-json-home-06, August 2017
17. Pautasso, C., Wilde, E.: Why is the web loosely coupled? A multi-faceted metric for service design. In: Quemada, J., León, G., Maarek, Y.S., Nejdl, W. (eds.) 18th International World Wide Web Conference, Madrid, Spain, pp. 911–920. ACM Press, April 2009
18. Pautasso, C., Zimmermann, O.: The web as a software connector: integration resting on linked resources. IEEE Software **35**(1), 93–98 (2018)
19. Robie, J., Sinnema, R., Wilde, E.: RADL: RESTful API description language. In: Kosek, J. (ed.) XML Prague 2014, Prague, Czech Republic, pp. 181–209. February 2014
20. Snell, J.M.: Atom License Extension. Internet RFC **4946**, July 2007
21. Tata, S., Mohamed, M., Sakairi, T., Mandagere, N., Anya, O., Ludwig, H.: RSLA: a service level agreement language for cloud services. In: Proceedings of the 9th International Conference on Cloud Computing (CLOUD2016), pp. 415–422. IEEE (2016). https://doi.org/10.1109/CLOUD.2016.60
22. The Open API Initiative: OAI (2016). https://openapis.org/
23. Uriarte, R.B., Tiezzi, F., De Nicola, R.: SLAC: a formal service-level-agreement language for cloud computing. In: UCC, pp. 419–426. IEEE, December 2014
24. Verborgh, R., Steiner, T., Deursen, D.V., Coppens, S., Vallés, J.G., de Walle, R.V.: Functional descriptions as the bridge between hypermedia APIs and the semantic web. In: Alarcón, R., Pautasso, C., Wilde, E. (eds.) Third International Workshop on RESTful Design (WS-REST 2012), Lyon, France, pp. 33–40, April 2012. https://doi.org/10.1145/2307819.2307828
25. Wilde, E.: Surfing the API web: web concepts. In: 27th International World Wide Web Conference, Lyon, France, pp. 797–803. ACM Press, April 2018
26. Wilde, E.: Link Relation Types for Web Services. Internet Draft draft-wilde-service-link-rel-10, January 2019
27. Wilde, E.: The Use of Registries. Internet Draft draft-wilde-registries-02, April 2019

Towards a Generalizable Comparison of the Maintainability of Object-Oriented and Service-Oriented Applications

Justus Bogner[1,2(✉)], Bhupendra Choudhary[2], Stefan Wagner[2], and Alfred Zimmermann[1]

[1] University of Applied Sciences Reutlingen, Reutlingen, Germany
{justus.bogner,alfred.zimmermann}@reutlingen-university.de
[2] University of Stuttgart, Stuttgart, Germany
{justus.bogner,stefan.wagner}@iste.uni-stuttgart.de,
bhupendra.choudhary@gmx.de

Abstract. While there are several theoretical comparisons of Object Orientation (OO) and Service Orientation (SO), little empirical research on the maintainability of the two paradigms exists. To provide support for a generalizable comparison, we conducted a study with four related parts. Two functionally equivalent systems (one OO and one SO version) were analyzed with coupling and cohesion metrics as well as via a controlled experiment, where participants had to extend the systems. We also conducted a survey with 32 software professionals and interviewed 8 industry experts on the topic. Results indicate that the SO version of our system possesses a higher degree of cohesion, a lower degree of coupling, and could be extended faster. Survey and interview results suggest that industry sees systems built with SO as more loosely coupled, modifiable, and reusable. OO systems, however, were described as less complex and easier to test.

Keywords: Maintainability · Service orientation · Object orientation · Metrics · Experiment · Survey · Interviews

1 Introduction

The ability to quickly and cost-efficiently change applications and services due to new or redacted requirements is important for any company relying on custom software. The associated quality attribute is maintainability: the degree of effectiveness and efficiency with which software can be changed [5], e.g. to adapt or extend it. The introduction of Object Orientation (OO) lead to maintainability-related benefits like encapsulation, abstraction, inheritance, or increased support for modularization [3]. In today's enterprise world, however, systems built on Service Orientation (SO) are increasingly more common. By introducing a higher level of abstraction, Service-Based Systems (SBSs) consist of loosely coupled distributed components with well defined technology-agnostic interfaces [7].

© Springer Nature Switzerland AG 2020
M. Fazio and W. Zimmermann (Eds.): ESOCC 2018 Workshops, CCIS 1115, pp. 114–125, 2020.
https://doi.org/10.1007/978-3-030-63161-1_9

SO aims to promote interoperability, reuse of cohesive functionality at a business-relevant abstraction level, and encapsulation of implementation details behind published interfaces [4].

So while Service Orientation seems to surpass Object Orientation w.r.t. maintainability from a theoretical point of view, this comparison is very hard to generalize in a practical setting. Developers can build systems of arbitrary quality in both paradigms, although the inherent properties of both paradigms may make it easier or harder to build well maintainable systems. Very little empirical research exists on the topic of comparing the maintainability of OO and SO (see Sect. 2). Results from such studies can bring valuable insights into the evolution qualities of these two paradigms. Research in this area can also highlight potential deficiencies and weaknesses, which helps raising awareness for developers as well as providing decision support for choosing a paradigm for a project.

This is why we conducted a study to compare the maintainability of object-oriented and service-oriented applications from different perspectives. For a practical empirical point of view, we constructed two functionally equivalent systems (one based on OO and the other on SO) and compared them with metrics as well as by means of a controlled software development experiment. To gain insight into software professionals' subjective estimation of the two paradigms, we conducted an industry survey as well as expert interviews. In the remainder of this paper, we first introduce related work in this area. Then we present the details of our 4-part study including the methods, results, and limitations. Lastly, we conclude by summarizing our results and putting them into perspective.

2   Related Work

A small number of scientific publications exists that compare Service Orientation and Object Orientation. In 2005 when SBSs were still very young, Baker and Dobson [1] published a theoretical comparison of Service-Oriented Architecture (SOA) and Distributed Object Architectures (DOA) based on literature and personal experience. Their comparison is very high-level and not focused specifically on maintainability. While they highlight a large number of similarities, they also point out the more coarse-grained interfaces of SOA that lead to simplified communication and less cognitive overhead for developers of service consumers. Moreover, they point out the missing notion of inheritance and interface specialization in SOA, which they acknowledge as initially less complex, but potentially limiting in the long term.

Stubbings [10] provided another theoretical comparison that also emphasizes the direct line of evolution from OO to SO. Beneficial OO concepts like encapsulation and reuse have been adapted to a higher abstraction level in Service Orientation that is closer to the business domain. He further assessed the structural and technological complexity to be higher in a system based on Service Orientation. Concerning communication, he reported the focus for OO to be primarily internal while SO would be more aimed at external interoperability.

One of the few empirical studies on the subject was performed by Perepletchikov et al. [8] on two versions of a fictional Academic Management System (one service-oriented version, the other one object-oriented). To compare the maintainability of the two, they employed traditional source code metrics like *Lines of Code, Cyclomatic Complexity*, as well as the OO metrics suite from Chidamber and Kemerer. They focused on the structural properties size, complexity, coupling, and cohesion. As findings, they reported that the SO version provides better separation of business and implementation logic and a lower degree of coupling. The OO system, however, would be overall less complex.

Lastly, Mansour and Mustafa [6] conducted a similar empirical study. They constructed a service-oriented version of an existing OO Automated Teller Machine system and compared the two versions with a set of metrics, very similar to the ones in [8]. They reported that the SO version of their system inhibited a higher degree of reusability and a lower degree of coupling while the complexity of the OO version was lower. Additionally, they described difficulties when trying to apply OO metrics to a Service-Based System and advocated the need for a set of service-oriented maintainability metrics.

Existing studies are either of a theoretical nature or solely focused on metrics. While the presented empirical studies provide first valuable support for a comparison with metrics, they also reported difficulties due to a lack of mutually applicable metrics. Not all OO metrics can be used for SBSs. Moreover, additional metric evaluations with other systems will be of value while new approaches can bring different perspectives to the discussion.

3   Study Design

Based on the results and lessons learned of the related work, we therefore conducted a study with four different parts. First, we constructed a service-oriented and an object-oriented version of a simple Online Book Store (OBS) that provided functionality to register as a user as well as to browse and order books. The service-oriented version was implemented with RESTful NodeJS services using the Express framework[1] and an Angular frontend[2] while the object-oriented version is a Java monolith relying on JavaServer Pages (JSP) as a web UI. These two systems were compared using a set of **coupling and cohesion metrics**. To respect the two system versions, we needed metrics that can be applied both to service- as well as object-oriented systems. This is often difficult to achieve, since coupling and cohesion metrics are usually designed for either of the two paradigms. We therefore chose two metrics for each structural property that could be adapted to be mutually applicable.

For coupling, we chose *Absolute Importance of the Service* (AIS) and *Absolute Dependence of the Service* (ADS). Both have been specifically designed for SBSs and represent the number of clients invoking a service (AIS) and the number of

---

[1] https://expressjs.com.
[2] https://angular.io.

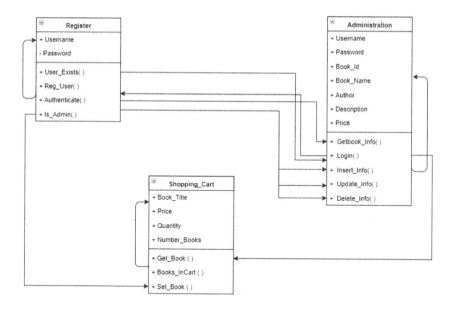

Fig. 1. Object-oriented version of OBS

other services a service depends on respectively (ADS) [9]. They can be easily adapted to object-oriented systems by substituting *services* with *classes*.

For cohesion, we selected two object-oriented metrics, namely *Tight Class Cohesion* (TCC) and *Loose Class Cohesion* (LCC) [2]. These metrics attempt to measure the relatedness of class functionality based on common class attributes that the methods operate on. TCC represents the relative number of directly connected methods while LCC also includes indirectly connected methods (via other intermediate methods). To adapt these metrics to a service-oriented context, class methods are substituted by service operations.

While the majority of maintainability metrics use structural properties as a proxy, industry is really interested in something else: how fast can changes or features be implemented for the system? To account for this, the same systems were used in a **controlled experiment**. Software practitioners had to implement search functionality for books while the time was measured. We then analyzed whether the version made a noticeable difference. 8 software developers participated in the experiment, four per system version of OBS. 7 of the 8 developers were from Germany. They had an average of ∼4.1 years of experience (OO AVG: 4.5 years, SO AVG: 3.75 years). All of them had worked with their respective paradigm before. We measured the time necessary to complete the exercise as well as the changed Lines of Code for the backend part.

To complement these two empirical approaches, we also conducted an **industry survey** to capture the general sentiment of developers towards the two paradigms. Software professionals filled out an online questionnaire where they

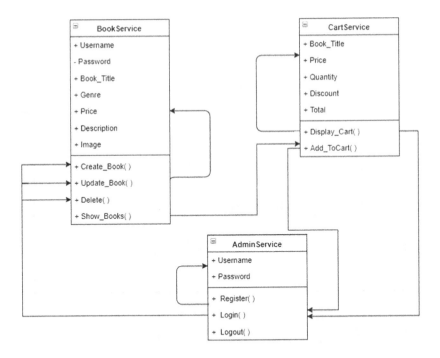

Fig. 2. Service-oriented version of OBS

were asked to compare structural and maintainability-related properties of the two paradigms based on their personal experience. 32 participants completed our web-based questionnaire that was distributed via personal industry contacts, mailing lists, and social media. The survey was hosted from 2018-04-19 until 2018-05-06 and consisted of 12 questions, mostly with Likert scale answers. Most participants were from Germany and India and all had at least three years of professional experience. They had to comment on the average condition of different structural properties (e.g. coupling) and subquality attributes of maintainability in SW projects based on either OO or SO. Lastly, they had to answer some questions where they ranked the three paradigms *Object Orientation, Service Orientation*, and *Component-Based* for similar attributes.

As a more in-depth follow-up to the survey, we conducted **qualitative interviews** with several experts to complement the broader scope of the survey and to dive more deeply into some of the topics. Similar to the survey, we also asked for their personal experience and preference w.r.t. the maintainability of the two paradigms under study. This was the fourth and final part of our study. All 8 experts had an IT or Engineering background and had previously worked with object-oriented as well as service-oriented systems. 7 of the 8 experts were older than 30 years, i.e. had considerable professional experience. The interviews started with an introduction of the two OBS versions and a discussion about their strengths and weaknesses. This was followed by similar questions as in the survey about properties of the two paradigms and the participants' experience.

Please refer to our GitHub repository for the source code of the systems as well as the detailed survey questions and results[3].

4   Results

For the metric-based part of the study, we measured all four **component-level metrics** for both the object-oriented (Fig. 1) and the service-oriented version (Fig. 2) of the Online Book Store (OBS). Since each version of the system includes three components (services or classes respectively), we have a total of 12 measurements (see Table 1). When looking at the AVG values per version and metric (see Fig. 3), we can see that the service-oriented version overall has slightly better values, i.e. on average lower coupling and higher cohesion per component.

Table 1. Coupling and cohesion metric values per component

	Component	AIS	ADS	TCC	LCC
OO Version	Administration	1	2	0.00	0.40
	Register	1	2	0.16	0.50
	Shopping_Cart	2	0	0.33	0.33
SO Version	AdminService	1	1	0.67	0.67
	BookService	1	1	0.33	0.50
	CartService	1	1	1.00	1.00

During the **controlled experiment**, it took less time and effort to extend the service-oriented version of OBS (see Fig. 4). The mean duration for the SO version was 0.8 h while it was 0.99 h for the OO version. Respectively, the mean effort was 7.25 LoC for SO and 12.5 LoC for OO. When analyzing the significance of the mean differences in our sample with an unpaired t-test, we found two-tailed p-values smaller than 0.05 (p-value$_{duration}$: 0.0479, p-value$_{effort}$: 0.005).

The following part highlights the results of the **survey questions**. For Likert scale question, we also present the aggregated score per paradigm (Strongly Disagree: -2, Disagree: -1, Neutral: 0, Agree: 1, Strongly Agree: 2).

Question: *In my experience, software based on <paradigm> has a comparatively low degree of **coupling**.*

---

[3] https://github.com/xJREB/research-oo-vs-so.

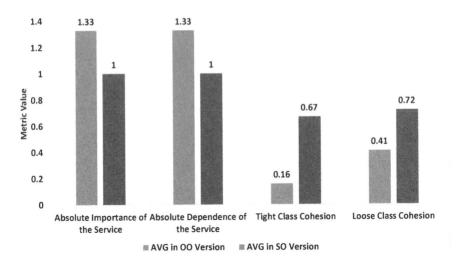

Fig. 3. Average coupling and cohesion metric values per version

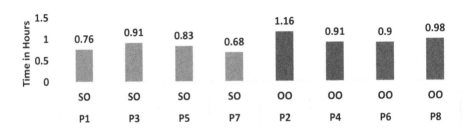

Fig. 4. Experiment: duration per participant

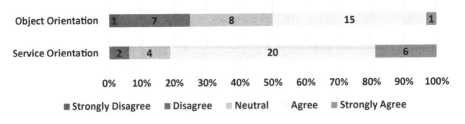

Fig. 5. Question: In my experience, software based on <paradigm> has a comparatively low degree of **coupling**.

For coupling, participants clearly favored Service Orientation (score: 30) over Object Orientation (score: 8). Over 80% reported that service-oriented systems were in their experience of a more loosely coupled nature while only 50% reported the same for object-oriented systems (see Fig. 5). This result was to be expected, since loose coupling and the reduction of dependencies is a major driver in SBSs.

Question: *In my experience, software based on <paradigm> facilitates a comparatively high degree of **cohesion**.*

When it came to cohesion, the results were less decisive (SO: 18, OO: 14). Overall, roughly 13% more participants agreed with this statement for Service Orientation (SO: ∼63%, OO: 50%). This does not seem to be a lot, when we consider the prevalence of the "cohesive services grouped around business capabilities" theme in an SOA and especially in a Microservices context.

Question: *In my experience, software based on <paradigm> promises a significant extent of **reusability**.*

Participants reported higher reusability for their service-oriented software than for their object-oriented software. While the scores were pretty even (SO: 25, OO: 22), ∼78% of participants agreed to this statement for SO while only ∼59% agreed for OO. Absolute scores are so close because two more people disagreed for SO and one more strongly agreed for OO (see Fig. 6). Overall, these results seem to support the SO principle of business-relevant reuse granularity.

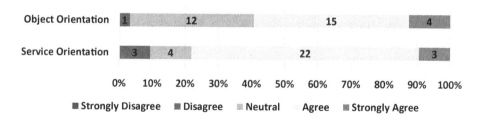

Fig. 6. Question: In my experience, software based on <paradigm> promises a significant extent of **reusability**.

Question: *In my experience, software based on <paradigm> reduces the complexity of **testing**.*

In the case of testability, Object Orientation (score: 24) was seen as more beneficial than Service Orientation (score: 14) to reduce complexity. Roughly 72% of participants agreed with this statement for OO while only ∼53% agreed for SO together with 6 disagreements (see Fig. 7). This is the first category where OO decisively wins out in the opinion of participating developers.

Lastly, developers were asked to rank the three paradigms *Object Orientation*, *Service Orientation*, and *Component-Based* from their experience for three further properties: modifiability, encapsulation/abstraction, and size/complexity. Ranking a paradigm first provided three points, ranking it second provided two,

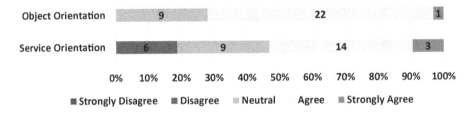

Fig. 7. Question: In my experience, software based on <paradigm> reduces the complexity of **testing**.

Table 2. Question: In your experience, which of the three paradigms provides on average the most favorable degree of <attribute>?

	Object Orientation	Component-Based	Service Orientation
Modifiability	63	43	86
Encapsulation and Abstraction	58	43	85
Size and Complexity	74	39	73

ranking it last provided one point respectively. The results (see Table 2) indicate that participants experienced systems based on Service Orientation as more modifiable and with a better degree of encapsulation and abstraction as for the other two paradigms. For size and complexity, however, participants reported that they believed the manageability of these properties to be roughly equal for OO and SO, with OO winning out by one point.

We compiled results from the **qualitative interviews** in several areas. For the topic of *modifiability*, 5 of the 8 experts reported that on average in their experience service-oriented systems are more beneficial than object-oriented ones when it comes to evolving already developed systems. Participants emphasized the advantages of service-based modularity, which would increase independence in the system and reduce costs in the long run. Some experts highlighted that SO is more convenient when requirements frequently change.

Concerning *complexity*, most experts indicated based on their past software projects that systems based on Object Orientation are on average less complex than SBSs from a structural and technological point of view. They also mentioned mature tool support in the field of object-oriented SW development that would ease some of the difficulties. In the service-oriented space, however, tool support would be lacking.

When comparing the average *analyzability* of the two paradigms, the majority of participants favored Service Orientation over Object Orientation. The structure of the system would be easier to grasp when referring to services as coarse-grained components. Moreover, experts experienced less dependencies in SBSs, which also helped to comprehend the structure of a system.

Lastly, in addition to the lack of mature tool support for Service Orientation, participants reported the danger of ripple effects when changing services, especially with service interface changes that require updates of all service consumers. Some experts also stressed that Object Orientation was a valuable paradigm to be used for the inner low-level design of single services and that it would nicely complement the service-based high-level architecture of a system. So the choice would not always be either Service or Object Orientation.

5   Threats to Validity

Several things have to be mentioned to put our results into appropriate perspective. For the **metric-based evaluation**, the tested systems were artificially constructed and are not real industry or open source systems. While we tried to design and implement them as close to a real use case as possible, we also needed something of manageable size and complexity, which may impact the generalizability of the comparison (e.g. the AVG metric values were computed from only three components). The chosen technology for both versions may also be a limitation. Results with other programming languages or frameworks could be different. Moreover, we only used a small number of metrics and targeted only two structural properties (coupling and cohesion). Other metrics, e.g. for size or complexity, could have yielded additional insights, but were neglected due to project time constraints. Finally, we calculated the metric values manually due to missing tool support. Since the systems are of limited size and we double-checked each value, the error probability should still be very small.

In the case of the **controlled experiment**, the same limitations of the constructed systems as described above hold true. The two different programming languages (Java and NodeJS/JavaScript) also limit the comparability of the LoC effort. Additionally, we only had a small number of participants. Potentially different development experience and skill levels could not be accounted for when assigning the participants to the two versions of OBS. Lastly, the experiment consisted of only one exercise, which can only test the modifiability of certain parts of the system.

As with most **quantitative surveys**, a number of limitations have to be mentioned. First, the number of participants (32) only provides limited generalizability, as a different population subset may have different views on the subject. Moreover, we could not guarantee that the participating developers indeed had sufficient experience with all three software paradigms. Lastly, the subjective estimation of the inherent qualities of a paradigm may be skewed by a particularly bad experience with a suboptimally designed system. Overall, it is important to keep in mind that personal preference of developers is not necessarily of a rational nature.

As opposed to our survey participants, we could select our **interview experts** based on their experience with the two paradigms under evaluation, at least up to a certain degree. However, there is still a chance that some experts were less proficient with one of the paradigms or were heavily influenced by one specific project of theirs. Moreover, there is a chance that we slightly influenced the experts by posing questions that should direct the conversation to the properties under evaluation. Lastly, our interviews were conducted and analyzed in a fairly loosely structured manner without a rigorous methodology.

6   Conclusion

To provide additional evidence for a generalizable comparison of the maintainability of Service Orientation and Object Orientation, we conducted a study with four parts: a metric-based comparison of two functionally equivalent systems (one SO and one OO version); a controlled experiment where practitioners had to extend the same systems; an industry survey with comparative questions about OO and SO; and expert interviews as a more in-depth follow-up to the survey.

The empirical results indicate that the service-oriented version of our Online Book Store system consists of more cohesive and more loosely coupled components and could also be extended faster and with less effort (LoC) by experiment participants. Survey and interview results seem to go in the same direction: industry professionals experienced higher modifiability, lower degrees of coupling, higher reusability, and stronger encapsulation and abstraction in their service-oriented projects. For their average object-oriented systems, however, they reported comparatively lower complexity and better testability.

While these results can aid in the decision process for a paradigm and can highlight important maintainability-related focus points when designing systems with either paradigm, it is still important to remember that we can build software of arbitrary quality in both paradigms. Moreover, Object Orientation can be a useful complement for the inner architecture of services.

Acknowledgments. This research was partially funded by the Ministry of Science of Baden-Württemberg, Germany, for the Doctoral Program "Services Computing" (http://www.services-computing.de/?lang=en).

References

1. Baker, S., Dobson, S.: Comparing service-oriented and distributed object architectures. In: Meersman, R., Tari, Z. (eds.) OTM 2005. LNCS, vol. 3760, pp. 631–645. Springer, Heidelberg (2005). https://doi.org/10.1007/11575771_40
2. Bieman, J.M., Kang, B.K.: Cohesion and reuse in an object-oriented system. In: Proceedings of the 1995 Symposium on Software reusability - SSR 1995, pp. 259–262. ACM Press, New York (1995)
3. Booch, G.: Object Oriented Analysis & Design with Application. Pearson Education, London (2006)
4. Erl, T.: Service-Oriented Architecture: Concepts, Technology, and Design. Prentice Hall PTR, Upper Saddle River (2005)
5. International Organization For Standardization: ISO/IEC 25010 - Systems and software engineering - Systems and software Quality Requirements and Evaluation (SQuaRE) - System and software quality models. Technical report (2011)

6. Mansour, Y.I., Mustafa, S.H.: Assessing internal software quality attributes of the object-oriented and service-oriented software development paradigms: a comparative study. J. Software Eng. Appl. **04**(04), 244–252 (2011)
7. Papazoglou, M.: Service-oriented computing: concepts, characteristics and directions. In: Proceedings of the 7th International Conference on Properties and Applications of Dielectric Materials (Cat. No.03CH37417), pp. 3–12. IEEE (2003)
8. Perepletchikov, M., Ryan, C., Frampton, K.: Comparing the impact of service-oriented and object-oriented paradigms on the structural properties of software. In: Meersman, R., Tari, Z., Herrero, P. (eds.) OTM 2005. LNCS, vol. 3762, pp. 431–441. Springer, Heidelberg (2005). https://doi.org/10.1007/11575863_63
9. Rud, D., Schmietendorf, A., Dumke, R.R.: Product Metrics for Service-Oriented Infrastructures. In: IWSM/MetriKon (2006)
10. Stubbings, G.: Service-orientation and object-orientation: complementary design paradigms. SPARK: ACES J Postgrad. Res. **1**, 1–9 (2010)

ESOCC 2018 PhD Symposium

ESOCC PhD Symposium Preface

The ESOCC PhD symposium is an international forum for PhD students working in any of the areas addressed by the ESOCC conference. The following papers collect all accepted research reports as submitted by the students. As a result, five out of the eight submitted papers are included in the following. The decision which of these reports to include in the symposium proceedings was based on the quality of the report, presentation, and short pitch by the student during the symposium.

As the organizers of this event, we would like to thank the students for their high quality submissions, the Program Committee for their reviews and feedback during and after the presentations, and the conference organizers for creating this space of idea exchanges.

March 2020

Vasilios Andrikopoulos
Massimo Villari

ESOCC PhD Symposium Organization

Program Committee

Marco Aiello	University of Stuttgart, Germany
Antonio Brogi	University of Pisa, Italy
Flavio De Paoli	University of Milano-Bicocca, Italy
Friederike Klan	Friedrich Schiller University Jena, Germany
Welf Loewe	Linnaeus University, Sweden
Alexander Pokahr	University of Hamburg, Germany
Emilio Tuosto	University of Leicester, UK
John Wittern	IBM Research, USA

Towards an Evolvability Assurance Method for Service-Based Systems

Justus Bogner[1,2]($\boxtimes$), Alfred Zimmermann[1], and Stefan Wagner[2]

[1] University of Applied Sciences Reutlingen, Reutlingen, Germany
`justus.bogner@reutlingen-university.de`
[2] University of Stuttgart, Stuttgart, Germany
`justus.bogner@informatik.uni-stuttgart.de`

Abstract. To enable software professionals to design and evolve long-living Service-Based Systems (SBSs) in sustainable fashion, we are developing a continuous assurance method to identify and remediate potential evolvability-related issues. With the rational of broad applicability within service-based architectural styles, we focus on the commonalities of Service-Oriented Architecture (SOA) and Microservices. The method is based on structural service-oriented metrics (e.g. coupling or cohesion), service evolution scenarios, as well as service-oriented design patterns to increase modifiability. Tool support should enable convenient usage and adoption of the method for practitioners. The final evaluation is planned as an industry case study in combination with action research.

Keywords: Evolvability · Maintainability · Service-Based Systems · Microservices · Metrics · Scenarios · Patterns

1 Introduction and Motivation

In a world of digital transformation where change is the only constant, it is essential for companies to quickly and efficiently adapt their software to new or changed requirements. The associated quality attribute (QA) is *maintainability*, the degree of effectiveness and efficiency with which software can be changed [21]. While requirements are stable, *corrective* or *perfective* maintenance can be performed. With changes in the set of requirements, we perform *adaptive* or *extending* maintenance [31]. The quality attribute for the latter types of maintenance is also referred to as *evolvability*. The importance and complexity of this quality attribute have been known for a long time and have been for example conceptualized in Lehman's laws of software evolution [23]. Nonetheless, evolvability is often overshadowed by the need for new features or other QAs with more end-user visibility, e.g. performance. Choosing expedient solutions that work in the short term but may pose significant issues for software evolution in the long run leads to the accrual of *technical debt* [4]. Lastly, it is very difficult to quantify and generalize evolvability, as one system may be very robust towards a certain type of change, but may be completely inflexible towards other changes.

© Springer Nature Switzerland AG 2020
M. Fazio and W. Zimmermann (Eds.): ESOCC 2018 Workshops, CCIS 1115, pp. 131–139, 2020.
https://doi.org/10.1007/978-3-030-63161-1_10

The introduction of Service-Oriented Computing (SOC) [28] allegedly brought several maintainability-related advantages like effective encapsulation and abstraction, loose coupling, increased reusability and composition, or a high degree of interoperability. However, Service-Based Systems (SBSs) also come with high technological and structural complexity and make end-to-end testing more difficult [16]. Industry dissatisfaction with Service-Oriented Architecture (SOA) in general and SOAP Web Services in particular (e.g. due to heavyweight and complex technology, vendor product lock-in, or governance overhead) led to the rise of a more agile and lightweight service-based architectural style, namely *Microservices* [26]. The combination of DevOps tools and principles [5], fine-grained loosely coupled services, and decentralization of management and control is also supposed to increase long-term maintainability and especially evolvability of these systems. Several studies indicate that increased maintainability is one of the primary drivers for migrating to a Microservice Architecture (MSA) [14,19,27]. While Microservices seem to work very well for companies stocked with top talent like Amazon, Netflix, or Spotify, they are certainly no silver bullet and also introduce a high complexity in the outer architecture [11].

Moreover, several publications report a high trust of practitioners in the inherent evolution qualities of service orientation (e.g. [1,34]), in fact to such a degree that they may deliberately reduce maintainability control efforts. In our industry survey (n = 60) [7], only 25% of participants indicated that they were actually content with the degree of maintainability of their software, while simultaneously $\sim$67% reported to not treat systems based on service orientation any different w.r.t. maintainability assurance. As reasons, most admitted that they did not know what to change or that they had never thought about addressing SBSs differently. A "blind" belief in the base-level maintainability of service orientation without being aware for the preconditions of these inherent qualities can lead to serious evolution issues in the long-term.

While the evolvability assurance of Service- and Microservice-Based Systems is of a complex nature due to, for example, a high degree of technological heterogeneity, a higher level of abstraction for metrics, a large number of components in different source code repositories, or indirect dependencies between services, there are very few publications on the topic from a holistic perspective. Likewise, available tool support to aid in the assurance process is also lacking. In the context of the presented problem space, the planned contribution of this research is therefore to develop a lightweight assurance method to support the identification and remediation of evolvability-related issues in Service-Based Systems.

This paper presents the specifics of the mentioned method by first explaining the scope and guiding questions for this research. The section thereafter provides an overview of completed and planned research contributions to design the method. To put our contribution into perspective, the related work section presents existing research of similar intent. Lastly, a conclusive section summarizes the paper and presents an outlook on the next steps.

2   Scope and Research Questions

While existing related work (see Sect. 4) holds value and may partially address evolvability-related issues in systems based on service orientation, there is currently no lightweight and practical method that is specialized for modern forms of service orientation and approaches evolvability from several perspectives at once. To address this gap, our goal is to develop a holistic assurance method with the following characteristics.

Targeted at Service-Based Systems in General. The method is specifically designed for service orientation. We consciously chose the more neutral term *Service-Based Systems* as opposed to *SOA* or *Microservices*. The rationale for this is that we focus on the commonalities of the two prevalent service-based architectural styles. Moreover, we believe that there are several SBSs in practice that are neither fully classifiable as SOA nor as Microservices, which seems to be confirmed by [33]. Nonetheless, we focus on modern containerized service- and web-based applications that use RESTful HTTP or lightweight messaging (e.g. AMQP) as opposed to heavyweight SOAP/WSDL.

An Efficient Method for Continuous Software Engineering. We aspire our method to be of a lightweight and flexible nature that is relevant for industry. It should be usable in agile organizations in line with the philosophy of continuous software engineering [18]. Within a continuous integration pipeline, timely automatic feedback for evaluating services will be provided.

Structural Metrics for Fast Feedback. The method enables the automatic gathering of structural metrics for system properties like coupling, cohesion, or granularity. This provides a quantitative evaluation of the base-level evolvability of the system.

Evolution Scenarios for Specific Changes. To complement the metric-based evaluation, we will provide qualitative evaluation in the method via lightweight scenarios. This tool-supported but manual analysis helps to prepare for specific changes and has been adapted for modifiability of service-based systems from scenario-based methods like ATAM or ALMA.

Service-Oriented Evolvability Patterns. As remediations to identified problems in the architecture (*hot spots*), we suggest selected service-oriented design patterns that are beneficial for modifiability.

Tool Support to Bring it All Together. As the central end-user interface, we plan to provide tool support for convenient visualization of the analysis results and remediation suggestions.

The research questions that frame and provide guidance for this project are as follows. RQ1a and RQ1b are of exploratory and analytical nature to accumulate knowledge while RQ2 is design-related and focused on the final artifact.

RQ1a: What are existing approaches to measure and improve maintainability and evolvability for Service-Based Systems?

RQ1b: Are these approaches also applicable to Microservice-Based Systems and what are potential limitations?

RQ2: What is a feasible and efficient method for continuous evolvability assurance of Service-Based Systems?

3   Research Activities

To build up the necessary knowledge and define the separate building blocks for the method, we already conducted a number of research activities, which we describe in this section together with ongoing and planned research. The method and building blocks are also visualized in Fig. 1.

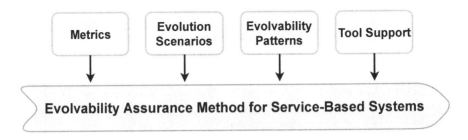

Fig. 1. Final contribution: evolvability assurance method

3.1   Metrics

The higher abstraction level in SBSs requires a set of new metrics, since object-oriented or traditional source code metrics are only of limited use [24,29]. To discover existing metric candidates specifically designed for systems based on service orientation, we conducted a literature review [8]. We identified nearly 50 metrics from 8 different publications and also analyzed their applicability to Microservices. With the exception of centralization metrics, the majority of metrics are indeed applicable.

As a follow-up, we started an experimentation and selection process with some of the metrics that yielded a maintainability model as an intermediate result [9]. Further research is however necessary to analyze which metrics are best suited for the planned method. Currently, several research projects center around metric evaluation as well as the development of tool support for their automatic gathering. Considered input artifacts are for example architecture models (e.g. SoaML[1]) and Swagger/OpenAPI[2] specification files.

---

[1] https://www.omg.org/spec/SoaML/About-SoaML.
[2] https://swagger.io/specification.

3.2   Scenarios

While metrics are valuable, they still mostly rely on structural attributes as a proxy. Scenario-based evaluation methods like ATAM [22] or ALMA [6] enable a more detailed analysis of potential future changes. However, they require lots of manual effort and are not specialized for service orientation. In our current research, we aim to synthesize a lightweight service-oriented scenario template from existing approaches that exploits the classifiability of change in these systems (e.g. service implementation vs. service interface changes). Furthermore, we are working on flexible tool support to document and evaluate scenarios based on this template.

3.3   Patterns

Design patterns are established solutions to structure software and help to address recurring problems. While there is a significant body of service-oriented patterns (e.g. [17]), patterns for Microservices are still forming [30]. To analyze the relevance of SOA patterns for Microservices, we conducted a qualitative analysis on the basis of Microservice principles [12]. Similar as with the metrics, a large part of SOA patterns was fully or partly applicable, notable exceptions being governance and centralization patterns.

Since the complex relation between design patterns and quality attributes is controversially discussed in literature and not a lot of research exists for service-oriented patterns, we used architectural modifiability tactics as a proxy for pattern candidate selection [10] (e.g. the tactic *Use an Intermediary* can be realized by the SOA pattern *Service Façade* or the Microservices pattern *API Gateway*). To further select service-based modifiability patterns in a reliable fashion, we are currently conducting research projects with functionally equivalent systems (one pattern version, one non-pattern version). These systems are analyzed with metrics as well as via controlled software development experiments. Our final goal within the method is to propose patterns based on the individual metric and scenario results.

4   Related Work

Brcina et al. [13] present a general method to maintain evolvability on an architectural level over the life-cycle of a system. Their approach is based on a quality model and an optimization process that employs generic metrics like *Number of Features* or *Number of Insulated Artifacts* as well as traceability links between features and architectural components.

Several publications exist also for the context of SOA or Microservices. Andrikopoulos [2] conceptualized a theoretical framework based on formal modeling to support SOA evolution in a non-breaking fashion. He focused on shallow changes that are local to a service, but may lead to ripple effects to consumers. The framework provides models for versioned service interfaces and compatible contract-based evolution.

Andrzej et al. [3] provided a high-level change-management-driven process to organize the evolution of service-oriented systems. The included phases and tasks are compliant with ISO 20000. The core of the method consists of models for business processes and service compositions as well as a traceability model to support change impact analysis.

Sabir et al. [32] analyze the specifics of the maintenance and evolution of Service-Based Systems. They point out key differences and research challenges such as dependency and impact analysis, tools and techniques to support multi-language system analysis and maintenance, or service-oriented evolution patterns.

In the domain of Microservices, Granchelli et al. [20] presented an approach to recover the potentially unknown evolved architecture of Microservice-Based Systems. The approach relies on model-driven reverse engineering, static source code analysis, as well as dynamic runtime analysis and is supported by the tool MicroART.

Similarly, Mayer and Weinreich [25] developed an approach to analyze the architecture and to visualize the dependencies of RESTful Microservice-Based Systems at runtime. Initially, a deployed service is added to the model based on static OpenAPI specification files. Later on, the model is enriched with communication data. The architecture is presented in a web-based dashboard together with some operational and QoS indicators.

Lastly, Engel et al. [15] used the Goal Question Metric (GQM) approach to come up with evaluation criteria for Microservice Architectures. Based on principles identified from literature, they select a set of metrics to quantify the maintainability of the architecture. To calculate these metrics, the architectural model is reconstructed from operational data using the Open Tracing API. Results are visualized in a web-based tool (MAAT).

5   Conclusion

To support software professionals in the development of Service-Based Systems with very high requirements w.r.t. evolvability, we are working on a continuous assurance method to identify and remediate hot spots in the architecture. The method is targeted at modern service- and web-based systems and applications and focuses on the commonalities of SOA and Microservices. To identify hot spots, we rely on quantitative analysis with structural metrics specifically designed for SBSs as well as qualitative analysis with service-oriented evolution scenarios. To increase the modifiability of identified hot spots, selected service-based patterns are suggested. Applying the method is supported by a web-based tool with convenient visualization of results and suggestions.

During the construction of the method, we put great emphasis on the industry's perspective and analyze the current state of practice as well as existing pain points via surveys and expert interviews. For the final evaluation of the assurance method, industry case studies and action research are planned.

Acknowledgments. This research was partially funded by the Ministry of Science of Baden-Württemberg, Germany, for the Doctoral Program "Services Computing" (http://www.services-computing.de/?lang=en).

References

1. Ameller, D., Galster, M., Avgeriou, P., Franch, X.: A survey on quality attributes in service-based systems. Softw. Qual. J. **24**(2), 271–299 (2015). https://doi.org/10.1007/s11219-015-9268-4
2. Andrikopoulos, V.: A theory and model for the evolution of software services. Ph.D. thesis, Tilburg University (2010)
3. Andrzej, Z., Marcin, S., Szymon, K.: An evolution process for service-oriented systems. Comput. Sci. **13**(4), 71 (2012)
4. Avgeriou, P., Kruchten, P., Ozkaya, I., Seaman, C., Seaman, C.: Managing technical debt in software engineering. Dagstuhl Rep. **6**(4), 110–138 (2016)
5. Bass, L., Weber, I., Zhu, L.: DevOps: a software architect's perspective, 1st edn. Addison-Wesley Professional, Boston (2015)
6. Bengtsson, P., Lassing, N., Bosch, J., van Vliet, H.: Architecture-level modifiability analysis (ALMA). J. Syst. Softw. **69**(1–2), 129–147 (2004)
7. Bogner, J., Fritzsch, J., Wagner, S., Zimmermann, A.: Limiting technical debt with maintainability assurance - an industry survey on used techniques and differences with service- and microservice-based systems. In: Proceedings of the 1st International Conference on Technical Debt (TechDebt 2018), Gothenburg, Sweden. ACM (2018)
8. Bogner, J., Wagner, S., Zimmermann, A.: Automatically measuring the maintainability of service- and microservice-based systems. In: Proceedings of the 27th International Workshop on Software Measurement and 12th International Conference on Software Process and Product Measurement on - IWSM Mensura 2017, pp. 107–115. ACM Press, New York (2017)
9. Bogner, J., Wagner, S., Zimmermann, A.: Towards a practical maintainability quality model for service-and microservice-based systems. In: Proceedings of the 11th European Conference on Software Architecture Companion Proceedings - ECSA 2017, vol. 3, pp. 195–198. ACM Press, New York (2017)
10. Bogner, J., Wagner, S., Zimmermann, A.: Using architectural modifiability tactics to examine evolution qualities of service- and microservice-based systems. SICS Softw.-Intensiv. Cyber-Phys. Syst. **34**, 141–149 (2019). https://doi.org/10.1007/s00450-019-00402-z
11. Bogner, J., Zimmermann, A.: Towards integrating microservices with adaptable enterprise architecture. In: IEEE 20th International Enterprise Distributed Object Computing Workshop (EDOCW), pp. 1–6. IEEE, September 2016
12. Bogner, J., Zimmermann, A., Wagner, S.: Analyzing the relevance of SOA patterns for microservice-based systems. In: Proceedings of the 10th Central European Workshop on Services and their Composition (ZEUS 2018), Dresden, Germany, pp. 9–16. CEUR-WS.org (2018)
13. Brcina, R., Bode, S., Riebisch, M.: Optimisation process for maintaining evolvability during software evolution. In: 16th Annual IEEE International Conference and Workshop on the Engineering of Computer Based Systems. pp. 196–205. IEEE, April 2009

14. Dragoni, N., et al.: Microservices: yesterday, today, and tomorrow. Present and Ulterior Software Engineering, pp. 195–216. Springer, Cham (2017). https://doi.org/10.1007/978-3-319-67425-4_12

15. Engel, T., Langermeier, M., Bauer, B., Hofmann, A.: Evaluation of microservice architectures: a metric and tool-based approach. In: Mendling, J., Mouratidis, H. (eds.) CAiSE 2018. LNBIP, vol. 317, pp. 74–89. Springer, Cham (2018). https://doi.org/10.1007/978-3-319-92901-9_8

16. Erl, T.: Service-Oriented Architecture: Concepts, Technology, and Design. Prentice Hall PTR, Upper Saddle River (2005)

17. Erl, T.: SOA Design Patterns. Pearson Education, Boston (2009)

18. Fitzgerald, B., Stol, K.J.: Continuous software engineering: a roadmap and agenda. J. Syst. Softw. **123**, 176–189 (2017)

19. Francesco, P.D., Malavolta, I., Lago, P.: Research on architecting microservices: trends, focus, and potential for industrial adoption. In: IEEE International Conference on Software Architecture (ICSA), pp. 21–30. IEEE, April 2017

20. Granchelli, G., Cardarelli, M., Francesco, P.D., Malavolta, I., Iovino, L., Salle, A.D.: Towards recovering the software architecture of microservice-based systems. In: IEEE International Conference on Software Architecture Workshops (ICSAW), pp. 46–53. IEEE, April 2017

21. International Organization For Standardization: ISO/IEC 25010 - Systems and software engineering - Systems and software Quality Requirements and Evaluation (SQuaRE) - System and software quality models. Technical report (2011)

22. Kazman, R., Klein, M., Clements, P.: ATAM : method for architecture evaluation. Technical report, August 2000

23. Lehman, M.M., Ramil, J., Wernwick, P., Perry, D., Turski, W.: Metrics and laws of software evolution - the nineties view. In: Proceedings of the Fourth International Software Metrics Symposium, pp. 20–32 (1997)

24. Mansour, Y.I., Mustafa, S.H.: Assessing internal software quality attributes of the object-oriented and service-oriented software development paradigms: a comparative study. J. Softw. Eng. Appl. **4**, 244 (2011)

25. Mayer, B., Weinreich, R.: An approach to extract the architecture of microservice-based software systems. In: IEEE Symposium on Service-Oriented System Engineering (SOSE), pp. 21–30. IEEE, Mar 2018

26. Newman, S.: Building microservices: designing fine-grained systems, 1st edn. O'Reilly Media, Newton (2015)

27. Pahl, C., Jamshidi, P.: Microservices: a systematic mapping study. In: Proceedings of the 6th International Conference on Cloud Computing and Services Science, vol. 1. SCITEPRESS - Science and and Technology Publications (2016)

28. Papazoglou, M.: Service-oriented computing: concepts, characteristics and directions. In: Proceedings of the 7th International Conference on Properties and Applications of Dielectric Materials. IEEE (2003)

29. Perepletchikov, M., Ryan, C., Frampton, K.: Comparing the impact of service-oriented and object-oriented paradigms on the structural properties of software. In: Meersman, R., Tari, Z., Herrero, P. (eds.) OTM 2005. LNCS, vol. 3762, pp. 431–441. Springer, Heidelberg (2005). https://doi.org/10.1007/11575863_63

30. Richardson, C.: Microservices Patterns. Manning Publications, Shelter Island (2018)

31. Rowe, D., Leaney, J., Lowe, D.: Defining systems architecture evolvability - a taxonomy of change. In: International Conference and Workshop: Engineering of Computer-Based Systems, pp. 45–52, December 1998

32. Sabir, B., Perveen, N., Qamar, U., Muzaffar, A.W.: Impact analysis on evolution patterns of service oriented systems. In: International Conference on Engineering, Computing & Information Technology (ICECIT 2017), pp. 61–67 (2018)
33. Schermann, G., Cito, J., Leitner, P.: All the services large and micro: revisiting industrial practice in services computing. In: Norta, A., Gaaloul, W., Gangadharan, G.R., Dam, H.K. (eds.) ICSOC 2015. LNCS, vol. 9586, pp. 36–47. Springer, Heidelberg (2016). https://doi.org/10.1007/978-3-662-50539-7_4
34. Voelz, D., Goeb, A.: What is different in quality management for SOA? In: 14th IEEE International Enterprise Distributed Object Computing Conference, pp. 47–56. IEEE, October 2010

Predictive Management of Fog Applications

Stefano Forti[✉]

Department of Computer Science, University of Pisa, Pisa, Italy
stefano.forti@di.unipi.it

Abstract. Deploying and managing multi-component IoT applications in Fog computing scenarios is challenging due to the heterogeneity, scale and dynamicity of Fog infrastructures, as well as due to the complexity of modern software systems. When deciding where/how to (re-)allocate application components over the continuum from the IoT to the Cloud, application administrators need to find the "best" deployment, satisfying all application (hardware, software, QoS, IoT) requirements over the contextually available resources, also fulfilling non-functional desiderata (e.g., financial costs, security).

Keywords: Fog computing · App deployment · App management

1 Introduction

Fog computing [3] aims at better supporting the growing processing demand of (time-sensitive and bandwidth hungry) IoT applications by selectively pushing computation closer to where data is produced and relying on a geographically distributed multitude of heterogeneous devices (e.g., personal devices, gateways, micro-data centres, embedded servers) spanning the IoT-Cloud continuum. A substantial amount of computation, storage and networking is therefore expected to happen closer to where data is produced and to cyber-physical systems, contiguously to and interdependently with the Cloud. In general, Fog computing platforms are expected to guarantee that processing always occurs wherever it is *best-placed* for any given IoT application, thereby accelerating the velocity of decision making, by enabling prompter responses to sensed events [20].

Modern large-scale applications are not monolithic anymore. Indeed, an application running in a Fog computing infrastructure is a set of independently deployable components (or services, or micro-services) that work together and must meet some (hardware, software, IoT and QoS) requirements. Deploying and managing such applications in Fog computing scenarios is therefore a challenging task. Indeed, it requires to dynamically map each of the (possibly many) application components (i.e., functionalities) to the computational node(s) that will host them at runtime. Whilst some application functionalities are naturally

S. Forti—PhD Thesis Supervisor: Prof. Antonio Brogi, University of Pisa, Italy.

© Springer Nature Switzerland AG 2020
M. Fazio and W. Zimmermann (Eds.): ESOCC 2018 Workshops, CCIS 1115, pp. 140–147, 2020.
https://doi.org/10.1007/978-3-030-63161-1_11

suited to the Cloud (e.g., service back-ends) and others are naturally suited to edge devices (e.g., industrial control loops), there are applications for which functionality segmentation is not as straightforward (e.g., short to medium term analytics). Future tools for the deployment and management of IoT applications should consider application requirements (i.e., hardware, software, IoT, QoS), infrastructure capabilities (i.e., hardware, software, IoT devices, network conditions, security) and deployers' desiderata (i.e., business and security policies, cost constraints) to efficiently support adaptive segmentation of functionalities from the Cloud to the IoT.

In this context, we are investigating the design, prototyping and validation of novel models, and predictive algorithms and methodologies which will be useful to *(i)* process data about the application, the infrastructure and their monitored performance so to informedly suggest how to (re-)distribute application components, *(ii)* identify and validate the best sequence of actions to (re-)distribute components to different Fog or Cloud nodes based on specified policies, and *(iii)* choose when/how to (re-)deploy, (re-)configure or scale components in response to workload or network variations, churn and failures.

2   State of the Art

Fog computing introduces new challenges, mainly due to its pervasive geo-distribution and heterogeneity, need for QoS-awareness, dynamicity and support to interactions with the IoT, that were not thoroughly studied in previous works addressing the problem of application deployment to the Cloud [25,28]. Among the first proposals investigating these new lines, [15] proposed a Fog-to-Cloud search algorithm as a first way to determine an eligible deployment of (multi-component) DAG applications to tree-like Fog infrastructures. Their placement algorithm attempts the placement of components *Fog-to-Cloud* by considering hardware capacity only. An open-source simulator – iFogSim – has been released to test the proposed policy against Cloud-only deployments. Building on top of iFogSim, [18] refines tries to guarantee the application service delivery deadlines and to optimise Fog resource exploitation. Also [27] used iFogSim to implement an algorithm for optimal online placement of application components, with respect to load balancing. Recently, exploiting iFogSim, [14] proposed a distributed search strategy to find the best service placement in the Fog, which minimises the distance between the clients and the most requested services, based on request rates and free available resources. [16,23] proposed (linearithmic) heuristic algorithms that attempts deployments prioritising placement of applications to devices that feature with less free resources.

From an alternative viewpoint, [1] gave a Mixed-Integer Non-Linear Programming (MINLP) formulation of the problem of placing application components so to satisfy end-to-end delay constraints. The problem is then solved by linearisation into a Mixed-Integer Linear Programming (MILP), showing potential improvements in latency, energy consumption and costs for routing and storage that the Fog might bring. [22] designed a hierarchical modelling of Fog infrastructures and adopted an ILP formulation of the problem of allocating computation to Fog nodes so to optimise time deadlines on application execution. A simple linear model for the Cloud costs is also taken into account. Regrettably, none of the discussed ILP/MILP approaches came with the code to run the experiments. Conversely, the authors of [9] released an open-source extension of Apache Storm that exploits ILP to perform component placement, while improving the end-to-end application latency and the availability of deployed applications. Finally, also dynamic programming (e.g., [21]), genetic algorithms (e.g., [22]) and deep learning (e.g., [24]) were exploited promisingly in recent works.

The management of Fog applications is also time-consuming and error-prone to be tuned manually, still lacking of adequate support. [19] proposed a MAPE-K loop to identify action plans to minimise SLA violations while maximising the use of allocated resources- [12] highlighted the need to check for inconsistencies that can arise within or between different stages of a deployment plan. [12] proposed a deployment management system model to enable the automated generation of deployment plans for distributed infrastructures after identifying (with static analysis techniques) possible flaws in deployment plan specifications. The use of formal models to verify properties of application deployments to Cloud infrastructure has been advocated by various authors. [17], for instance, defined a process calculus to specify deployment, migration and security policies of virtual machines (VMs) across different Clouds, in order to enable the verification of security policies after live VM reconfigurations. [2] proposed a similar approach to preserve data consistency when migrating deployed applications in Fog scenarios. [11] proposed a pseudo-dynamic testing approach, which combines emulation, simulation, and existing real testbeds. While various proposals exist to automate the management of applications, to verify the correctness of deployments to the Cloud, to the best of our knowledge, none of the existing approaches addresses the validation of application management for the Fog.

3   Thesis Objectives

This section aims at illustrating the objectives of this thesis work, towards supporting the QoS-aware deployment and management of Fog applications, with suitable models (Sect. 3.1), algorithms and methodologies (Sect. 3.2).

3.1   Modelling

First, with this thesis we aim at contributing to the modelling of the Fog scenario with particular focus on:

1. describing arbitrary *multi-component applications* topologies considering their processing (e.g., hardware, software and IoT devices), QoS (e.g., latency, bandwidth, security) requirements and component inter-dependencies, along with the possibility for their components to scale both vertically and horizontally, according to workload demand and behaviour models,

2. describing accordingly *Fog infrastructures* in terms of their capabilities (i.e., Cloud data-centres, Fog nodes, Things) and their (expected or current) performance[1] (e.g., QoS of communication links, nodes utilisation, reliability of nodes and links), considering IoT-Fog, Fog-Fog and Fog-Cloud interactions,

3. accounting for *dynamicity* and *churn* of the infrastructure (e.g., variations in the QoS of communication links, mobility of IoT devices and Fog nodes, failures) and in the users' demand, as well as for *application scalability* on heterogeneous devices so to be able to plan for scalable, reliable and dependable application deployments,

4. including the possibility of expressing *preferences* on application deployment that have to be enforced due to particular end-user targets (e.g., QoS-assurance, financial budget, resource usage) or deployment needs (e.g., security, trust, reliability, energy consumption),

5. identifying and devising appropriate *metrics* and *performance indicators* (e.g., QoS-assurance, resource consumption, reliability) to characterise eligible application deployments and plans, also considering their behaviour over time, as well as financial costs and energy consumption to keep the application up and running.

3.2 Algorithms and Methodologies

To complement and make use of the models described in the previous section, we intend to devise algorithms and methodologies in order to:

1. efficiently *determine eligible* context- and QoS-aware *deployments* of application components to Fog infrastructures, according to different strategies and by adopting proper heuristics to reduce the search space, whilst selecting cost-/energy-aware matchings between application requirements (viz., hardware and software) and available Fog/Cloud offerings,

2. *simulate* and *predict* the (expected) behaviour of different eligible deployments under the proposed metrics at varying *(i)* QoS of available communication links, *(ii)* available resources in the current state of the infrastructure, *(iii)* workload and users demand, also considering historical data about the monitored infrastructure and feedback about previous deployments,

3. *compare* and recommend and/or automatically select *best candidate deployments* – among the eligible ones – based on predicted metrics and declared targets, by plotting results to empower experts to make informed choices, and by exploiting multi-objective optimisation or learning techniques,

4. *determine* and *optimise plans* that take into account dependencies between components so to perform application deployment to a given infrastructure, envisioning deployment (vertical and horizontal) scalability on heterogeneous devices and optimal resources exploitation (e.g., hardware, energy), and considering alternative backup deployments to tackle dynamicity issues (e.g., increasing workload, mobility, QoS variations, churn and failures),

---

[1] Data on monitored infrastructure capabilities – collected either through centralised or self-attesting distributed mechanisms – can be aggregated and used to this end.

5. understand when to trigger and how to (optimally) perform *reconfiguration actions* (e.g., enactment of an alternative plan), scaling of application components, or components re-allocation to different nodes so to guarantee QoS or SLA constraints will be met by enacted deployments, whilst avoiding (or minimising) the likelihood of service disruption.

4   First Results

First results of this work have been described in some conferences and journals.

Deployment. In [4], we proposed a simple, yet general, model of multi-component IoT applications and Fog infrastructures. After proving that the problem of determining eligible deployments is NP-hard, we devised a greedy backtracking search algorithm to solve it. In [5], we combined an exhaustive version of our search algorithm with Monte Carlo simulations so to consider variations in the QoS of communication links (modelled by probability distributions) and to predict how likely a deployed application is to comply with the desired network QoS (viz., latency and bandwidth) and how much Fog resources it will consume in the Fog layer. In [6], we further enhanced the proposed methodology by proposing a cost model that extends Cloud cost models to Fog scenarios and integrates them with costs coming from the IoT. It is worth noting that, with respect to the majority of related work, our approach works on arbitrary application and infrastructure graph topologies and considers interactions between applications and the IoT.

All proposed predictive methodologies have been implemented in an open-source prototype[2], FogTorchΠ, and are described in detail in [7], which also offers a comparison with one of the first tools for simulating Fog scenarios (iFogSim [15]). FogTorchΠ (Fig. 1) can be used to determine, simulate and compare eligible deployments of an application to a given (probabilistic) infrastructure in a QoS- (with respect to network variations), context- (with respect to the considered hardware and IoT resources), and cost-aware (estimating monthly revenues and outflows) manner.

Indeed, based on FogTorchΠ output deployments, which can be plotted as shown in Fig. 1, application deployers can choose their application deployment looking for the best trade-off among predicted QoS-assurance, Fog resource consumption and estimated monthly cost.

Management. CISCO FogDirector [10] (FD) is among the first available management tools for large-scale production deployments of Fog applications. In [13] we presented a simple operational semantics of all basic functionalities of FD, describing the effects of the operations that client programs can perform to publish, deploy, configure, start, monitor, stop, undeploy and retire their applications in a given infrastructure, using the REST APIs offered by the tool. Based on such modelling, we introduced a prototype simulation environment[3],

---

[2] Available at: https://github.com/di-unipi-socc/FogTorchPI/.

[3] Available at: https://github.com/di-unipi-socc/FogDirMime/.

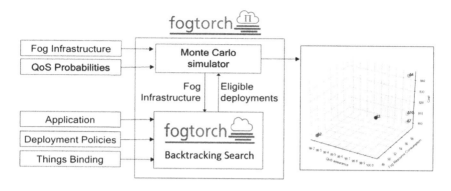

Fig. 1. Bird's-eye view of FogTorchΠ.

FogDirMime (Fig. 2), that also considers probabilistic (hardware and network QoS) variations of the infrastructure that happen independently from the considered application management. On one hand, the proposed semantics constitutes a concise and unambiguous reference of the (basic) behaviour of FD that can be used to quickly understand its functioning and to check correctness of management scripts at design time. On the other hand, FogDirMime can be fruitfully exploited to experiment and compare different application management policies, so to predict their effectiveness and tune them in a simulated environment, according to user-defined metrics (Fig. 2 (b)).

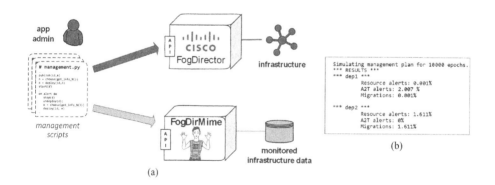

Fig. 2. (a) Bird's-eye view of FogDirMime and (b) output example.

5   Conclusions and Future Work

We consider our preliminary results as first promising steps to support decision-making when deploying or managing IoT applications to Fog infrastructures. Yet, such results clearly show some limitations with respect to the objectives of this thesis, as set in Sect. 3. In our future work, we intend to:

1. extend our methodologies to include more aspects of the life-cycle of application management, including new features such as components upgrade, reconfiguration and scaling, while envisioning the possibility for a component to be deployed in different flavours like in *Osmotic Computing* [26],

2. consider new metrics and dimensions that will be important in Fog scenarios (e.g., security, mobility, energy consumption) and propose a way to automatically and efficiently select best candidate (re-)deployments – i.e., matching deployers' desiderata – using AI and multi-objective optimisation, and

3. prototype, validate and assess all new methodologies as extensions to our prototypes or as new open-source tools that can synergically work with them, and assess them in controlled settings (e.g., over the simple Fog application we proposed in [8]) as well as, possibly, in lifelike Fog environments.

References

1. Arkian, H.R., Diyanat, A., Pourkhalili, A.: MIST: fog-based data analytics scheme with cost-efficient resource provisioning for IoT crowdsensing applications. J. Netw. Comput. Appl. **82**, 152–165 (2017)

2. Bao, W., et al.: Follow me fog: toward seamless handover timing schemes in a fog computing environment. IEEE Commun. Mag. **55**(11), 72–78 (2017)

3. Bonomi, F., Milito, R., Natarajan, P., Zhu, J.: Fog computing: a platform for internet of things and analytics. In: Bessis, N., Dobre, C. (eds.) Big Data and Internet of Things: A Roadmap for Smart Environments. SCI, vol. 546, pp. 169–186. Springer, Cham (2014). https://doi.org/10.1007/978-3-319-05029-4_7

4. Brogi, A., Forti, S.: QoS-aware deployment of IoT applications through the fog. IEEE Internet Things J. **4**(5), 1185–1192 (2017)

5. Brogi, A., Forti, S., Ibrahim, A.: How to best deploy your fog applications, probably. In: Rana, O., Buyya, R., Anjum, A. (eds.) Proceedings of 1st IEEE International Conference on Fog and Edge Computing, Madrid (2017)

6. Brogi, A., Forti, S., Ibrahim, A.: Deploying fog applications: how much does it cost, by the way? In: Proceedings of the 8th International Conference on Cloud Computing and Services Science, CLOSER 2018, Funchal, Madeira, Portugal, 19–21 March 2018, pp. 68–77 (2018)

7. Brogi, A., Forti, S., Ibrahim, A.: Predictive analysis to support fog application deployment. In: Buyya, R., Srirama, S.N. (eds.) Fog and Edge Computing: Principles and Paradigms, chap. 9, pp. 191–222. Wiley (2019)

8. Brogi, A., Forti, S., Ibrahim, A., Rinaldi, L.: Bonsai in the fog: an active learning lab with fog computing. In: Third International Conference on Fog and Mobile Edge Computing (FMEC), pp. 79–86. IEEE (2018)

9. Cardellini, V., Grassi, V., Lo Presti, F., Nardelli, M.: Optimal operator placement for distributed stream processing applications. In: Proceedings of the 10th ACM International Conference on Distributed and Event-based Systems, DEBS 2016, pp. 69–80. ACM, New York (2016)

10. CISCO: Cisco Fog Director Reference Guide (v. 1.5) (2017). https://www.cisco.com/c/en/us/td/docs/routers/access/800/software/guides/iox/fog-director/reference-guide/1-5/fog_director_ref_guide.html

11. Ficco, M., Esposito, C., Xiang, Y., Palmieri, F.: Pseudo-dynamic testing of realistic edge-fog cloud ecosystems. IEEE Commun. Mag. **55**(11), 98–104 (2017)

12. Fischer, J., Majumdar, R., Esmaeilsabzali, S.: Engage: a deployment management system. SIGPLAN Not. **47**(6), 263–274 (2012)
13. Forti, S., Ibrahim, A., Brogi, A.: Mimicking FogDirector application management. Softw.-Intensiv. Cyber-Phys. Syst. **34**(2–3), 151–161 (2019). https://doi.org/10.1007/s00450-019-00403-y
14. Guerrero, C., Lera, I., Juiz, C.: A lightweight decentralized service placement policy for performance optimization in fog computing. J. Ambient Intell. Humanized Comput. **10**(6), 2435–2452 (2018). https://doi.org/10.1007/s12652-018-0914-0
15. Gupta, H., Vahid Dastjerdi, A., Ghosh, S.K., Buyya, R.: iFogSim: a toolkit for modeling and simulation of resource management techniques in the internet of things, edge and fog computing environments. Softw. Pract. Exp. **47**(9), 1275–1296 (2017)
16. Hong, H.J., Tsai, P.H., Hsu, C.H.: Dynamic module deployment in a fog computing platform. In: 2016 18th Asia-Pacific Network Operations and Management Symposium (APNOMS), pp. 1–6 (2016)
17. Jarraya, Y., Eghtesadi, A., Debbabi, M., Zhang, Y., Pourzandi, M.: Cloud calculus: security verification in elastic cloud computing platform. In: International Conference on Collaboration Technologies and Systems (CTS), pp. 447–454 (2012)
18. Mahmud, R., Ramamohanarao, K., Buyya, R.: Latency-aware application module management for fog computing environments. ACM Trans. Internet Technology (TOIT) **9**, 1–21 (2018)
19. Maurer, M., Brandic, I., Sakellariou, R.: Adaptive resource configuration for Cloud infrastructure management. Future Gener. Comput. Syst. **29**(2), 472–487 (2013)
20. OpenFog: OpenFog Reference Architecture (2016)
21. Rahbari, D., Nickray, M.: Scheduling of fog networks with optimized knapsack by symbiotic organisms search. In: 21st Conference of Open Innovations Association (FRUCT), pp. 278–283 (2017)
22. Skarlat, O., Nardelli, M., Schulte, S., Dustdar, S.: Towards QoS-aware fog service placement. In: IEEE 1st International Conference on Fog and Edge Computing (ICFEC), pp. 89–96 (2017)
23. Taneja, M., Davy, A.: Resource aware placement of IoT application modules in fog-cloud computing paradigm. In: IFIP/IEEE Symposium on Integrated Network and Service Management (IM), pp. 1222–1228 (2017)
24. Tang, Z., Zhou, X., Zhang, F., Jia, W., Zhao, W.: Migration modeling and learning algorithms for containers in fog computing. IEEE Trans. Serv. Comput. **12**(5), 712–725 (2018)
25. Varshney, P., Simmhan, Y.: Demystifying fog computing: characterizing architectures, applications and abstractions. In: IEEE 1st International Conference on Fog and Edge Computing (ICFEC), pp. 115–124 (2017)
26. Villari, M., Fazio, M., Dustdar, S., Rana, O., Ranjan, R.: Osmotic computing: a new paradigm for edge/cloud integration. IEEE Cloud Comput. **3**(6), 76–83 (2016)
27. Wang, S., Zafer, M., Leung, K.K.: Online placement of multi-component applications in edge computing environments. IEEE Access **5**, 2514–2533 (2017)
28. Wen, Z., Yang, R., Garraghan, P., Lin, T., Xu, J., Rovatsos, M.: Fog orchestration for internet of things services. IEEE Internet Comput. **21**(2), 16–24 (2017)

How to Manage Efficiently Clinical Big-Data by Means of Cloud Computing

Antonino Galletta$^{(\boxtimes)}$ and Massimo Villari

MIFT Department, University of Messina, Messina, Italy
{angalletta,mvillari}@unime.it

Abstract. Nowadays, Information and Communication Technologies (ICT) are widely adopted in hospitals. Increasingly often medical devices are computer-assisted. Hospital Information Systems (HISs) are not designed to manage the huge amount of data produced by these devices. New paradigms, such as Cloud Computing, by means of its features represents a valid tool to handle this kind of problem. Cloud Computing is very powerful, but it arises issues concerning data privacy. For this reason, clinical operators are reluctant to adopt it in HISs. In this paper, considering two real use-cases coming from the IRCCS "Bonino Pulejo", a clinical and research center in Messina, we discuss a Cloud Computing architecture able to manage amounts vast of medical data. From a technical point of view, the proposed solution is based on microservices each of them realized for performing a specified task, such as the anonymizer. A microservice that is able to obfuscate users' sensitive data in order to assure data privacy and to make the system compliant with GDPR.

Keywords: Telemedicine · GDPR · Cloud computing · MRI · Internet of Things · Big data

1 Introduction

Nowadays, we are observing a revolution in hospital and clinical centers. Indeed, often old medical devices are replaced by innovative computer assisted ones. These new kind of equipment widely adopt Internet of things (IoT) approach. Statista [1] predicted that the number of connected devices will grow up to about 75 billion in 2025. These new kind of devices allow physicians to make more accurate and precise diagnoses. However, they produce a huge amount of data. These data are different for type and structure, therefore, the way to manage them is also different. Considering as example Magnetic Resonance (MR). It produces Digital Imaging and COmmunications in Medicine DICOM files: series of jpg images with a specific header. Instead equipments for rehabilitation such as CAREN and Lokomat produce raw data that can be stored in internal Hard-Disks or exported as Comma-separated values (CSV) files. Traditional

M. Villari—Supervisor.

© Springer Nature Switzerland AG 2020
M. Fazio and W. Zimmermann (Eds.): ESOCC 2018 Workshops, CCIS 1115, pp. 148–157, 2020.
https://doi.org/10.1007/978-3-030-63161-1_12

Hospital Information Systems are not able to manage these data. Innovations in ICT provide a very powerful tool suitable for solving such a problem: Cloud Computing. Use Cloud Computing in HIS provides several advantages for clinical centers. Indeed, it allows to create high available specific workflows that can scale up or down based on the workload. However, it presents several issues related to users' data privacy especially in the GDPR era. Such a problem makes difficult the proliferation of Cloud based systems in HIS. In this paper, we discuss about of the experience done during the first two years of the doctorate course at the University of Messina and the IRCCS Centro Neurolesi "Bonino Pulejo". In particular, considering two real medical use-cases coming from the IRCCS, one related to Magnetic Resonance (MR) and another related to rehabilitation, we discuss about of a Cloud Computing microservice architecture able to manage the huge amount of produced data. In our solution we widely adopt the Hybrid Cloud approach: sensitive data are stored in a secure manner into the Private Cloud, data that have to be shared with foreign users are stored into the Public Cloud. From a technical point of view, the proposed solution is based on microservices each of them realized for performing a specified task, such as the anonymizer. A microservice that is able to obfuscate users' sensitive data in order to assure data privacy and to make the system compliant with GDPR. The rest of the paper is organized as follows. In Sect. 2, we present other works related to telemedicine, BigData visualization and mechanisms to share data over the Cloud. In Sect. 3 we focus on our motivations for this work. The Sect. 4, describes the architecture designed for managing effectively clinical Big Data. Finally, in Sect. 6 we conclude the work discussing about of future steps.

2 Background and Related Work

Nowadays, ICT is present in all fields from the industry to the agriculture to the health care. Innovations in ICT word led to creation to new systems and protocols. Such as telemedicine, physicians by using it are able to provide assistance to remote bedridden patients. Benefits and drawbacks of telemedicine were discussed in [2].

The consequence of the introduction of these new systems was an explosion of data. The management of these data is very complicated, indeed traditional techniques and systems are not adequate to manage them. Another problem in Big Data is the analysis of them in order to extract insight.

In [3], authors presented a way for processing electroencephalography data. Their work is based on three steps: in the first step they convert data from European Data Format (EDF) to the JavaScript Object Notation (JSON); in the second they gather JSON data; in the latter, by means of smartphones, they perform real-time interactions with signal data.

A tool able to show the relationship among heterogeneous data is presented in [4]. This tool, based on three data structures (Tree Structure, Graph Structure and Graph-Tree Structure), shows the relationship of data stored into relational databases.

4 visualization tools for physicians were discussed [5]. These visualization tools show the behavior of measured parameters considering different time interval: the "Continuous Month" which groups measurement by month representing them day by day; the "Continuous Day" which groups measurement by day representing them hour by hour; the "Circular Day" which represents by means of a pie chart same parameters of the "Continuous Day"; the "Multi-Circular Day" tool, instead, allows to compare the behavior of specified parameter over several days.

In Big Data another challenge is the sharing of them among several users.

In [6], authors considering a Network Storage Environment (NSE) discussed a file partitioning method optimization. In particular, considering serviceability, reliability and availability, they proposed an algorithm for distributing files inside a cluster.

An approach for improving the file reliability is discussed in [7]. In particular, authors split data into chunks. The main idea is to increase the reliability of the system adding redundancy. In such a way, they can assure by means of data correction procedures. In PRESIDIO [8], is discussed a similar strategy.

Authors in [9] discussed a file partitioning strategy. In particular, they presented BerryStore: a distributed object storage system designed for Cloud service especially for the massive small files storing. By means of a distributed coordinated controller, BerryStore is able to assure concurrency, scalability, and fault-tolerance.

The management of Big Data is a very complex task. The common idea of all aforementioned scientific works is to create a specif tool per each type of data. In this work, we aim to create a single architecture that can be specialized based on the type of data.

3   Motivation

Nowadays, Information and Communication Technologies (ICT) are widely adopted in hospitals. Indeed more often medical devices are computer-assisted (e.g., Magnetic Resonance, Lokomat, CAREN). Data produced from these devices are different for dimension, form and quantity. For instance, considering the Magnetic Resonance (MR) it produces Magnetic Resonance Images (MRIs): series of jpg images with a specific header. Usually, these images are stored and processed as DICOM files. CAREN and Lokomat produce raw data related to rehabilitation activities of patients, these data are stored into internal Databases (DBs) and can be exported as CSV files. The difference among the structure of these kind of data reflects also differences in the management. Indeed in the first case the object storage is needed.

The research activities presented in this paper can be divided into two main branches: the first one related to the management of MRIs, the latter related to the management of rehabilitation data coming from CAREN, Lokomat and wearables. With reference to MRI branch, physicians need a system that allow them to share DICOMs in a safe manner with other practitioners, physicians and patients.

Share content among different practitioners is very important for a clinical point of view, indeed, it allows to merge the experience of different physicians and to have more accurate diagnosis. Instead, with reference to rehabilitative data, physicians need a telemedicine Big-Data visualization tool that allows them to analyse patients' health status simply looking at data representation.

The enabler technology that allows us to create a system able to manage effectively these kinds data is the Cloud Computing. In particular, in order to reach our goals, we adopted a Hybrid Cloud Computing approach. We used public Cloud Storage providers for storing anonymized DICOM images and Private Cloud in order to save personal and rehabilitative data. Public Cloud may arise many treats in terms of data security, privacy and availability. Indeed, Cloud Storage services might discontinued (such as copy https://copy.com/), or attacked by hackers (such as Dropbox. Indeed in 2012 68 Million of account was compromised [10]). If we also consider the GDPR the scenario become very complex. The end users of our system, physicians and patients, often are not accustomed to use this kind of tools, therefore they need an user friendly tool that allows them to manage these data. Considering the assumptions that we made before, we aim to realize an user friendly tool that allows physicians to manage clinical data in a secure manner.

The design of our Cloud based clinical Big Data management solution have to satisfy the following requirements:

1. single core that can be specialized based on users' requirements;
2. high scalability: capability to adapt the execution of different services to the workload;
3. compliance with GDPR;
4. ability to manage both real time acquisitions and historical data coming from different data sources;
5. user friendly interface suitable for Personal Computers and mobiles.

4   Our Approaches

In this Section, we discuss about of approaches adopted in order to manage effectively medical data. In particular, considering requirements described in the Sect. 3, we designed and developed two specific software prototypes based on microservices. The design of these prototypes starts from the same core that can be specialized based on users' requirements. We decided to adopt a microservice-based architecture in order to fulfill the scalability requirement. Indeed, each microservice can be migrated based on the workload from a machine with lower computation capabilities to a more powerful one.

In the following Subsection we discuss about of the design of these prototypes.

4.1   Big MRI Share

In this Subsection we discuss about of the software prototype designed for managing MRIs and share them with practitioners, physicians and patients.

Figure 1, shows whole architecture of the system for managing and sharing MRIs. The system is compound of 8 blocks:

1. Magnetic Resonance (MR) the source of MRIs;
2. OwnCloud, the Private Cloud adopted for storing MRIs;
3. Anonymizer, the GDPR compliant microservice that anonymizes sensitive patient's data;
4. MongoDB a Document Oriented Big Data database used as system database;
5. Splitter, the microservice that executes the data decomposition algorithm and spread data chunks over the Public Cloud Storage providers;
6. Public Cloud Storage providers, the public repository;
7. Meteor based app, a web-app that executes the data recomposition algorithm and displays MRIs to end users;
8. practitioners, the consumers of MRIs.

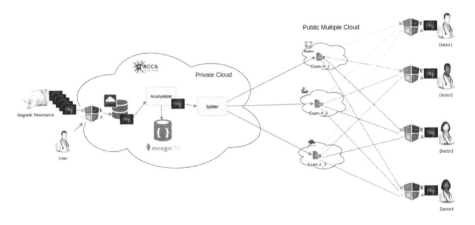

Fig. 1. Big MRI sharing architecture

Producer and Consumers generate and analyse DICOM files containing MRIs. With reference to the architecture showed above, the producer is the MR. In our system we could have two kind of consumers that need to analyse MRIs: foreign and internal practitioners. Each DICOM file is composed of thousands of images that are organized in series. In our system, we store each series into a specific OwnCloud directory. At this level, the data privacy is guaranteed by OwnCloud, indeed only authorized users can gain the access to the stored files.

External practitioners, do not have any way to access directly to data stored inside the Private Cloud. Only internal authorized physicians can share contents for a limited time period.

As discussed in Sect. 3, share clinical sensitive data on Public Cloud Storage services arises several privacy threats. We remark that one of the requirement is the compliance with GDPR. In order to satisfy this requirement and increase the security of the whole system we created a specific microservice able to anonymize users' sensitive data.

The anomymization process updates the sensitive data contained into the header of DICOM files and store metadata inside MongoDB. More specifically this process updates the name of the patient, the user ID and the date of birth. The patient name is replaced by an UUID that depends on the DICOM series; the user ID is updated with a random number; regarding the date of birth the algorithm updates only day and month because the year could be useful in order to make diagnosis.

Anonymized DICOM files, from Anonymizer are sent to the Splitter microservice. It, by means of splitting algorithms such as the RRNS [11], divides the original file into chunks and spread them over the Public Cloud Storage services. The exact location of each chunk is stored into a Map-File, a special XML file composed of two main nodes: the header, that contains metadata (such as hospital and practitioner) and the data node that contains public paths to anonymized DICOM chunks.

The Map-File is very important during the recomposition phase. Indeed, it is passed as input to the Meteor web-app that runs the recomposition algorithm. The Meteor web-app represent the interface for external practitioners, it provides different functionalities such as DICOM visualization, identification and display of Region of Interest ROI etc.

4.2 Big Rehabilitative Data Visualization

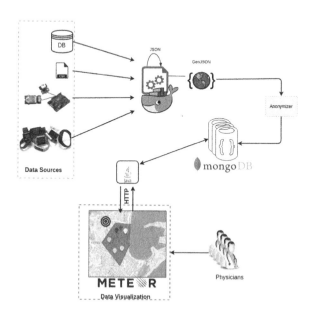

Fig. 2. Big rehabilitative data visualization architecture

In Fig. 2, is shown the overall architecture of the system able to manage rehabilitative data. Also in this case the architecture is based on microservices, in such a way several component, such as Anonimyzer and MongoDB, can be shared among different solutions.

The system is composed of seven blocks:

1. Data sources such as CAREN, Lokomat and wearable;
2. GeoJSON converter, the microservice that uniforms and transforms incoming data to GeoJSON;
3. Anonymizer, the GDPR compliant microservice that anonymizes sensitive patient's data;
4. MongoDB a Document Oriented Big Data database used as system database;
5. Mongo Interface, the microservice that acts as interface between front-end and back-end;
6. Meteor based app, a web-app that shows charts related to patients' data;
7. Practitioners, the consumers of data.

In our system we could have different data sources such as CAREN Lokomat and Wearables. Data produced from these sources can be stored into specific files or gathered in a real time fashion. We remark that the fourth requirement discussed into the Sect. 3 is the ability to manage both real time acquisitions and historical data coming from different data sources. In order to fulfill it, we created a microservice that by means of specific interfaces is able to interact with different data sources. Data acquired from these sources will be converted in GeoJSON, a standard for encoding geographic data structures.

We adopted this format because it is natively stored inside the database system, therefore we can make queries in a simple way.

The fifth requirement is related to the user friendliness of the system. In order to satisfy it, we created a Meteor web-app that shows data for physicians-defined geographical zones in two modalities: general overview or patient-specific [12].

For security concerns, MongoDB is not directly exposed to the external word. Thus we created a specific microservice that act as interface. It runs a Java application that is able to make query on MongoDB by means of the official MongoDB drivers and to receive command from the Meteor web-app.

5 Highlights and Discussions

In this Section we analysed our system from a numerical point of view. In order to validate the system, we made specific analyzes for each proposed approach. Our analyses can be divided into three categories: common aspect of presented architectures (scalability analysis of the anonymization process), MRI (in term of disk usage) and rehabilitative data (in term of time needed to make queries).

Our testbed is composed of microservices running on a web server with the following hw/sw characteristics: CPU Intel(R) Core(TM) i5-5200U CPU @ 2.8 8 GHz with 2 cores and 2 threads, RAM 8 GB, GFLOPS 66, OS: Ubuntu server

16.04 LTS 64 BIT. In order to have more reliable results we performed 30 consecutive iterations and considered confidence at 95%. In Fig. 3 the behavior of the anonymizer is shown. As the reader can observe the system scales up linearly with the increasing of the number of processed elements.

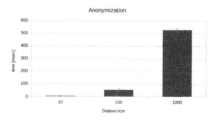

Fig. 3. Performance analysis of the anonymization module considering increasing dataset sizes.

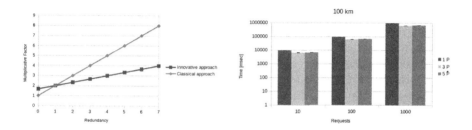

Fig. 4. Performance analysis of MRI management (a) and rehabilitative data (b)

In Fig. 4(a) is shown a comparison, in term of disk usage for store MRIs, between RAID 1 approach and RRNS. As the reader can observe, the capacity of the disk required from RAID 1 approach increase linearly with the redundancy. RRNS, instead, scales following a different behavior. Indeed, considering the case without redundancy it is less convenient of RAID 1, but considering the case with 7 degrees of redundancy it is more powerful, indeed it reduces the space required of a factor 1.75. For further the reader can refer to [13] and [14].

Considering the Big rehabilitative data, hereby we analyse performance of the general overview visualization mode. Our testbed is composed of 400k on random patients stored inside a specific MongoDB collection. As reference case, we considered a circular area of interest of 100 km. In our analyses, we considered three different configurations. In order to analyse the robustness of the system, we made 10, 100 and 1000 subsequent requests. Figure 4(b), show the behavior of the deployed system. As the reader can observe, time performances increase linearly with the number of subsequent requests that we performed.

Requests with a single patient's parameter are the simplest but time performance are slower. This behavior is due to the huge amount of data that flows from MongoDB to practitioners. Requests with five patient's parameters have intermediate performance, indeed they present the more complex query but return back less results. From a numerical point of view, the better trade off is implemented by the request with three parameters, indeed it presents computation time lower than other scenarios. For further the reader can refer to [12].

6 Conclusions and Future Work

In this scientific work, we discussed about of the management of clinical Big-Data. In particular, considering two real use-cases one related to MRI and another one related to the rehabilitation, that were defined from the IRCCS Centro Neurolesi "Bonino Pulejo" of Messina, we described a Cloud based software architecture. During the design of this architecture, we considered five requirements such as i) the presence of a single core that can be specialized based on users' requirements; ii) high scalability of the system; iii) compliance with GDPR; iv) ability to manage both real time acquisitions and historical data coming from different data sources; v) user friendliness interface.

The architecture that fulfills above described requirements is based on microservices, each of them with a specific function such as the such as the anonymizer. A microservice that is able to obfuscate users' sensitive data in order to assure data privacy and to make the system compliant with GDPR.

In this report we discussed about of the experience done during the first two years of the doctorate course at the University of Messina and the IRCCS Centro Neurolesi "Bonino Pulejo". For the last year the plan is to spend six month at Karlstads University in order to work on the design of SDN-based geologically distributed solutions for Big Data analytics.

References

1. statista: Iot number of connected devices worldwide. https://www.statista.com/statistics/471264/iot-number-of-connected-devices-worldwide/. Accessed Jan 2018
2. Hjelm, N.M.: Benefits and drawbacks of telemedicine. J. Telemed. Telecare **11**, 60–70 (2005)
3. Serhani, M.A., Menshawy, M.E., Benharref, A., Harous, S., Navaz, A.N.: New algorithms for processing time-series big EEG data within mobile health monitoring systems. Comput. Methods Programs Biomed. **149**, 79–94 (2017)
4. Liu, Q., Guo, X., Fan, H., Zhu, H.: A novel data visualization approach and scheme for supporting heterogeneous data. In: 2017 IEEE 2nd Information Technology, Networking, Electronic and Automation Control Conference (ITNEC), pp. 1259–1263 (2017)
5. Frink, T.M., Gyllinsky, J.V., Mankodiya, K.: Visualization of multidimensional clinical data from wearables on the web and on apps. In: 2017 IEEE MIT Undergraduate Research Technology Conference (URTC), pp. 1–4 (2017)

6. Hai-Jia, W., Peng, L., Wei-wei, C.: The optimization theory of file partition in network storage environment. In: 2010 9th International Conference on Grid and Cooperative Computing (GCC), pp. 30–33 (2010)
7. Bhagwat, D., Pollack, K., Long, D.D.E., Schwarz, T., Miller, E.L., Paris, J.F.: Providing high reliability in a minimum redundancy archival storage system. In: Proceedings of the 14th IEEE International Symposium on Modeling, Analysis, and Simulation. MASCOTS 2006, Washington, DC, USA, pp. 413–421. IEEE Computer Society (2006)
8. You, L.L., Pollack, K.T., Long, D.D.E., Gopinath, K.: Presidio: a framework for efficient archival data storage. Trans. Storage **7**, 6::1–6:60 (2011)
9. Fan, K., Zhao, L., Shen, X., Li, H., Yang, Y.: Smart-blocking file storage method in cloud computing. In: 2012 1st IEEE International Conference on Communications in China (ICCC), pp. 57–62 (2012)
10. BBC: Dropbox hack' affected 68 million users'. https://www.bbc.com/news/technology-37232635. Accessed 30 July 2018
11. Celesti, A., Fazio, M., Villari, M., Puliafito, A.: Adding long-term availability, obfuscation, and encryption to multi-cloud storage systems. J. Netw. Comput. Appl. **59**, 208–218 (2016)
12. Galletta, A., Carnevale, L., Bramanti, A., Fazio, M.: An innovative methodology for big data visualization for telemedicine. IEEE Trans. Ind. Inf. **15**(1), 490–497 (2018)
13. Galletta, A., Celesti, A., Tusa, F., Fazio, M., Bramanti, P., Villari, M.: Big MRI data dissemination and retrieval in a multi-cloud hospital storage system. In: DH (2017)
14. Galletta, A., Bonanno, L., Celesti, A., Marino, S., Bramanti, P., Villari, M.: An approach to share MRI data over the cloud preserving patients' privacy. In: 2017 IEEE Symposium on Computers and Communications (ISCC), pp. 94–99 (2017)

The Slingshot Approach
Model-Driven Engineering the Coordination of Autoscaling Mechanisms for Elastic Cloud Applications

Floriment Klinaku[(✉)] and Steffen Becker

University of Stuttgart, Stuttgart, Germany
{floriment.klinaku,steffen.becker}@iste.uni-stuttgart.de

Abstract. Distributed software systems composed of two or more self-adaptive components require the presence of a coordination mechanism to ensure the fulfilment of overall system objectives over time. Exploiting elasticity, for example, is one important objective for operating software systems in the cloud. The recently adopted architectural style of independent Microservices, each with its autoscaling mechanism, creates a class of software systems that are composed of several self-adaptive components which provision and release resources in an autonomous manner. Manually evaluating the impact of coordinating actions among autoscaling mechanisms can be complicated because of their large configuration space. So, to aid software engineers in designing and evaluating coordinating actions for achieving overall elastic applications, we propose the Slingshot approach which leverages model-driven quality prediction and search-based software engineering techniques. The approach has three facets: (1) the decomposition of a software architecture into elastic layers where the impact of adaptations propagates in a top-down order; (2) the extension of self-adaptive performance modelling approaches to allow engineers to specify and analyze dependencies between layers; and (3) finding the optimal adaptation strategy of a lower layer for a fixed upper layer context. In this paper, we present a road-map consisting of research objectives and expected benefits of the proposed approach.

Keywords: Elasticity · Cloud · Coordination

1 Introduction

The primary purpose of engineering self-adaptive software systems [10] is that the software system will adjust without the need to intervene manually. An elastic software system should be able to adjust its autoscaling mechanisms [3] seeking for an optimal elasticity whenever its *context*, for which it is designed, evolves in terms of *workloads* entering the system (, a new tenant[1] joins the system) or other changes in its *environment* (, the cloud provider increases the prices or non-functional requirement change). Similar as in physics, where a constant

---

[1] A group of users that share the same SLA against a SaaS.

© Springer Nature Switzerland AG 2020
M. Fazio and W. Zimmermann (Eds.): ESOCC 2018 Workshops, CCIS 1115, pp. 158–165, 2020.
https://doi.org/10.1007/978-3-030-63161-1_13

factor quantifies the elasticity of a material which determines the proportionality of deformation under given stress, there exist several proposals to quantify elasticity for a given software system [6]. For example, Herbst et al. [7] measure the timeshare in which a system is over-provisioning or under-provisioning resources altogether with the magnitude of the over-provisioning and under-provisioning, respectively.

The variety of autoscaling mechanisms, their large configuration space, and the different type of available resources in cloud increases the complexity and makes it costly to evaluate the impact of their use and their different configurations [4]. The complexity grows when the system is composed of several components where each has its autoscaling mechanism, and coordinated actions need to be taken to reach overall system objectives. On top of that, depending on the context, system owners might weight differently the system objectives, some might want to ensure *performance* while allocating more operational *budget* while others would rather sacrifice *reliability* for a *cost-efficient* solution. Such objectives affect the choice of the autoscaling mechanism, its configuration and actions that coordinate autoscaling mechanisms across components. Since the space of well-suited configuration rules and coordinating actions is too large, it is usually costly and inefficient to find a solution which optimizes between multi-objective goals [3].

State-of-the-art approaches in simulation-based model-driven quality predictions [1] can help engineers to evaluate the impact of autoscaling mechanisms for modelled software architectures at design-time. However, even in cases where existing approaches support elasticity analyzes, they require a high modelling effort to specify elasticity mechanisms and to express coordinated actions in-between. Currently, the high effort out-weights the support in evaluating design-decisions concerning elasticity. On the other hand, when the coordination is not known beforehand, engineers seek to find suitable actions that ensure an optimal elasticity. Several works tackle this optimization problem through search-based software engineering techniques for searching optimal configurations which balance between different trade-offs. However, they do not explore the dependencies which may exist across autoscalers.

To tackle the high modelling effort in evaluating the impact of autoscaling configurations and coordinated actions across components and to reduce the search space for finding optimal rules, we propose the Slingshot approach. The approach is composed of three facets: (1) the decomposition of software architectures with respect to elasticity into layers of adaptations where one upper layer impacts one at the bottom, (2) the extension of self-adaptive performance modelling approaches to reduce the effort for engineers to specify and analyze the coordination across layers and (3) finding the optimal adaptation strategy of a lower layer for a fixed upper layer context.

The rest of this work is structured as follows: in Sect. 3 we present a running example which motivates the problem and the proposed solution, in Sect. 2 we describe the foundations for the proposed approach, in Sect. 4 we describe the three facets that constitute the Slingshot approach, and correspondingly the necessary work packages and expected outcomes. Finally, in Sect. 5 we summarize and conclude this paper.

2   Foundations

Three related research threads lay the groundwork for our proposal. In the area of quality predictions for software systems, traditional approaches predict quality attributes like performance or reliability for *static software systems* (, non-adaptive). One prominent approach is the Palladio Component Model [2] where engineers can model a software system through several viewpoints, and then different types of analyzes can predict different quality attributes based on different viewpoints of the modelled system. Palladio is later extended through SimuLizar to enable the performance prediction of *self-adaptive software systems* [1]. Engineers can model reactive adaptations based on threshold conditions and evaluate how they impact the performance of a system. To reduce the modelling effort and capture the knowledge for common architectural patterns into reusable templates, Lehrig et al. [8] propose the Architectural Template engineering method for efficient design-time analysis.

Another thread constitutes the variety of mechanisms and approaches for engineering self-adaptive software in general and elastic software systems in specific. One instance of such approaches for developing self-adaptive systems is called EUREMA (Executable Runtime Megamodels) which focuses on easing the development of adaptation engines through a model-driven engineering approach [11]. One of the many requirements they tackle which is relevant for this proposal is the operation of feedback loops in multiple layers where a loop at a higher layer can adapt a loop at the layer below. On the other hand, a recent survey on autoscaling mechanisms [3] shows the high variety of solutions to exploit elasticity. One relevant outcome of the survey is that the use of multiple loops can potentially bring new benefits by having fine-granular adaptations with localized objectives. Since the ultimate goal is to predict the elasticity of a software system containing dependencies between adaptation mechanisms it is important to consider the dependency between the same and different types of elasticity management mechanisms.

Last but not least, the third fundamental research thread is work that combines search-based software engineering techniques [5] and model-driven quality predictions discussed above. One prominent example is the PerOpteryx approach [9]. They apply a multi-criteria genetic algorithm to software architectures, modelled via the Palladio Component Model, to automate the search of good candidates which constitute the Pareto front with regards to quality attributes such as performance, reliability, and cost. The relevance of this thread is to determine if the proposed layered approach reduces the search space and increases the efficiency of employing search-based software engineering for deriving dependencies between elasticity mechanisms.

3   Running Example

As a running example, we consider a software deployed in the cloud which processes data from field sensors. As Fig. 1 shows, the software is composed of two components: a front-end (FE) and a back-end (BE).

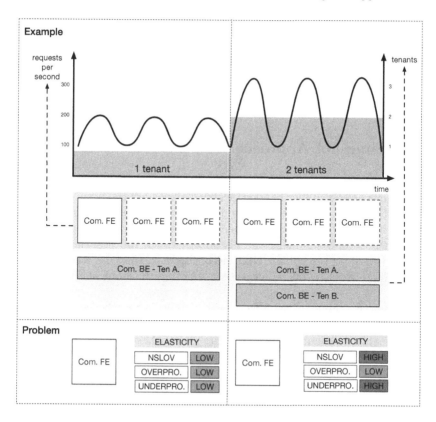

Fig. 1. Example: A cloud solution made of two self-adaptive components FE and BE processing requests from IoT devices. Component FE adapts based on the requests per second entering the system while Component BE based on the number of tenants (group of devices). **Problem**: When a new tenant joins, the self-adaptation strategy of the FE component is not able to deliver the same elasticity as before.

The front-end component processes incoming requests from IoT devices and invokes the BE component to store the result. The BE component stores the results for a fixed amount of sensors (tenant). Whenever there is a new group of sensors deployed in the field the BE adapts by creating an additional shard for the new group. This way the system can ensure service level objectives (SLOs) for each tenant. Contrary to the BE, the FE component is stateless and adapts through horizontal replication based on lower level signals such as the number of incoming requests per second or when the average CPU utilization is exceeded above a threshold. The FE is entirely agnostic to the notion of grouped sensors.

As Fig. 1 depicts, both components, FE and BE, cost-efficiently handle a single tenant. Once another group of sensors is deployed, the FE component experiences degradation of elasticity which results either in quality degradation or inquires unnecessary costs. Various reasons can lead to elasticity degradation. Since in the new context the slope at which requests arrive is higher, the adaptation process and its configuration is not optimal for the new context. It may be the case that the adaptation process *slowly* adapts the FE and the under-provisioning timeshare increases, or, no violation of SLOs occur since the adaptation process in the new context over-provisions most of the time. In both cases, there is the need to update self-adaptation rules or conditions so that the software system as a whole maintains the desired elasticity.

4   The Slingshot Approach

A slingshot is a composite of two materials, one Y-shaped wooden or plastic frame and one elastic rubber band attached at the end of the branched-out edges of the plastic casing. Its only objective is to shoot or displace an object, usually a stone, with a high velocity at a specific target. When deforming the plastic frame (, increasing or reducing the distance between the branched-out edges), one needs to adjust the rubber band accordingly so that the whole composite can continue to meet its overall objective: shooting the stone at the same speed as before.

Based on this analogy, we introduce the Slingshot approach to model and analyze dependencies between self-adaptations so that we can reason on and predict the elastic behaviour of a software system based on its dynamic architectural model as a composite at design-time. At the root of the approach is the decomposition of the software architecture, concerning self-adaptations, into two parts: the *plastic* and the *elastic* part. Both parts entail unique characteristics with respect to the *context* against they adapt, the *rental costs*, the *adaptations reversibility* and their *granularity*.

For example, the BE component in our running example self-adapts whenever a group of sensors join the system. The FE component, unlike the BE component, adapts based on the number of requests in the system and independently of the number of tenants in the system. Another characteristic which differentiates the plastic part from the elastic one is the rental costs: once a new tenant is part of the system the service provider has fixed costs for the BE component and variable cloud expenses for the FE component. They also differ concerning adaptations granularity and reversibility: there are less frequent variations in the number of tenants than in the number of requests that enter the system; thus fewer adaptations for the BE component during some period. As a consequence, we have prolonged periods where the plastic part does not change and against which the elastic part can adjust to offer a high quality of elasticity: saving costs while still being performant and reliable.

Once decomposed, one can identify and model dependencies between the plastic and the elastic part. This dependency is a directed edge from the self-adaptive mechanism of the plastic part to the self-adaptive mechanism of the elastic part. This edge can be seen as an *event-condition-action* rule where the *event* represents an adaptation event on the plastic part, the *condition* can be an arbitrarily condition and the *action* modifies the autoscaling mechanism of the elastic part.

We distinguish three different cases concerning the dependency between the plastic and the elastic part. Based on these three cases we design our research road-map consisting of research objectives, work packages and expected outcomes.

No Edge Specified. It is possible to employ independent autoscaling mechanisms for components in the software architecture. Considering our running example, it means that the BE and the FE can adapt independently against different *contexts* and resolve the impact of each other adaptations without specifying explicit actions. Further, it means that the software architecture may be elastic against all context changes (, changes in load, changes in the number of tenants) as a whole and meet the expected and weighted objectives for a target bounded context.

This case marks out our first work package which involves investigating candidates that represent state-of-the-art self-adaptive software architectures with a particular focus on the coordination of adaptation actions. Possible candidates are messaging queues which play a significant role in many cloud solutions primarily for the recently adopted Function as a Service (FaaS) model. For the selected candidates, first, we intend to identify existing adaptations at the component level and classify them based on the context against which they adapt. The second step involves determining the dependencies between adaptations. Illustrating this with our running example it means identifying all directed edges such as the one from the adaptation mechanism of the BE to the adaptation mechanism of the FE. The expected result from this work package is to obtain a layered data structure where for every two layers the upper one represents the plastic part which when adapted impacts the lower layer—the elastic layer. At this stage, we also investigate the rules/constraints for edges to be drawn between layered components, if the adaptation of two components part of a plastic layer impact the adaptation of the same component at the elastic layer then only one edge is necessary to be drawn and analyzed.

Known Edge. In the second case, engineers know the dependency between the plastic and the elastic part. Considering the running example, the edge between the plastic component BE, and the elastic component FE in an *event-condition-action* structure would look like: whenever BE replicates (*event*), increase the size of an FE instance, select another image from the cloud provider (*action*). We distinguish three different classes of *actions* which adapt the self-adaptive mechanism of the elastic part: re-configuring the adapted element, choosing a different size of VM; adjusting autoscaling parameters, selecting different thresholds in threshold-based autoscalers, or re-configuring both the adapted element and the adaptation rules. With such dependency specified, one is interested to know the impact in the overall elasticity of the system.

This case determines the second work package of our approach which consists in extending SimuLizar to allow engineers and interested parties to model and evaluate such dependencies between self-adaptive components and evaluate the elasticity of the composite at design-time. With regards to assessing the elasticity, engineers will be able to predict the elasticity of a software system architecture for any context alternation. Since we distinguished three different classes of *actions*, it is essential to extend SimuLizar's approach formally. Through this extension it is clear what an elasticity analysis should yield for each of the action classes: for example, if the dependency modifies the adapted element, as previously described, by changing its size, then when evaluating the elasticity of the system with respect to the number of tenants the analysis should consider the time until all FE instances match the size specified in the dependency.

Unknown Edge. The last case which determines our last part of the proposed research is when the existence of the impact between layers is known, but the optimal actions are not known; thus an optimal action has to be searched when the plastic part adapts. The main question is to evaluate the feasibility of using model-driven simulation and search based software engineering techniques as in PerOpteryx [9] to automatically obtain a set of candidates for the dependencies between two layers which deliver the same quality of elasticity. Since elasticity is related to performance, reliability, and costs, it is of interests to find and classify the degrees of freedom which retain one property but impact the other.

Evaluation Methods. The proposed approach relies on the assumption that an elastic software system can be designed through a layered approach where the impact of adaptations propagate in a top-down order. To verify this assumption, we plan to conduct lab experiments and simulations, complemented by empirical research evidence on publicly accessible data. To verify if the modelling abstractions aid engineers to model and analyze dependencies between two self-adaptive components, we plan to obtain qualitative and quantitative feedback by designing and conducting an industrial case study. Through the designed case study, we will evaluate the method itself, the modelling abstractions it offers, and the outcome of its application. The expected evaluation result is to show that the Slingshot approach supports engineers and software architects in designing autonomous cloud software system where its elastic behaviour is designed, evaluated and can be explained throughout its lifetime through the modelled part and the weighted objectives.

5   Conclusion

In this research proposal, we tackle the problem of designing and evaluation coordinated actions across autoscalers and components to reach the desired quality of elasticity throughout the lifetime of a software system. We propose the Slingshot approach which decomposes the software architecture into elastic layers where provisioning actions in an upper layer impact the provisioning mechanism of a layer below. To understand the impact of such dependencies, we plan to extend SimuLizar, the state-of-the-art performance modelling and analysis approach for self-adaptive software systems. This way we enable engineers and interested parties to evaluate the impact of coordinating actions at design-time and evaluate the elasticity of the architecture as a whole. Last but not least, in cases where the specific impact of an upper layer adaptation is not known, we intend to use search-based software engineering methods in the modelled architecture to derive the optimal action for the new context.

References

1. Becker, S., Brataas, G., Lehrig, S.: Engineering Scalable, Elastic, and Cost-Efficient Cloud Computing Applications: The CloudScale Method. Springer, Cham (2017). https://doi.org/10.1007/978-3-319-54286-7
2. Becker, S., Koziolek, H., Reussner, R.: The palladio component model for model-driven performance prediction. J. Syst. Softw. **82**(1), 3–22 (2009). Special Issue: Software Performance - Modeling and Analysis
3. Chen, T., Bahsoon, R., Yao, X.: A survey and taxonomy of self-aware and self-adaptive cloud auto scaling systems. In: CSUR (2018)
4. Evangelidis, A., Parker, D., Bahsoon, R.: Performance modelling and verification of cloud-based auto-scaling policies. Future Gener. Comput. Syst. **87**, 629–638 (2018)
5. Harman, M., Briand, L., Wolf, A.: The current state and future of search based software engineering (2007)
6. Herbst, N., et al.: Ready for Rain? A View from SPEC Research on the Future of Cloud Metrics. Technical report. SPEC-RG-2016-01, SPEC Research Group – Cloud Working Group (2016)
7. Herbst, N.R., Kounev, S., Reussner, R.: Elasticity in cloud computing: What it is, and what it is not. In: Proceedings of the 10th International Conference on Autonomic Computing (ICAC 2013), pp. 23–27. USENIX, San Jose (2013)
8. Lehrig, S., Hilbrich, M., Becker, S.: The architectural template method: templating architectural knowledge to efficiently conduct quality-of-service analyses. Softw. Pract. Exp. **48**(2), 268–299 (2018)
9. Martens, A., Koziolek, H., Becker, S., Reussner, R.: Automatically improve software architecture models for performance, reliability, and cost using evolutionary algorithms. In: Proceedings of the First Joint WOSP/SIPEW International Conference on Performance Engineering, pp. 105–116. ACM, New York (2010)
10. Salehie, M., Tahvildari, L.: Self-adaptive software: landscape and research challenges. ACM Trans. Auton. Adapt. Syst. **4**(2), 141–1442 (2009)
11. Vogel, T.: Model-driven engineering of self-adaptive software. Ph.D. thesis, Universität Potsdam (2018)

Analysing and Deploying (Micro)service-Based Applications

Davide Neri[(⊠)]

Department of Computer Science, University of Pisa, Pisa, Italy
davide.neri@di.unipi.it

Abstract. Microservices propose to develop applications as suites of small independent services communicating via lightweight mechanisms. Microservices are usually packaged into containers created ad-hoc, which help in deploying applications onto cloud platforms. Even if microservices and containers are already pervading enterprise IT, how to design, refactor and deploy microservice-based applications are key open problems. This paper illustrates our research project aimed at addressing two main research challenges deriving from the above mentioned problems, i.e., (i) analysing and (ii) deploying microservice-based applications.

1 Introduction

Arising from SOA [26], microservices are an approach to developing a single application as a suite of small services, each running in its own process and communicating with lightweight mechanisms, often an HTTP resource API. These services are built around business capabilities and are independently deployable by fully automated deployment machinery. There is a bare minimum of centralized management of these services, which may be written in different programming languages and use different data storage technologies [12].

Microservices are typically deployed in the cloud by exploiting container technologies [21]. Containers are a virtualisation mechanism used for application packaging, distribution and orchestration on cloud platforms and fog infrastructures [19]. Containers enable the deployment of microservices into multiple execution environments with a centralized management [17]. In the last years, Docker (www.docker.com) has emerged as the de-facto platform for containers [20].

In this paper, we discuss our research project aimed at enhancing the current support for microservices. Our project focuses on two main research challenges, in-line with the currently open problems of microservices [9,11,13,22,23] i.e., analysis and deployment of microservices. In order to introduce the reader to the concrete problems, we hereafter discuss a motivating example.

Motivating Example. Figure 1 shows the microservice-based architecture of a toy application, which allows users to search and order items from a catalog.

Supervisor: Antonio Brogi, University of Pisa, Italy.

© Springer Nature Switzerland AG 2020
M. Fazio and W. Zimmermann (Eds.): ESOCC 2018 Workshops, CCIS 1115, pp. 166–173, 2020.
https://doi.org/10.1007/978-3-030-63161-1_14

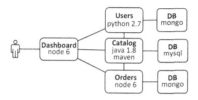

Fig. 1. Microservice-based architecture of an e-commerce application.

The application provides a service (viz., *Dashboard*) that gathers information from three services (viz., *Users*, *Catalog*, and *Orders*), each equipped with its own database. *Users* manages the users of the application, *Catalog* maintains the catalogue of the saleable items, and *Orders* manages the orders of the users. The services communicate with each other using HTTP resource APIs, and each service requires a different runtime environment (viz., *Users* requires *Python 2.7*, *Orders* requires *Node v6*, *Catalog* requires both *Java 1.8* and *Maven*, and *Dashboard* requires *Node v6*). Given our toy application, a system architect may wish to answer to the following questions:

– Is the *Users* service horizontally scalable? If not, how can we refactor the application to make it so? What about the other microservices?
– Can we automatically package the *Catalog* service in a container that satisfies its requirements (i.e., a container that supports both *Java 1.8* and *Maven*)?

□

2   Research Objectives

Our research project aims at supporting microservice-based architectures by addressing two research challenges:

– **(R1) Analysing microservice-based architectures**. Microservice-based architectures are usually composed by a huge amount of interacting services. The lack of an appropriate modelling makes it hard to analyse and refactor such complex architectures [23]. For example, it is hard to check whether a microservice-based architecture enjoys some of the key microservice principles (e.g., independent deployability, horizontal scalability), or to refactor an existing architecture [24]. This is because all such kinds of analyses are currently done manually, or by setting ad-hoc runtime test. This research objective aims at developing design-time methodologies for supporting the analysis and the refactoring of microservice-based architectures.
– **(R2) Deploying microservice-based architectures**. Microservice-based architectures are usually deployed using container-based virtualisation. However, it is currently not possible to automatically select the container satisfying the requirements of a microservice (e.g., operating system and software distributions needed by the microservices). Microservices hence need proper

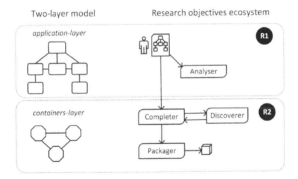

Fig. 2. Two-layers modelling and research objectives ecosystem.

solutions for automatically deploying each microservice in a container capable of satisfying its deployment requirements.

To address our research challenges, a suitable **modelling** is needed. Such modelling should allow to describe the structure of microservice-based architectures and the interactions among microservices (i.e., the *application-layer*), and to represent the containers deployement (i.e., the *containers-layer*). The availability of such modelling would allow to **analyse** microservice architectures (e.g., to check whether they meet some properties and or to suggest refactorings) and to propose refactorings, and to automatically **package** the components of an application into containers (e.g., finding containers satisfying services' requirements).

Figure 2 shows our two research challenges (i.e., R1 and R2) along with the two-layered model (left) and the research objectives ecosystem (right). R1 includes the selection of a proper model for describing microservice architecture and the development of the `Analyser` module, which is in charge to run the methodologies for analysing and refactoring microservice-based architectures. R2 includes the development of tools (i.e., `Completer`, `Discoverer`, and `Packager`), which are in charge of packaging microservices into containers. In the following, we expand the discussion concerning the research challenges R1 and R2.

(R1) Analysing Microservice-Based Architectures. A support for the design of microservice-based architectures requires to find a suitable representation of such complex architectures. A comparative assessment of existing models will allow us to proceed with the selection of the metamodel that we consider more suited for representing microservice-based architectures under various comparative dimensions—e.g., expressive power of each metamodel, its ease of use, its non-ambiguity, etc. In this perspective, we will choose one among the following possibilities: (i) employ one of the emerging standard proposals, (ii) extend one of the existing proposal, or (iii) design and develop a new model.

After the definition of a suitable representation for microservice-based architectures, we would like to propose methodologies to (i) analyse microservice-based architectures, to (ii) suggest architecture refactoring for resolving identified problems, and to (iii) validate the microservice-to-container packaging.

The proposed analysis methodologies can be then exploited by the `Analyser` module (Fig. 2). The `Analyser` takes as input the two-layered modelling of a microservice-based architecture, it executes the analysis methodologies, and it suggests refactorings of the microservice-based architecture (if needed).

(R2) Deploying Microservice-Based Architectures. Currently, developers are required to manually deploy the services of an application into containers by following the whole packaging process (e.g., copying the source code inside a container, installing or updating the software dependencies). This process of packaging microservices into containers is time-consuming and error-prone, and it has to be manually repeated whenever the requirements of a microservice change. We plan to design tools that, given the requirements of microservices, can automatically discover the containers that satisfy such requirements, and automatically package services inside the discovered containers.

For addressing R2, we plan to develop three modules (`Completer`, `Discoverer`, and `Packager`—Fig. 2) whose purpose is the following. `Completer` receives the description of a microservice-based architecture (where each service is described with its requirements) and it completes the description by selecting the containers that can satisfy its requirements (e.g., *Python 2.7* runtime). To accomplish such completion, it can either call the `Discoverer` module or it can built containers from scratch. `Discoverer` receives a list of services requirements and it returns the containers satisfying such requirements. The `Discoverer` should also perform a pre-processing phase that consists of finding the containers (e.g., from a central repository like Docker Hub hub.docker.com) offering the requirements (e.g., *Python 2.7*) and store them in a local database.The requirements describe the characteristics offered by the containers. `Packager` receives the description of a microservice-based architectures (including the mapping of microservice on the containers that will host them), and it translates such description in a format that is executable by orchestrator engines (e.g., Docker Compose [10], Kubernetes [15]).

3   Related Work

In this section we discuss the state of the art regarding the two research objectives we outlined in Sect. 2.

Analysing Microservice-Based Architectures. Due to space limitations, we only discuss the approaches that focus on modelling and analysing cloud applications and microservice-based architectures. *TOSCA* [18] is an emerging standard whose main goals are to enable the specification of portable cloud applications and to automate their deployment and management. To do so, TOSCA provides modelling language that allows to formalise the structure of a cloud application as a typed topology graph, and the deployment/management tasks as plans.

Docker Compose [10] is a tool for defining and running multi-container Docker applications. With Docker Compose, developers define a YAML file (i.e., *Compose file*) that describes their services in their applications. Each service in a

Docker Compose configuration file is described by a list of attributes (e.g., Docker image, number of replicas, and placement constraints) that are used to properly build and deploy the service in a Docker containers.

Kubernetes [15] is a container orchestration platform. Kubernetes takes care of the deployment, scaling and management of containerized applications across a distributed cluster of nodes. The applications packed into Docker containers can be seamlessly deployed using Kubernetes.

System-Z [2] is a tool developed by Spotify for supporting their microservice-based architecture. *System-Z* creates a dependency graph of components by tracking the outgoing calls that the microservices perform. The dependency graph can be used to model and analyse the structure of a microservice-based architecture, e.g., by finding information about components, by discovering the dependencies among microservices, or by detecting wrong communications.

spigo [1] is a tool developed by Adrian Cockcroft that is able to simulate the interactions of microservice-based architectures. The architecture in *spigo* is described as a JSON file that lists the components and the dependencies among them. *spigo* simulates the call of the microservices in an architecture and it generates statistics of the simulated execution.

Finally, it is worth discussing also two solutions for modelling the behaviour of service-based applications. *Aeolus* [8] and management protocols [3] permit describing the characteristics of the components of cloud applications (e.g., states, management operations, and dependencies), as well as the fact that component interfaces might vary depending on the internal component state. They both provide mechanisms for automatically analysing and planning the deployment and management of an application.

Although the aforementioned approaches are interesting, none of them provides the two layered model for supporting the analysis and deployment of microservices.

Deploying Microservice-Based Architectures. In this section, we discuss some solutions for enhancing the discovery and packaging of software components in virtual environments. Docker eases images distribution by permitting sharing them through so-called Docker registries, like Docker Hub (hub.docker.com) and Docker Store (store.docker.com). Docker Hub permits searching Docker image "by name" (i.e., it permits specifying a term to be matched within the name, description, or username associated to an image). Docker Store is a web-based application that extends the search capabilities provided by the Docker Hub by also allowing to filter images by category (e.g., database images, programming languages images). The main limitations of Docker registries are twofold. They only allow to search for images based on their name and category. It is not possible to look for images based on the software distributions they support, or on other attributes that developers may wish to specify to find the images(s) they need.

JFrog's artifactory [14] is an universal artefact repository working as a single access point to software packages created by any language or technology (including Docker). JFrog users can look for Docker images by indicating their name, tag or image digest. Users can also assign custom properties to images, which can then be exploited to specify and resolve queries. JFrog, however, requires users to manually assign properties to images, as it does not to automatically assign properties to images that satisfy a certain software requirements.

Wettinger et al. [25] contribute to the general objective of easing the discovery of DevOps "knowledge" (which includes Docker images). More precisely, [25] proposes to build the knowledge-base (which includes Docker images) in a semi-automated way, by (automatically) crawling heterogeneous artefacts from different sources, and by requiring DevOps experts to share their knowledge and (manually) associate metadata to the artefacts in the knowledge-base. However, the process proposed by [25] requires to manually assign custom metadata.

4   First Results and Future Work

In this section we outline our first results, and how we plan to proceed towards achieving the research objectives introduced in Sect. 2.

First Results. We focused our initial efforts more on R2. Indeed, we have already developed solutions that implement some of the `Discoverer` and `Completer` funcionalities. For the `Discoverer` module we developed two tools (`DockerFinder`, and `DockerAnalyser`). `DockerFinder` [7] is a tool that permits searching for (images of) Docker containers based on multiple attributes (e.g., images size, supported software distributions). `DockerAnalyser` [6] generalises `DockerFinder` by allowing to customise the function that is used to analyse the crawled images allowing users to create their own analysers of Docker images.

For the `Completer` we developed `TosKeriser` [4,5] a tool that can automatically complete TOSCA application specifications, by discovering Docker-based runtime environments. More precisely, `TosKeriser` take as input a TOSCA-based representation of an application, which specifies the microservices forming such application, the dependencies among them, and the software support that each microservice requires to effectively run. Then, `TosKeriser` automatically completes the TOSCA application specification, by discovering and including the Docker containers providing the software support needed by the microservices forming such application.

Ongoing Research. We are currently working on R1 for determining an appropriate model which permits specifying all information needed for describing the two layers we wish to consider (viz., application and containers). Currently, we are developing a simple modelling that permits describing an application as a directed graph (whose node are the software components and the edges are the interactions among them). Based on this simple model, we are developing analyses based on antipatterns that permit to discover portions of an architecture that are not compliant to microservice principles (i.e., bounded context, independent deployability, and horizontal scalability) and to propose refactorings that can solve the identified problems (e.g., split the database in order to obtain bounded contexts, refactor the interactions among services in order to obtain independently depoyable services, add a load balancer for obtaining horizzontally scalable services). Given that microservices are ever-evolving architectures, we plan to obtain such direted graph in completely automatic way by exploiting existing tools that extract the architecture of microservice-based systems (such as [16]).

We are also working at the container-layer of the model. Microservices are packaged onto containers that are deployed by orchestration engines. Orchestration engines provide additional functionalities (e.g., load balancing, service discovery) that can impact on whether/how microservice-based architectures comply with microservice principles. To cope with such a kind of situations, we plan to permit modelling the packaging of microservices onto containers, as well as to consider the additional functionalities provided by orchestration engines while analysing and refactoring microservice-based architectures.

All the methodologies developed in the scope of R1 will be included in the `Analyser` module shown in Fig. 2, so as to allow developers to concretely analyse and refactor their microservice-based architectures.

Next Steps. There are two main steps towards R1 and R2 that we plan to pursue. For R1, we plan to formalise our current two-layer model for microservice-based architectures (by also allowing to specify the behaviour of services), and to develop techniques for analysing and refactoring them. For R2, we plan to extend the work in [4,6,7] and by developing the `Packager` module (Fig. 2). The `Packager` will be in charge to translate the description of a microservice-based architecture (packaged in proper containers by the `TosKeriser` tool) into a format (e.g., Compose file [10]) which can hence be used by other orchestration engines to run the containerised application in an infrastructure. We also plan to evaluate our approach by studying the advantages and disadvantages of our model under different dimensions (e.g., the effort required to use our model with respect to analyse an architecture manually).

References

1. Adrian Cockcroft: Simulate Protocol Interactions in Go. https://github.com/adrianco/spigo. Accessed 17 July 2018
2. Petter Måhlén: Modelling Microservices at Spotify. https://clusterhq.com/2016/03/22/microservices-spotify-petter-mahlen/. Accessed 17 July 2018
3. Brogi, A., Canciani, A., Soldani, J.: Fault-aware management protocols for multi-component applications. J. Syst. Softw. **139**, 189–210 (2018)
4. Brogi, A., Neri, D., Rinaldi, L., Soldani, J.: From (incomplete) TOSCA specifications to running applications, with Docker. In: Cerone, A., Roveri, M. (eds.) SEFM 2017. LNCS, vol. 10729, pp. 491–506. Springer, Cham (2018). https://doi.org/10.1007/978-3-319-74781-1_33
5. Brogi, A., Neri, D., Rinaldi, L., Soldani, J.: Orchestrating incomplete TOSCA applications with Docker. In: Science of Computer Programming (2018, in press)
6. Brogi, A., Neri, D., Soldani, J.: A microservice-based architecture for (customisable) analyses of Docker images. Softw. Pract. Exp. **48**(8), 1461–1474 (2018)

7. Brogi, A., Neri, D., Soldani, J.: DockerFinder: multi-attribute search of Docker images. In: 2017 IEEE International Conference on Cloud Engineering (IC2E), pp. 273–278 (2017)
8. Di Cosmo, R., Mauro, J., Zacchiroli, S., Zavattaro, G.: Aeolus: a component model for the cloud. Inf. Comput. **239**, 100–121 (2014)
9. Di Francesco, P.: Architecting microservices. In: 2017 IEEE International Conference on Software Architecture Workshops (ICSAW), pp. 224–229. IEEE (2017)
10. Docker Inc.: Docker Compose. https://docs.docker.com/compose/. Accessed 17 July 2018
11. Fazio, M., Celesti, A., Ranjan, R., Liu, C., Chen, L., Villari, M.: Open issues in scheduling microservices in the cloud. IEEE Cloud Comput. **3**(5), 81–88 (2016)
12. Fowler, M., Lewis, J.: Microservices. ThoughtWorks. https://martinfowler.com/articles/microservices.html. Accessed 17 July 2018
13. Jamshidi, P., Pahl, C., Mendonça, N.C., Lewis, J., Tilkov, S.: Microservices: the journey so far and challenges ahead. IEEE Softw. **35**(3), 24–35 (2018)
14. JFrog Ltd.: Docker: Secure Clustered HA Docker Registries With A Universal Artifact Repository. https://www.jfrog.com/support-service/whitepapers/docker/. Accessed 17 July 2018
15. Linux Foundation: Kubernetes - Production-Grade Container Orchestration. https://kubernetes.io/. Accessed 17 July 2018
16. Mayer, B., Weinreich, R.: An approach to extract the architecture of microservice-based software systems. In: 2018 IEEE Symposium on Service-Oriented System Engineering (SOSE), pp. 21–30, March 2018
17. Newman, S.: Building Microservices: Designing Fine-Grained Systems. O'Reilly Media Inc., Sebastopol (2015)
18. OASIS: Topology and OrchestrationSpecification for Cloud Applications (TOSCA) Simple Profile in YAML Version 1.0 (2015). http://docs.oasis-open.org/tosca/TOSCA-Simple-Profile-YAML/v1.0/csprd01/TOSCA-Simple-Profile-YAML-v1.0-csprd01.pdf
19. Pahl, C., Lee, B.: Containers and clusters for edge cloud architectures - a technology review. In: 2015 3rd International Conference on Future Internet of Things and Cloud, pp. 379–386 (2015)
20. Pahl, C., Brogi, A., Soldani, J., Jamshidi, P.: Cloud container technologies: a state-of-the-art review. IEEE Trans. Cloud Comput. (2017, in press)
21. Pahl, C., Jamshidi, P.: Microservices: a systematic mapping study. In: CLOSER 2016, pp. 137–146. SCITEPRESS - Science and Technology Publications, Lda (2016)
22. Pautasso, C., Zimmermann, O., Amundsen, M., Lewis, J., Josuttis, N.: Microservices in practice, part 1: reality check and service design. IEEE Softw. **34**(1), 91–98 (2017)
23. Pautasso, C., Zimmermann, O., Amundsen, M., Lewis, J., Josuttis, N.: Microservices in practice, part 2: service integration and sustainability. IEEE Softw. **34**(2), 97–104 (2017)
24. Taibi, D., Lenarduzzi, V.: On the definition of microservice bad smells. IEEE Softw. **35**(3), 56–62 (2018)
25. Wettinger, J., Andrikopoulos, V., Leymann, F.: Automated capturing and systematic usage of DevOps knowledge for cloud applications. In: 2015 IEEE International Conference on Cloud Engineering, pp. 60–65 (2015)
26. Zimmermann, O.: Microservices tenets. Comput. Sci. Res. Dev. 301–310 (2016). https://doi.org/10.1007/s00450-016-0337-0

ESOCC 2018 EU Projects Track

EU Project Space Track Preface

The ESOCC 2018 program included a special track devoted to presenting results and perspectives of EU research projects on service-oriented and cloud computing. The track session was held on September 12, 2018. It featured a good opportunity for eight EU projects (TheyBuyForYou[1], EW-Shopp[2], I-BiDaaS[3], SmartSDK[4], FIRST[5], ElasTest[6], RECAP[7], and DOSSIER-Cloud[8]) to disseminate their results and for participants to get an updated view of the ongoing research on service-oriented and cloud computing.

The topics covered by the projects were wide. The first group of projects focused on big data platforms, two were specific purpose platforms – e-procurement for TheyBuyForYou and targeted marketing for EW-Shopp – while I-BiDaaS focused on self provisioning aspects of big data solutions. Two other projects explored platforms for smart services, covering cities in the case of SmartSDK and factories for FIRST. Another two projects presented technologies to support cloud-based services development: large scale end-to-end application testing, in the case of ElasTest, and cloud-to-edge scalability simulators in the case of RECAP. Finally DOSSIER-Cloud project presented lessons learnt in knowledge transfer activities for cloud and dev-ops technologies.

The chairs wish to thank the track Program Committee members for their hard work in the careful assessment of the submitted papers. Further thanks go to the authors of contributed papers, in particular, for their efforts in the preparation of their submissions, the camera-ready versions, as well as the presentations at the event. The chairs finally thank the entire organization team of the ESOCC 2018, who actively contributed to the organization and the success of the event.

March 2020

Federico Facca
Dumitru Roman

---

[1] https://theybuyforyou.eu/.

[2] http://www.ew-shopp.eu.

[3] https://www.ibidaas.eu/.

[4] https://www.smartsdk.eu/.

[5] https://www.h2020first.eu/.

[6] https://elastest.eu/.

[7] http://recap-project.eu/.

[8] http://web.cut.ac.cy/dossier/.

EU Project Space Track Organization

Track Program Committee

Anna Fensel — Semantic Technology Institute (STI) Innsbruck, University of Innsbruck, Austria

Carlos A. Iglesias — Universidad Politécnica de Madrid, Spain

Ahmet Soylu — Norwegian University of Science and Technology, Norway

Sean Murphy — Zurich University of Applied Sciences (ZHAW), Switzerland

Attilio Vaccaro — MBI Srl, Italy

Maria Maleshkova — University of Bonn, Germany

Hugo Estrada — INFOTEC, Mexico

Manolis Koubarakis — National and Kapodistrian University of Athens, Greece

Vladimir Alexiev — Ontotext, Bulgaria

Matteo Palmonari — University of Milano-Bicocca, Italy

TheyBuyForYou: Enabling Procurement Data Value Chains

Elena Simperl[1], Oscar Corcho[2], Marko Grobelnik[3], Dumitru Roman[4],
Ahmet Soylu[4(✉)], María Jesús Fernández Ruíz[5], Stefano Gatti[6],
Chris Taggart[7], Urška Skok Klima[8], Annie Ferrari Uliana[9], Ian Makgill[10],
Philip Turk[4], and Till Christopher Lech[4]

[1] University of Southampton, Southampton, UK
[2] Universidad Politécnica de Madrid, Madrid, Spain
[3] Jožef Stefan Institute, Ljubljana, Slovenia
[4] SINTEF Digital, Oslo, Norway
`ahmet.soylu@sintef.no`
[5] Ayuntamiento de Zaragoza, Zaragoza, Spain
[6] Cerved Group Spa US, Milan, Italy
[7] OpenCorporates Ltd., London, UK
[8] Ministrstvo za javno upravo, Ljubljana, Slovenia
[9] OESIA Networks SL, Madrid, Spain
[10] OpenOpps Ltd., London, UK

Abstract. The release of a growing amount of open procurement data means that we are increasingly able, and even have the obligation, to scrutinize and analyse public spending for delivering better quality of public services, optimizing costs, preventing fraud and corruption, and building healthy and sustainable economies. The TheyBuyForYou project addresses this challenge by developing an integrated technology platform, with a cross-lingual and cross-border procurement knowledge graph, core services, open APIs, and online tools, and validating them in several business cases in public/corporate procurement in Slovenia, Spain and Italy. This paper gives an overview about the project's goals and challenges.

Keywords: Knowledge graph · Public procurement · Ontology · Interaction design · Data analytics · Cross-lingual document comparison

1 Introduction

The interaction between governments and their suppliers needs to be subjected to new levels of scrutiny to ensure the efficient delivery of public services and to protect the interests of taxpayers. With a spending in the range of trillions of euros[1], governments are facing a real responsibility to ensure that this money is

---

[1] http://ec.europa.eu/DocsRoom/documents/20679.

This work is funded by EU H2020 TheyBuyForYou project (780247).

© Springer Nature Switzerland AG 2020
M. Fazio and W. Zimmermann (Eds.): ESOCC 2018 Workshops, CCIS 1115, pp. 179–186, 2020.
https://doi.org/10.1007/978-3-030-63161-1_15

used in the best way possible and that decisions are made considering inclusive, long-term goals and strategies. The release of a growing amount of open procurement data means that we are increasingly able, and even have the obligation, to scrutinize and analyse public spending for delivering better quality of public services, optimizing costs, preventing fraud and corruption, and building healthy and sustainable economies [1].

The recently started TheyBuyForYou project[2] (Enabling procurement data value chains for economic development, demand management, competitive markets and vendor intelligence) addresses this challenge by developing an integrated technology platform, with a cross-lingual and cross-border procurement knowledge graph, core services, open APIs, and online tools, and validating them in several business cases in public/corporate procurement in Slovenia, Spain and Italy. This paper gives an overview about the project's goals and challenges.

The rest of the paper is structured as follows. Section 2 discusses the related work, while Sect. 3 presents the project background through project's objectives and challenges. Section 4 describes the TheyBuyForYou approach and Sect. 5 presents customer scenarios and business cases. Finally, Sect. 6 reports the current state of the project.

2 Related Work

Many of the tools in use by governments are often not optimised for government use, or are subject to restrictive contracts which unnecessarily complicate publishing open data. Other contracts, such as contracts for tender advertising portals are hampering the progress of transparency because the portals are claiming copyright over all data published in the portals, even though their public-sector clients are the authors and the data on tender opportunities are required to be published openly by law. The technical landscape for managing such contracts is very heterogeneous: for example, even in medium-sized cities, contracts are handled using different tools and formats across departments, including relational databases, Excel spreadsheets, and Lotus Notes. This makes it difficult to have a high-level overview of processes and decisions.

There are various initiatives whose purpose is to create de-jure and de-facto standards for electronic procurement, including such as Open Contracting Data Standard (OCDS)[3] and TED eSenders[4]. However, these are mostly oriented to achieve interoperability (i.e., addressing communication between systems), document oriented (i.e., the structure of the information is commonly provided by the content of the documents that are exchanged), and provide no standardised practices to refer to third parties, companies participating in the process, or even the main object of contracts. This at the end generates a lot of heterogeneity. Procurement domain can take advantage of applying the Semantic Web approach by

---

[2] https://theybuyforyou.eu.

[3] http://standard.open-contracting.org/latest/en/.

[4] http://simap.ted.europa.eu/.

reusing existing vocabularies, ontologies, and standards [1]. Specifically in the procurement domain, these include among others PPROC ontology [6] for describing public processes and contracts, LOTED2 ontology [3] for public procurement notices, PCO ontology [7] for contracts in public domain, and MOLDEAS ontology [9] for announcements about public tenders. LOTED2 is considered as a legal ontology and is comparatively more complex and detailed with respect to MOLDEAS, PCO, and PPROC. The latter is concerned on reaching a balance between usability and expressiveness.

3   Background

TheyBuyForYou explores how procurement and public spending data, paired with data management, analytics, and interaction design, could be used to innovate four key areas:

(i) economic development by delivering better economic outcomes from public spending, in particular for SMEs (to get better access to public tenders, competing with more established players etc.);
(ii) demand management by spotting trends in spending and supplier management to achieve long-term goals such as cost savings and efficiency gains;
(iii) competitive markets by identifying areas for cost cuts through healthier competition;
(iv) and, procurement intelligence by producing advanced analytics to inform decision support, risk monitoring and supply market analysis for procurement managers.

3.1   Objectives

Our first objective is to build a technology platform, consisting of a set of modular, Web-based services and APIs to publish, curate, integrate, analyse, and visualize an open, comprehensive, cross-border and cross-lingual procurement knowledge graph, including public spending and corporate data from multiple sources across the EU.

Our second objective is to support the realisation of the four innovation areas discussed, through a series of online tools and public portals, which allow suppliers, buyers, data journalists, data analysts, control authorities and regular citizens to explore and understand how public procurement decisions affect economic development, efficiencies, competitiveness and supply chains. For private buyers looking to overhaul their procurement and purchasing decisions, we will deliver vendor intelligence solutions with advanced analytics capabilities around risk monitoring, collusive tendering, and bespoke decision support.

Finally, our third objective is validation in the procurement market to investigate how the knowledge graph published can be used to support the four main innovation scenarios. While the economic development and procurement intelligence scenarios target SMEs and big industries looking for subcontractors, the other two offer decision support to public buyers and other parties interested in an analysis of the public spending market.

3.2   Challenges

The first challenge to meet is the heterogeneity of the underlying data, which covers structured (e.g., statistics, financial news) as well as unstructured (e.g., text, social media) sources in different languages and using their own terminology and formats (CSV, PDF, databases, websites, APIs etc.). To be truly useful, our technology will have to offer its services in real-time, including the thousands of new tenders published on official portals such as TED (Tenders Electronic Daily)[5] every week, as well as general-purpose corporate data streams such as business-centric social networks and stock market data.

The second challenge will be in turning this vast array of information into a semantic knowledge graph [12], an interconnected knowledge organization structure using Web URIs and linked data vocabularies, which can be analysed in depth to identify patterns and anomalies in procurement processes and networks. Finally, we need to find means to communicate the results of our analysis and inform decisions, which convey useful information while scaling well to complex data shapes and large volumes of data.

4   TheyBuyForYou Approach

The TheyBuyForYou approach has three layers. First, data and technology layer enables developers to create fully functional, robust, and scalable data integration pipelines, from sourcing the data; pre-processing, augmenting, and interlinking it; to learning patterns and anomalies; making predictions; and communicating the insights to specific audiences. Second, tools and products layer offers end-user tools and procurement APIs such as for visualisation, and document comparison. Finally, validation layer realises a set of selected business cases over online portals, one for suppliers and one for buyers, built on tools and products layer. The TheyBuyForYou approach is mapped to a high-level architecture as described in Fig. 1.

4.1   Procurement Knowledge Graph

The knowledge graph primarily integrates supplier data and procurement data. Core company data is provided by OpenCorporates[6]. Tenders and contracts data is provided by OpenOpps[7] in the OCDS (Open Contracting Data Standard) format[8], whose primary source of data is the TED data feed. The data is curated (e.g., missing and duplicate records), normalised, and integrated through a common ontology [5,6,11]. The entities in the knowledge graph (e.g., tenders and suppliers) are linked and reconciled. The data will be made available through SPARQL end-points, open APIs, and linked data interfaces.

---

[5] http://ted.europa.eu.

[6] https://opencorporates.com.

[7] https://openopps.com.

[8] http://standard.open-contracting.org/latest/en.

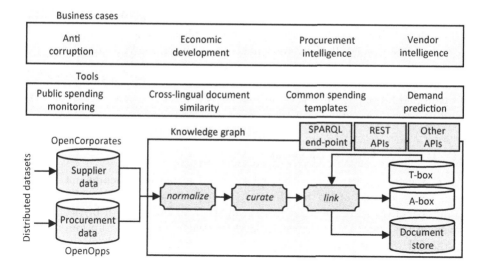

Fig. 1. TheyBuyForYou high level architecture.

4.2 Cross-lingual and Real-Time Analytics

A real-time monitoring and analysis framework is to be developed for public and private procurement information that is published over several different sources and in different languages. The framework needs to scale to the millions of documents available (calls, news, events etc.). Since most procurement documents are available in the native language of the issuing authority or organisation, cross-language support is a key [4]. A methodology for discovery of common order and spending patterns is also to be developed, which will offer additional insight into public procurement practices [2].

4.3 Data Interaction and Story Telling

TheyBuyForYou will develop tools, using such as interactive visualizations, configurable infographics, and automatically generated data stories, to explore procurement data and to support sense making and decision making based on this data. Three features will be at the core of the designs: encouraging exploration, as a means to master the high-dimensionality of the knowledge graph; emphasizing provenance trails for the data and accountability of analytics insights; and contextualizing visualizations and analytics findings via data narratives [8]. To make the creation of data narratives manageable, we will learn storytelling templates, which could be assembled into configurable infographics.

5   Customer Scenarios and Business Cases

We will develop a series of tools across four innovation scenarios (i.e., economic development, demand management, competitive markets, and procurement intelligence), discussed in Sect. 3, to ensure the project impact. These scenarios will result in two open online portals: one for suppliers/bidders and a second one for buyers. Tools and APIs delivered will be used to implement initially three business cases (see Fig. 1) targeting the main customer segments in procurement. Two business cases will be with public administrations at the national and local levels in Spain and Slovenia, while the third one is a corporate business case and will result in a new commercial product.

5.1   Business Case 1: Slovenia

The first case targets competitive markets and advanced procurement intelligence scenarios and is led by Ministrstvo za javno upravo (The Ministry of Public Administration, Slovenia) with support from Jozef Stefan Institute. The Slovenian business case is centred around the theme of anti-corruption, including the following aspects: definition of selection criteria for tenders; monitoring diversity of requirements in similar procurement calls and issuing of an alert when relevant anomalies are identified; providing support in the post procurement process, so as to prevent unnecessary changes to the original contract; and offering transparency data to help ensure they are working with the most suitable and reliable suppliers.

5.2   Business Case 2: Spain

The second case targets economic development, demand management, and competitive markets scenarios and is led by Ayuntamiento de Zaragoza (City of Zaragoza, Spain) with support from Oesia. They together with other regional public administrations in Spain launched the PPROC ontology within W3C for the standardisation of public procurement information according to the Spanish legislation. City of Zaragoza and Oesia aim to improve their procurement business by focusing on easier access to smaller companies for specific types of tenders, better understanding of demand from public organizations both inside and outside Spain, and identifying opportunities to cut costs.

5.3   Business Case 3: Italy

The third case targets advanced procurement intelligence and is led by Cerved. Cerved will develop a new product for vendor intelligence targeting the entire procurement market. The product will use open data (e.g., knowledge graph created in this project); proprietary data (e.g., chamber of commerce data, balance sheet data etc.); and third-party data (e.g., website traffic statistics). An important goal is to provide a more nuanced supplier analysis and classify relevant companies into micro, small and medium-sized enterprises by cross-connecting multiple data sources. This will enable Cerved to target SMEs better and define appropriate similarity scores between tenders and potential bidders.

6 Current Status

At the time of writing, the project is in the middle of its first year and plan is to publish the first version of the knowledge graph at the end of first year. Currently data providers, i.e., OpenOpps and OpenCorporates, are expanding their data coverage by identifying, prioritising, and auditing new data sources with respect to some quality criteria (e.g., legal, practical, and technical) and the needs of the business cases. Some data curation and integration activities directly take place at the side of our data providers, while main integration tasks will be handled by DataGraft, a cloud-based platform for data transformation and publishing [10].

A cross-lingual document similarity service for automatic comparison of public orders and spending documents across different languages has been implemented and deployed through a RESTful API. A conceptual framework has been developed for describing dimensions of data visualisation, based on a review of background literature and media, for the purpose of informing the initial process of ideation prior to the creation of visualisation and narrative components. Finally, existing ontologies for suppliers and procurement data are being reviewed for re-use (cf. [1]) and requirements are being collected from business cases.

References

1. Alvarez-Rodríguez, J.M., et al.: New trends on e-Procurement applying semantic technologies: current status and future challenges. Comput. Ind. **65**(5), 800–820 (2014)
2. Chandola, V., et al.: Anomaly detection: a survey. ACM Comput. Surv. **41**(3), 15:1–15:58 (2009)
3. Distinto, I., et al.: LOTED2: an ontology of European public procurement notices. Semant. Web **7**(3), 267–293 (2016)
4. Fortuna, B., et al.: A kernel canonical correlation analysis for learning the semantics of text. In: Kernel Methods in Bioengineering, Communications and Image Processing (2006)
5. Kharlamov, E., et al.: Ontology based data access in Statoil. Web Semant. Sci. Serv. Agents World Wide Web **44**, 3–36 (2017)
6. Muñoz-Soro, J.F., et al.: PPROC, an ontology for transparency in public procurement. Semant. Web **7**(3), 295–309 (2016)
7. Necaský, M., et al.: Linked data support for filing public contracts. Comput. Ind. **65**(5), 862–877 (2014)
8. Portet, F., et al.: Automatic generation of textual summaries from neonatal intensive care data. Artif. Intell. **173**(7), 789–816 (2009)
9. Rodríguez, J.M.Á., et al.: Towards a pan-European e-procurement platform to aggregate, publish and search public procurement notices powered by linked open data: the MOLDEAS approach. Int. J. Softw. Eng. Knowl. Eng. **22**(3), 365–384 (2012)

10. Roman, D., et al.: DataGraft: one-stop-shop for open data management. Semant. Web **9**(4), 393–411 (2018)
11. Suchanek, F.M., et al.: Knowledge bases in the age of big data analytics. Proc. VLDB Endow. **7**(13), 1713–1714 (2014)
12. Yan, J., et al.: A retrospective of knowledge graphs. Front. Comput. Sci. **12**(1), 55–74 (2018)

EW-Shopp Project: Supporting Event and Weather-Based Data Analytics and Marketing Along the Shopper Journey

Matteo Palmonari[1], Michele Ciavotta[1(✉)], Flavio De Paoli[1], Aljaž Košmerlj[2], and Nikolay Nikolov[3]

[1] University of Milan-Bicocca, Milan, Italy
{matteo.palmonari,michele.ciavotta,flavio.depaoli}@unimib.it
[2] Jovžef Stefan Institute, Ljubljana, Slovenia
aljaz.kosmerlj@ijs.si
[3] SINTEF, Oslo, Norway
nikolay.nikolov@sintef.no

Abstract. EW-Shopp is an innovation project, the aim of which is to build a platform for support of data linking, integration, and analytics in companies from the e-commerce, retail, and marketing industries. The project consortium joins several business partners from different sectors of e-commerce including marketing, price comparison, and both web and brick-and-mortar stores. The project is developing several pilot services to test the platform and inform its further development.

Keywords: Machine learning · Data integration · e-commerce · Visual analytics

1 The Project

EW-Shopp[1] aims at providing support to companies operating in the fragmented European e-commerce ecosystem in order to connect, transform and integrate their data with external sources and use analytics to gain insights into their business. It is an innovation action project funded within the H2020 Research and Innovation program of the European Commission (*ICT-14-2016-2017, Big Data Public-Private Partnership: cross-sectorial and cross-lingual data integration and experimentation*). With its start in January 2017, it is now at the mid-point of its three-year duration.

The crux of the project is to foster small and medium-sized enterprises (SMEs), which represent 99% of all businesses in the EU, by building a platform which will deliver an end-to-end flexible solution to work with consumer and market data. In particular, to achieve novel customer and market insights, the platform will empower data manipulation, linking, and enrichment of business data

---

[1] http://www.ew-shopp.eu.

© Springer Nature Switzerland AG 2020
M. Fazio and W. Zimmermann (Eds.): ESOCC 2018 Workshops, CCIS 1115, pp. 187–191, 2020.
https://doi.org/10.1007/978-3-030-63161-1_16

with weather and event information, as a first enabler to create powerful analytical services. In fact, as a result of operating in a multi-lingual and multi-market environment, European companies (even those not operating through digital channels) commonly deal with large amounts of data, in multiple languages, acquired from different sources and sectors, or generated internally. Furthermore, their businesses are strongly impacted by external factors such as weather and global, as well as local events. To compete with international e-commerce giants, these companies must increasingly leverage this business data using modern analytics technologies to power and improve their services. Unfortunately, managing and integrating this heterogeneous data is prohibitively costly and time-consuming for a large number of companies, whose workforce generally does not possess the necessary skills. This is especially true for SMEs. Further, language barriers, lack of common models and shared systems of identifiers to interlink data, make these data integration tasks even more challenging.

The EW-Shopp platform attempts to simplify and streamline these tasks and level the playing field. We firmly believe this to be possible and give as an example the case of a project partner that, by using a predictive model built on top of integrated data about click-through rate of products, weather, and events, could design a service able to increase advertising of top-gear sport equipment in the days before a sunny weekend during the Tour De France.

2   The Consortium

The majority of the consortium consists of private companies from various sectors of e-commerce, covering the entire shopper journey from advertising and market research to sales and customer relations management for both online as well as brick-and-mortar stores. This includes: Ceneje Ltd. (SI), the manager of the largest price comparison shopping platform in Slovenia, Croatia, Serbia, and Bosnia and Herzegovina; BrowseTel Limited (UK), a provider of multi-channel communication services for customer relation management; GFK Eurisko (IT), the Italian branch of the fourth largest market research company in the world; Big Bang Ltd. (SI), the largest electronics retailer in Slovenia; Measurence (IR), a provider of sensor-based analytics solutions for physical locations; and JOT Internet Media (SP), a digital marketing solutions company.

Providing the technical and research expertise for the development of the platform the consortium includes: Engineering Ingegneria Informatica S.p.A (IT), the leading Italian software and services group; University of Milano-Bicocca (IT), focusing on semantic and interactive technologies for data linking; SINTEF (NO), the leading Norwegian research institute supporting data integration through their DataGraft[2] platform, and Jožef Stefan Institute (SI), the largest research institute in Slovenia overseeing all project analytics efforts and providing the event data source through the Event Registry[3] global media monitoring platform.

---

[2] https://datagraft.io.
[3] http://eventregistry.org.

3   Innovation

The data sources combined in the project offer numerous possibilities for innovative applications of knowledge discovery and data mining methodology. By linking and integrating the data sets of business partners and external data sources regarding weather and events, models can be constructed that power real-time responsive services for digital marketing, reporting-style services for market research, advanced data and resource management services for retail and e-commerce companies and their technology providers, as well as enhanced location intelligence services.

To guide the development of the platform and provide a basis for its evaluation, several pilot services are in development:

- **Pilot I - Enrichment of purchase information for web platforms:** By building a predictive model of user interaction on an online shopping portal in relation to external weather and event factors, we will enable the portal to run a reactive sense-of-urgency information service. For example, before a heatwave, we inform consumers that air conditioning sales commonly spike in such conditions and delivery could be delayed significantly.
- **Pilot II - Integrated platform for category and marketing optimization:** Combining data from a price comparison platform and a retailer will enable analysis and modeling of business actions such as marketing campaigns and discounts. This analysis will power a business-to-business service that will allow a retailer to use the wider market view of the price comparison platform to inform its category and marketing management.
- **Pilot III - External data access API and decision-making systems supporting customized campaigns:** Using weather and event-based predictive models for predicting customer response rate in a call center and managing marketing campaigns.
- **Pilot IV - Location Intelligence:** Modeling seasonal dependencies of visits to physical store locations to support activity planning and management.
- **Pilot V - Campaign-driven purchasing intentions:** Modeling the dynamics of web search engine keywords (e.g.. Google Adwords[4]) with respect to weather and event factors to support marketing campaign management.

All the pilot services will be tested by business partners in the scope of their regular operations. Their feedback will guide development in the second half of the project.

As it is still undergoing development, we are unfortunately not able to show a full end-to-end interaction with the platform. Currently, we can demonstrate a selection of analytics results from the pilots and show the business insights they offer. These results will be presented with a strong focus on interactive visualizations, as one of the guiding principles of the project is an emphasis on intuitive and interactive visualizations in platform reporting services. Because they contain sensitive business information, we are unable to share these visualizations publicly before the conference.

---

[4] http://adwords.google.com.

4   Platform

In this section, we present the characteristic elements of the EW-Shopp platform, for the design of which the consortium members have completed a requirements collection phase based mainly on the needs of the business partners (through the work done on the pilots) and on the best practices of the Big Data architectures.

At the end of this process, the need for an *open source* platform, capable of managing data in *tabular format* and of generating *linked data* to be used for analytics and visualization, became clear. In addition, two possible use cases have emerged. In the first case, small amounts of data have to be manipulated, the platform has to be lean and *easy to install on a commodity machine* similarly to tools like OpenRefine[5]. In the second scenario, the platform needs to manage big data, which means that a domain expert user must be able to describe the transformations through a user-friendly and interactive interface and to execute it in an automated way as a *batch* process (as in Karma[6] and Trifacta Wrangler[7]).

In an attempt to give a syncretic response to the needs outlined in the requirements, the platform has been conceived as composed of three macro-components (Fig. 1):

Core Data Services (in light blue): These components provide access to corporate or third party data to be used in both data linking and extension processes. Figure 1 shows services to access the project's core data, i.e., weather (W), events (E) and products (P). Other enrichment sources include Wikifier[8], as well as freely accessible knowledge bases such as DBpedia[9].

Platform Services (in green): data preparation, analytics and visualization services. These services offer simple and intuitive user interfaces for creating (and executing if the working table is small enough) data wrangling, linking and extension pipelines.

Corporate Services (in red): These services implement platform components needed for data governance, i.e., ingestion, storage, processing, data flow and security management of massive data sets.

The platform components at application level in Fig. 1 are:

Data Wrangler that is the component that enables the user to define the transformations of data cleaning, linking and enrichment at design time, and possibly on a data sample. Such data preparation processes will then be carried out by the component referred to as Big Data Runtime on the full dataset.

Data Analyzer that is the component that provides a set of predefined tools for predictive and prescriptive algorithms on enriched data.

Data Reporter that is the component that allows the user to visualize and analyze the outcomes produced by the Analyzer from a business viewpoint.

---

[5] http://openrefine.org/.
[6] http://usc-isi-i2.github.io/karma/.
[7] https://www.trifacta.com/products/wrangler/.
[8] http://wikifier.org/.
[9] https://wiki.dbpedia.org/.

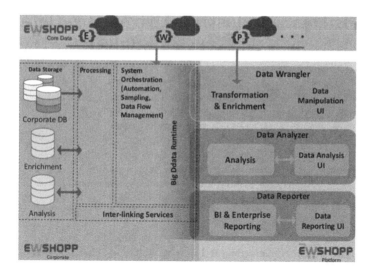

Fig. 1. General architecture (Color figure online)

With regards to the so-called Corporate services, these are gathered in a single macro-component called Big Data Runtime (BDR) that has the capability to execute transformation operations defined using the Platform services on genuine Big Data. In addition, it provides the data reporter with specific APIs for data access. Within the Big Data Runtime, we recognize a sub-component in charge of Data Storage and another dedicated to the Processing of such data.

5   Conclusions

The EW-Shopp ecosystem aims at fostering e-commerce, Retail and Marketing industries in improving their efficiency and competitiveness through providing a platform for supporting data linking, integration, and analytics in European e-commerce companies. It is developed in cooperation with businesses from all stages of a shopper's journey and will be tested in several pilot services to ensure that it addresses actual business needs. The project showcase will focus on selected analytics results collected during pilots' development and present them using rich interactive visualizations.

Acknowledgements. This paper has been written by the authors on behalf of the EW-Shopp Consortium. The work is supported by H2020 project EW-Shopp (Grant n. 732590).

I-BiDaaS: Industrial-Driven Big Data as a Self-service Solution

Giorgos Vasiliadis[1(✉)], Dusan Jakovetic[2], Ilias Spais[3], and Sotiris Ioannidis[1]

[1] FORTH, Heraklion, Greece
{gvasil,sotiris}@ics.forth.gr
[2] University of Novi Sad, Novi Sad, Serbia
dusan.jakovetic@dmi.uns.ac.rs
[3] AEGIS IT Research, Brunswick, Germany
hspais@aegisresearch.eu

Abstract. The convergence of Internet of Things (IoT), Cloud, and Big Data, creates new challenges and opportunities for data analytics. Human- and machine-created data is being aggregated continuously, transforming our economy and society. To face these challenges, companies call upon expert analysts and consultants to assist them.

In this paper, we present I-BiDaaS, a European Union Horizon 2020 research and innovation project that proposes a self-service solution for Big Data analytics. The solution will be transformative for companies that aim to extract knowledge from big data. It will empower their employees with the right knowledge, and give the true decision-makers the insights they need to make the right decisions. It will shift the power balance within an organization, increase efficiency, reduce costs, improve employee empowerment, and increase profitability. I-BiDaaS aims to empower users to easily utilize and interact with Big Data technologies, by designing, building, and demonstrating, a unified solution that significantly increases the speed of data analysis while coping with the rate of data asset growth, and facilitates cross-domain data-flow towards a thriving data-driven EU economy.

Keywords: Big Data · Batch processing · Stream processing

1 Introduction

Organizations leverage data pools to drive value, while it is variety, not volume or velocity, which drives big-data investments. The convergence of IoT, cloud, and big data, creates new opportunities for self-service analytics [3] towards big data analytics. Human and machine created data is being aggregated, transforming our economy and society. The aforementioned trends lead us to one of the main challenges of the data economy [5], Big-Data-as-a-Self-Service. A self-service solution will be transformative for organizations, it will empower their employees with the right knowledge, and give the true decision-makers

© Springer Nature Switzerland AG 2020
M. Fazio and W. Zimmermann (Eds.): ESOCC 2018 Workshops, CCIS 1115, pp. 192–196, 2020.
https://doi.org/10.1007/978-3-030-63161-1_17

the insights they need to make the right decisions. It will shift the power balance within an organisation, increase efficiency, reduce costs, improve employee empowerment, and increase profitability. The domains that can exploit such self-service solutions are numerous, including among others banking, manufacturing, and telecommunications.

In this paper we present the project I-BiDaaS [2], that aims to address the above challenges and deficiencies. I-BiDaaS targets to empower users to easily utilize and interact with big data technologies, by designing, building, and demonstrating, a unified framework that: significantly increases the speed of data analysis while coping with the rate of data asset growth, and facilitates cross-domain data-flow towards a thriving data-driven EU economy. I-BiDaaS will be tangibly validated by three real-world, industry-lead experiments with significant challenges and requirements: banking, manufacturing, and telecommunications.

I-BiDaaS is a European Union (EU)-funded H2020 3 year project that has started on January 1, 2018, and will last for 3 years. The project consortium comprises the following institutions: Foundation for Research and Technology Hellas, Greece (FORTH) – project coordinator; Barcelona Supercomputing Center (BSC), Spain; IBM Israel (IBM); Centro Ricierche FIAT SCPA Italy (CRF); Software AG (SAG), Germany; Caixabank, SA, Spain (CAIXA); The University of Manchester, UK (UNIMAN); Ecole Nationale des Ponts et Chausees, France (ENPC); ATOS, Spain (ATOS); AEGIS IT Research LTD, UK (AEGIS); Information Technology for Market Leadership, Greece (ITML); University of Novi Sad, Faulty of Sciences, Serbia (UNSPMF); and Telefonica Investigacion y Desarrollo SA, Spain (TID).

The main objectives of I-BiDaaS are:

- Develop, validate, demonstrate, and support, a complete and solid big data solution that can be easily configured and adopted by practitioners.
- Break inter- and intra-sectorial data-silos, create a data market and offer new business opportunities, and support data sharing, exchange, and interoperability.
- Construct a safe environment for methodological big data experimentation, for the development of new products, services, and tools
- Develop data processing tools and techniques applicable in real-world settings, and demonstrate significant increase of speed of data throughput and access.
- Develop technologies that will increase the efficiency and competitiveness of all EU companies and organisations that need to manage vast and complex amounts of data.

Current Project Stage. So far, the project work has focused on: 1) investigating the industrial challenges of the data economy in the fields of Finance, Manufacturing, and Telecommunications; 2) carrying out a through review of state of the art in the scientific and technological domains relevant to the project; and 3) defining initial data management policy for the data that will be consumed and generated within the project.

2   Approach and Methodology

Based on the challenges and requirements of the three critical domains (i.e., banking, manufacturing, and telecommunications), we aim to develop I-BiDaaS, a solution to enable Big Data as a self-service. It will offer an integrated, full-stack solution for processing and extracting actionable knowledge from big data, that includes: (i) configuration of the underlying infrastructure resources (commodity/public clusters or private clouds), (ii) efficient and automatic usage of computational and storage resources (resource provisioning, data transfers, etc.), (iii) data capture and integration from a variety of different sources and formats (unstructured, noisy, incomplete, etc.), (iv) batch and real-time data processing analytics for fast-growing data, and (v) simple, intuitive, and effective visualization and interaction capabilities for the end-users.

I-BiDaaS will offer Big Data as a Self-Service to enterprises by allowing seamless integration and injection of streaming and batch heterogeneous data, and facilitate the adoption of big data analytics to enterprises that possess big data, but may not have in-house expertise to extract the required actionable knowledge. To achieve this, it will allow the development of new applications or tasks via standard sequential programming, alleviating the burden of dealing with sophisticated analytics techniques (that requires data mining expertise), thus lowering enterprise costs. Also, the platform will be extendible to other application scenarios, as well as compatible with existing platforms such as OpenStack.

2.1   The Three-Layer Architecture: A Layer-by-Layer Description

We now present our layered system architecture, and provide a detailed workflow and user interface description. Conceptually, the architecture is divided into three principal layers: the infrastructure layer, the distributed large-scale layer, and the application layer.

Infrastructure Layer. The infrastructure layer includes the actual underlying storage and processing infrastructure of the I-BiDaaS solution, nominally provided and managed by ATOS and FORTH. This includes (i) a private cloud infrastructure provided by ATOS, (ii) a commodity cluster provided by FORTH (which consists of high-end GPUs, Intel Phi accelerators, and powerful multicore CPUs that contain secure enclaves that are able to protect the code and the sensitive data). We note that the I-BiDaaS solution will be deployable to other infrastructure premises as well; for instance, in the end user scenario that involves CAIXA, the platform will be deployed within CAIXA proprietary private cloud.

Distributed Large-Scale Layer. The distributed large-scale layer is responsible for the orchestration and management of the underlying physical computational and storage infrastructure. It allows the effective and efficient use of the infrastructures and enables the application layer to provide effective big data analytics. The distributed large-scale layer is responsible for the following tasks: (i) task and data dependency capturing, (ii) data transfer optimization, (iii) task and data scheduling, (iv) resource provisioning and management, and (v) capturing, integrating, and preparing data from heterogeneous, distributed sources,

Application Layer. The application layer sits on top of the distributed large-scale layer. It refers to the architecture aspects and components that are involved in the actual workflow of extracting actionable knowledge from the big data, starting from data preparation and analytics, to delivering results for supporting decision making. The data analytics include both batch and real time processing of streaming data. The data from heterogeneous sources are ingested in the solution. For early development scenarios when not sufficient real data is available, we will use the IBM's data fabrication platform [1].

In terms of interleaving batch and stream processing, the proposed solution goes beyond the traditional lambda architecture [4]. It uses a complex event analysis system, combined with a hardware-based implementation of streaming analytics that uses many different many-core accelerators (GPUs, Intel Phi, etc.). This design allows us to offload parts of the streaming analytics that can be parallelized and gives us the opportunity to partition the analytics queries, between the high-level stream processing engine and the low-level, hardware-optimized implementation. By carefully performing part of the queries at the lowest level (especially for the filtering), only the required data will be forwarded to the stream-processing engine for a more sophisticated analysis, while the remainder will be ignored at the earliest possible. The partition of the queries (between the complex event analysis system and the hardware-based streaming analytics) can be done either statically (i.e., during the implementation of a specific user query) or dynamically, at run-time (i.e., by monitoring the execution of a user-defined query, and deciding if the offloading to a manycore processor would lead to better performance.

User Interface. In order to make our solution ease to use by end-users, we will build a multi-purpose interface (AEGIS), that can be used by different categories of users. The interface will provide different levels of abstractions, tailored to different categories of user expertise. First, we will offer a programming API for access to every level of our software stack. This will give the flexibility to experienced IT users to utilise every aspect of our solution, and fine-tune their applications. The API will give access to the high-level application components—such as the advanced machine-learning modules and the streaming analytics—as well as to the low-level infrastructure layer, such as the scheduling and the resource management of the underlying infrastructure. Second, we will provide a domain language for access to the application layer. The purpose of this language is to offer an easy way to program data analytics (either batch or stream processing) without caring about scalability issues and infrastructure placement.

3   Conclusions

In this paper, we presented I-BiDaaS, a European Union Horizon 2020 project that proposes a solution for Big Data as a self-service. Once achieved, the solution will be transformative for enterprises that seek to extract actionable knowledge from Big Data, as it will allow their employees to easily utilize and interact with Big Data technologies. This can lead to increased efficiency, reduced costs, and increased profitability within an enterprise.

Acknowledgments. The authors thank all project partners for all the fruitful discussions on several aspects of the architecture. This work is supported by the I-BiDaaS project, funded by the European Commission under Grant Agreements No. 780787. This publication reflects the views only of the authors, and the Commission cannot be held responsible for any use which may be made of the information contained therein.

References

1. Creating secure test data to test systems. https://www.ibm.com/blogs/research/2014/07/creating-secure-test-data-to-test-systems/
2. I-BiDaaS: Industrial-Driven Big Data as a Self-Service Solution. https://www.ibidaas.eu
3. Self-Service Analytics. https://www.gartner.com/it-glossary/self-service-analytics/
4. Marz, N., Warren, J.: Big Data: Principles and Best Practices of Scalable Realtime Data Systems, 1st edn. Manning Publications Co., Greenwich (2015)
5. Passlick, J., Lebek, B., Breitner, M.H.: A self-service supporting business intelligence and big data analytics architecture. In: Wirtschaftsinformatik (2017)

SMARTSDK - A FIWARE-Based Software Development Kit for Smart Applications for the Needs of Europe and Mexico

Tomas Aliaga[1], Hugo Estrada[2], Miguel González Mendoza[3(✉)], and Daniele Pizzolli[4]

[1] Martel Innovate, Lugano, Switzerland
tomas.aliaga@martel-innovate.com
[2] INFOTEC, Mexico D.F., Mexico
hugo.estrada@infotec.mx
[3] ITESM, Atizapán de Zaragoza, Mexico State, Mexico
mgonza@itesm.mx
[4] CRATE-NET (FBK), Trento, Italy
dpizzolli@fbk.eu

Abstract. We present the goals, development and results of the SmartSDK project, a FIWARE initiative that aims to create a sustainable FIWARE ecosystem between Europe and Mexico by leveraging on existing FIWARE outcomes and building reference standards for common challenges, providing ready-to-use bundles to simplify the creation of Smart Software Services.

Keywords: FIWARE · Software development · Cloud computing · IoT · Docker · Open source · Smart cities

1 Fiware

FIWARE [3], a public-private partnership initiative supported by the European Commission, is nowadays considered the reference platform for Future Internet solutions. With the recent engagement of third-party actors not part of the original initiative, FIWARE rapidly evolved from being just a platform to become a complex and rich ecosystem. Nowadays this ecosystem spans across Europe and beyond thanks to the efforts of the FIWARE Mundus programme and the collaboration around Smart Cities with major worldwide initiatives such as the Global City Team Challenge, organized by NIST, and the Open & Agile Smart Cities (OASC) involving at the moment more than 100 cities around the world.

2 SMARTSDK

2.1 Introduction

SmartSDK is the FIWARE's "cookbook" for developing smart applications in the Smart City, Smart Healthcare and Smart Security domains. Concretely, this means that

© Springer Nature Switzerland AG 2020
M. Fazio and W. Zimmermann (Eds.): ESOCC 2018 Workshops, CCIS 1115, pp. 197–203, 2020.
https://doi.org/10.1007/978-3-030-63161-1_18

SmartSDK refines, combines and develops new FIWARE Generic Enablers (GEs) [4] and FIWARE Data Models [1] into a set of well-codified and ready-to-use solutions. This is very important to improve the uptake of FIWARE by new developers and facilitate the transition from proof-of-concept environments to production ones.

The "cookbook" is based on a set of architecture patterns (i.e. the basic cooking processes), a set of Generic Enablers (i.e. the basic ingredients) and a set of data models (i.e. the spices and flavors binding the ingredients through the cooking process). This idea is illustrated in Fig. 1.

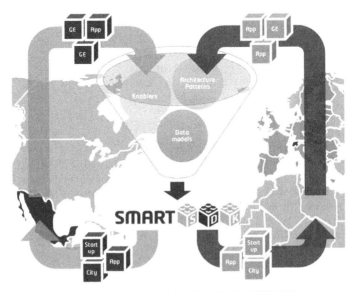

Fig. 1. SmartSDK as catalyzer of the EU - Mexico FIWARE ecosystem.

SmartSDK also proposes a Platform Manager (PM) which orchestrates resources provided by an underlying cloud computing platform, such as FIWARE Lab, where the PM is deployed. Then, with the PM users can deploy their container-based applications. Such applications are typically built with the reuse of open-source components, FIWARE Generic Enablers, Data Models and common architecture and recipes, realized through Docker[1] technologies to orchestrate the composing microservices. Figure 2 gives a good picture of these mentioned SmartSDK components.

The main project goals include enhancing Europe-Mexico collaboration and technology transfer within FIWARE, facilitating and increasing FIWARE adoption by providing ready-to-use reference service architectures and data models for IoT and data-intensive Future Internet scenarios (SmartCities, SmartSecurity and SmartHealthcare), and supporting the global uptake of validated FIWARE-based applications.

---

[1] https://www.docker.com.

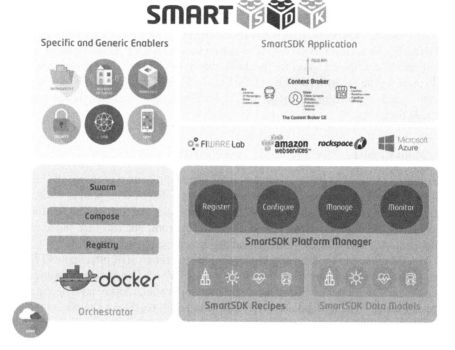

Fig. 2. SmartSDK architecture.

2.2 Project Organisation

The project responds to the European call H2020-ICT-2016-2017 and has been co-funded by the EU's Horizon2020 programme under agreement number 723174 - ©2016 EC and by CONACYT agreement 737373. It has been running from September 2016 and will find its closure at the end of 2018. The consortium comprises a total of 10 companies and research institutions from Mexico and Europe.

On the European side, the project counts with the collaboration of MARTEL INNO-VATE (Switzerland) acting as the project manager and developer of architectural software components and recipes. FBK CREATE-NET (Italy) works mostly on the Platform Manager and cloud infrastructure. UBIWHERE LDA (Portugal) brings its experience in geo-visualizations and smart cities, particularly helpful for the SmartCity demonstrator. Essential for the same demonstrator has been the work from HOP UBIQUITOUS SL on the open-hardware and IoT aspects of the platform. Halfway-through the project, TELE-FONICA I+D (Spain) left and the recently-formed FIWARE Foundation [2] (Germany) joined to contribute in standardization efforts and harmonization of data models created in the project.

With the support of European partners, the Mexican institutions have been more focused on the development of different applications acting as validators of SmartSDK in the three scenarios. Nevertheless, their work has also covered the development of platform software components and data models to be reused in different applications. The collaboration has been so good that it is difficult to trace hard boundaries for contribution efforts; however, it could be summarized as follows. INFOTEC has taken the lead of the "GreenRoute" application, focused on mobility in the SmartCities scenario. CICESE and INAOE have focused on the rehabilitation and monitoring applications in the case of SmartHealthCare. INAOE has lead the development of "VIVA", the video-surveillance application for the SmartSecurity scenario. Finally, ITESM and CENIDET have worked on orthogonal contributions to all scenarios, developing also data models and reusable software libraries.

2.3 Main Results

The project has accumulated a good number of successful outcomes during the last two years, both in the form of new technical contributions to FIWARE as well as through the collaboration between European and Mexican Institutions and SMEs. This section will briefly cover the results grouped in four areas: the platform, the software and hardware components, the validator applications and the dissemination activities.

With the release of the Platform Manager (PM) [6], SmartSDK offers now FIWARE users a harmonized and simplified way of deploying FIWARE Generic Enablers and other Open Source Components used to assemble user applications. Users no longer need to manually create Virtual Machines (VM) and install each required software component (each with a different procedure) and their dependencies; the PM simplifies all these tasks. For example, users just need an account in FIWARE Lab which comes with some assigned resources (RAM, IPs, VMs quotas, etc.) Then, they can log in the PM with their FIWARE Account, and easily create their environment. PM will automatically create the VMs in FIWARE Lab, provision them with Docker and use them to form a Swarm cluster. Then, with a simple click on the PM, users can deploy containerized GEs or applications of their choice on top of the Docker Swarm[2] Cluster, which is running on top of their cloud resources. PM is built using Rancher[3], the FIWARE Authentication services, Portainer[4], and an ad-hoc catalogue of recipes[5].

Having a cluster of machines and such a powerful tool as Docker Swarm, users are now empowered to profit from the benefits of more complex architectural patterns for the development and deployment of their applications. SmartSDK studied the composition of FIWARE Generic Enablers and created recipes aimed to enable the deployment of components with patterns such as Scalability, High Availability and Multisite in mind. This way, a simple Orion Context Broker could be automatically launched as shown in Fig. 3 without the need of user manual configuration. Figure 4 provides excerpts of how a recipe for the deployment of Fig. 3 would look like and marks in bold which kind of parameters are used to leverage different architecture patterns. These ideas are presented in more depth in deliverable 3.4 [7].

Worth mentioning are also the contributions to the FIWARE offerings in the form of software and hardware components. How these components fit into the overall FIWARE

---

[2] https://docs.docker.com/engine/swarm/.

[3] https://rancher.com/.

[4] https://portainer.io/.

[5] https://github.com/smartsdk/smartsdk-recipes.

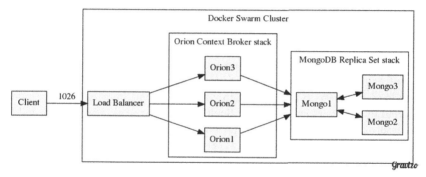

Fig. 3. Orion CB in HA.

```
version: '3'
services:
  orion:
    image: fiware/orion:${ORION_VERSION:-1.12.0}
    ports:
      - "1026:1026"
    command: -dbhost ${MONGO_SERVICE_URI:-"mongo"} -rplSet ...
    deploy:
      replicas: 3
    networks:
      - backend
      - frontend
    ...
  ...
  mongo:
    image: mongo:${MONGO_VERSION:-3.2}
    entrypoint: [ "/usr/bin/mongod", "--replSet", "${REPLICASET_NAME:-rs}",
...]
    networks:
      - backend
    deploy:
      mode: global
      restart_policy:
        condition: on-failure
      update_config:
        parallelism: 1
        delay: 1m30s
      ...
  controller:
    image: smartsdk/mongo-rs-controller-swarm:latest
    environment:
      - REPLICASET_NAME=${REPLICASET_NAME:-rs}
      ...
    entrypoint: python /src/replica_ctrl.py
    networks:
      - backend
    deploy:
      mode: replicated
      replicas: 1
      placement:
        constraints: [node.role==manager]
      restart_policy:
        condition: on-failure
      ....
```

Fig. 4. Recipes excerpts

reference architecture can be seen in Fig. 5. Moreover, all these components are open source and can be found at [5]. QuantumLeap, for example, has been proposed as a new incubated FIWARE Generic Enabler [4], to let users of NGSI data manipulate historical records on top of modern distributed databases tailored to work with timeseries. It has been used not only in the validator applications but also in different projects as well

[9]. Other component examples include a JavaScript library to exchange NGSI data in mobile applications, a library to encrypt and decrypt NGSI data and the integration of Cloudino and SmartSpot as IoT sensors for FIWARE solutions.

The Mexican partners, with the support from the European ones, have been developing a set of applications in the scenarios of Smart Cities (traffic-and-pollution-aware user mobility), Smart Security (intelligent video surveillance) and Smart Healthcare (mobile-sensing and in-house patient recovery). Such applications work as validators and first beneficiaries of the aforementioned components developed in the project. Moreover, the new and extended NGSI Data Models were contributed back to the official FIWARE Data Models catalogue [1].

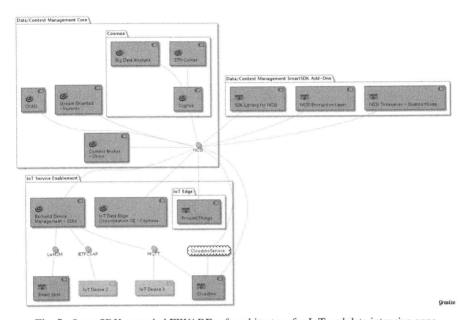

Fig. 5. SmartSDK extended FIWARE ref. architecture for IoT and data intensive apps.

Finally, dissemination activities were carried out with the aim of maintaining and coordinating the appropriate mechanisms and tools to ensure broad visibility and impact of the project's work and results, while expanding the FIWARE community reach in Mexico. Such activities have contributed towards the elaboration of a wide range of events, webinars, workshops, documentation materials and guided tours.

The official SmartSDK website [8] has been one of the main communication channels where ongoing results have been presented throughout the lifespan of the project. In the deliverables page [7], readers can find more details not only about the technical tasks, but also about results from the exploitation activities, including for example workshops in Mexico and new pieces of bilingual documentation and tutorials for FIWARE.

References[6]

1. Data Models. https://www.fiware.org/developers/data-models/
2. FIWARE Foundation. https://www.fiware.org/foundation
3. FIWARE. https://www.fiware.org
4. Generic Enablers. https://catalogue-server.fiware.org/enablers
5. Github project. https://github.com/smartsdk
6. Platform Manager. http://platform-manager.smartsdk.eu
7. Project Deliverables. https://www.smartsdk.eu/deliverables/
8. SmartSDK. https://www.smartsdk.eu
9. Orchestra Cities. https://www.orchestracities.com/

---

[6] All link references have been last accessed on 2018/09/28.

The FIRST (vF Interoperation suppoRting buSiness innovaTion) Project: Service Management for Virtual Factories

Yuewei Bai[1], Stephan Böse[2], Giacomo Cabri[3(✉)], Paul de Vrieze[4],
Norbert Eder[2], Alexander Lazovik[5], Federica Mandreoli[3], Massimo Mecella[6],
Hua Mu[7], and Lai Xu[4]

[1] Shanghai Second Polytechnic University, Shanghai, China
ywbai@sspu.edu.cn
[2] GK Software, Berlin, Germany
neder@gk-software.com
[3] Università degli Studi di Modena e Reggio Emilia, Modena, Italy
{giacomo.cabri,federica.mandreoli}@unimore.it
[4] University of Bournemouth, Poole, UK
{pdvrieze,lxu}@bournemouth.ac.uk
[5] University of Groningen, Groningen, NL, The Netherlands
a.lazovik@rug.nl
[6] Sapienza Università di Roma, Rome, Italy
mecella@dis.uniroma1.it
[7] KM Soft, Wuhan, China
muh@kmsoft.com.cn
http://www.sspu.edu.cn, http://www.gk-software.com,
http://www.unimore.it, http://www.bournemouth.ac.uk, http://www.rug.nl,
http://www.uniroma1.it, http://www.kmsoft.com.cn/

Abstract. The H2020 FIRST project addresses the virtual factories, which are digital abstractions of real factories. The exploitation of virtual factories enables interoperability between real components inside a factory as well as between different factories belonging to the same supply chain. Moreover, virtual factories can be exploited to manage and compose services inside a factory, defining dynamic adaptation of set of services depending on high-level goals.

In this paper we sketch the project results and its current state.

Keywords: Virtual factories · Interoperability · Service management

This work is funded by the EU H2020-RISE Project "FIRST: virtual Factory Interoperation suppoRting buSiness innovaTion" (Grant no. 734599).

© Springer Nature Switzerland AG 2020
M. Fazio and W. Zimmermann (Eds.): ESOCC 2018 Workshops, CCIS 1115, pp. 204–209, 2020.
https://doi.org/10.1007/978-3-030-63161-1_19

1   Introduction

The EU H2020 "vF Interoperation suppoRting buSiness innovaTion" (FIRST) is a project funded in the framework of H2020 RISE program, which promotes international and inter-sectoral collaboration through research and innovation staff exchanges, and through sharing of knowledge and ideas from academia to industry (and vice-versa)[1].

The FIRST project addresses the challenges related to virtual factories, digital abstractions of real factories, considering in particular manufacturing factories. Advanced manufacturing is entering a new era. It requires new ICT technologies and collaborative applications. Integration among traditional manufacturing practices and processes can increase flexibility in manufacturing, i.e. mass customisation speeds to markets with better design and quality. Virtual factory models need to be created before the real factory is implemented to better explore different design options, evaluate their performance and before commissioning the automation systems thus saving time-to. This foundational concept to future factories allow the flexible amalgamation of manufacturing resources in multiple organisations to model, simulate and test factory layouts and processes in a virtual reality environment, virtual factory design and virtual factories, finally create the real factory in shorter time, with demand driven product lines.

In this scenario the specific goals of the FIRST project are to provide new technology and methodologies to describe manufacturing assets; to compose and integrate existing services into collaborative virtual manufacturing processes; and to deal with evolution of changes. Moreover, the issues and gaps are investigated from a global view, i.e. among European member states and Chinese perspectives.

The work of the FIRST project can rely on a well-established body of research on virtual organisations in the services industry as well as on open product design, general service description, discovery, composition, adaption, interoperation and execution. Manufacturing assets, however, are not general (digital) services. Moreover, there are different practices and protocols in different countries. Member states are also sponsoring national initiatives such as Industrie 4.0 in Germany, the Factory of the Future in Italy, High Value Manufacturing Catapult in the UK, etc. It is essential to ensure the exchange of data between smart machines, systems and software within a networked value chain, as product design shares with all involved parties through "virtual factory", a product moves into and through the 'smart factory', as well as to allow flexible manufacturing processes through simple 'plug-and-play' techniques.

1.1   Project Facts

The project involves 7 partners, of which 5 are universities, 2 are companies, 5 are European, 2 are Chinese[2].

---

[1] https://www.h2020first.eu/.

[2] https://www.h2020first.eu/first/bin/view/Main/Partners.

The current number of secondment-months performed is 34^3.

In the context of the project 12 papers have been published in international journals and conference proceedings[4].

2   Project Results

In this section we present summaries of the main results of the project. Interested readers can refer to the cited publications to get more details about specific results.

A first result of the project is a review of concepts and research challenges of interoperability of virtual factory [6], which presents basic concepts of factories of the future, i.e. smart factory, digital factory and virtual factory, studies the relationships among smart factory, digital and virtual factory, and defines interoperability of virtual factories. The main challenges of interoperability of virtual factories are identified as the lack of standards of virtual factories; managing traceability of sensitive data, protected resources and applications or services are critical for forming and using virtual factories; handling multilateral solutions and managing variability of different solutions/virtual factory models are also impact to the usability of the virtual factory. In short, the interoperability of virtual factory is related to many newly developed ICT of the hardware and software innovation. An interoperation framework allows evolutional and handling changes, which is crucial for generating and maintaining virtual factories among different industrial sectors.

A second study concerned the compliance constrains processes to adhere to rules, standards, laws and regulations [2]. Non-compliance can lead enterprises to litigation and financial fines, so compliance verification is essential to deploy and implement collaborative business process systems. It ensures that processes are checked for conformance to compliance requirements throughout their life cycle. A proactive approach has been proposed, which aims to discuss the need for design time preventative compliance verification as opposed to after effect runtime detective approach.

Another result is a resilience analysis perspectives of SOA collaborative process systems [4], i.e., overall system perspective, individual process model perspective, individual process instance perspective, service perspective, and resource perspective. A real world collaborative process has been exploited for illustrating our resilience analysis. This research contributes to extend SOA collaborative business process management systems with resilience support, not only looking at quantification and identification of resilience factors, but also considering ways of improving the resilience of SOA collaborative process systems through measures at design and runtime. Resilience is defined as the combination of two aspects. The former aspect is the capability of the system to contain and minimize the effect of a disruption. The second aspect is the system capability of reducing the impact of disturbances over time including the use of

---

[3] https://www.h2020first.eu/first/bin/view/Main/Secondments.

[4] https://www.h2020first.eu/first/bin/view/Main/Publications.

temporary alternative until the resumption of normal operations. A disruption is an event that leads to failures of the processes coordinated by the process management system. Another way of looking at this perspective of resilience is as the impact of a disruption over time. The definition of resilience takes into consideration the following parameters:

- start of the disruption;
- equilibrium point at which the disruption causes no further performance degradation;
- slack time, i.e., maximum amount of time to post-disruption equilibrium that is acceptable before ensuring recovery;
- time to final recovery, i.e., new equilibrium state;
- time to complete initial recovery actions;
- decay in resilience attributable to time to new equilibrium.

An architecture of collaborative processes for managing short term, low frequency collaborative processes has been proposed [7]. A real-world case of collaborative processes is used to explain the design and implementation of the cloud-based solution for supporting collaborative business processes. Service improvement of the new solution and computing power costs are also analysed accordingly.

SSPU has closely cooperated with KMSoft in the field of smart manufacturing technology, particularly in Manufacturing Execution System (MES) Framework development, production scheduling algorithm based on virtual manufacturing network, and precision measurement system integration [3,5] (i.e., among coordinate measurement machine, motion controller, and measurement software systems). We have implemented some original requirement surveys with Bournemouth University of UK, which focused on the manufacturing asserts management in Shanghai Huida Mechanical Manufacture Co[5], Smart Manufacturing Lab of SSPU respectively. The related requirements of MES being used in multi-enterprises have been gathered and it's helpful for KM-MES (developed by KMSoft) Improvement in next step which has been applied in over twenty companies of three industries separately.

An interoperability architecture for digital factories has been proposed [1]. To this end, we analysed the main challenges that must be addressed to support an integrated and scalable factory architecture characterized by access to services, aggregation of data, and orchestration of production processes. Then, we revised the state of the art in the light of these requirements and proposes a general architectural framework conjugating the most interesting features of service-oriented architectures and data sharing architectures. Figure 1 reports the architectural layers of the proposed interoperable platform.

Besides the scientific results presented above, in the spirit of the RISE framework, the project has achieved also structural results for the companies.

In fact, FIRST has been a turning point for the GK company. It is the large opportunity to establish own and sustainable research and innovation infrastruc-

---

[5] http://www.huidajx.com.

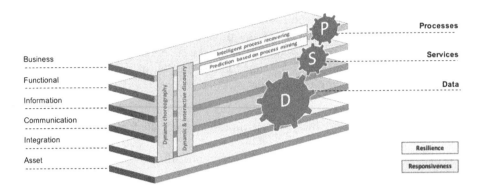

Fig. 1. Conceptual overview of the interoperable architectural layers

ture in order to meet the customer expectations and to secure future competitiveness. GK Software AG is working on the digitization of large retail companies with OmniPOS products to integration physical, online and mobile commerce. In order to have a maximum benefit of the project FIRST and facing the opportunities as the project's single industry partner receiving almost all secondments, GK Software AG decided to establish a new and own Innovation and Research unit, recruiting a new Head of Unit.

The Virtual Factories of FIRST and the OmniChannel Solutions of GK Software AG fit optimal together because the integration across the lifecycle - including the IoT information - and sales channel integration is a key aspect of modern manufacturing. Manufacturing is driven entirely from the sales channels and from omni-channel and customer journey approaches in the digital economy and society.

3   Conclusions and Future Work

In this paper we have presented the current results of the FIRST project.

In the context of virtual factories, services play an important role, both interfactory and intra-factory. In fact, proper and interoperable service management can lead not only to a control of the real factory processes, but also to dynamically adapt the factory processes to the factory goals. In addition, services can be exploited to enable and leverage interaction among factories belonging to the same supply chain, as well as to enable dynamic supply chains where factories can be added and changed depending on the needs. To achieve effective results, a global approach is deserved.

With regard to the future work, we aim at concretising the service composition sketched in the architectures we have defined, in order to enable factories to apply the virtual factory concept. Moreover, we will apply the defined approaches to real cases of factories, in order to test them and to have a useful feedback to continue our research.

References

1. Bicocchi, N., Cabri, G., Mandreoli, F., Mecella, M.: Dealing with data and software interoperability issues in digital factories. In: International Conference on Transdisciplinary Engineering (TE2018) (2018)
2. Kasse, J.P., Xu, L., deVrieze, P., Bai, Y.: The need for compliance verification in collaborative business processes. In: Camarinha-Matos, L.M., Afsarmanesh, H., Rezgui, Y. (eds.) PRO-VE 2018. IAICT, vol. 534, pp. 217–229. Springer, Cham (2018). https://doi.org/10.1007/978-3-319-99127-6_19
3. Pan, F., Nie, L., Bai, Y., Wang, X., Wu, X.: Geometric errors measurement for coordinate measuring machines. In: IOP Conference Series: Earth and Environmental Science, vol. 81, p. 012117. IOP Publishing (2017)
4. de Vrieze, P., Xu, L.: Resilience analysis of service-oriented collaboration process management systems. Serv. Oriented Comput. Appl. 12, 25–39 (2018). https://doi.org/10.1007/s11761-018-0233-5
5. Wu, X., Bai, Y., Nie, L., Pan, F., Liu, K., Yu, Y.: Tracking object in four dimensions by multi-exposure compressive in-line holography. In: Sixth International Conference on Optical and Photonic Engineering (icOPEN 2018), vol. 10827, p. 108270T. International Society for Optics and Photonics (2018)
6. Xu, L., de Vrieze, P., Yu, H., Phalp, K., Yuewei, B.: Interoperability of virtual factory: an overview of concepts and research challenges. Int. J. Mech. Manuf. Syst. 13, 3–27 (2020)
7. Xu, L., Vrieze, P.D.: Supporting collaborative business processes: a BPaaS approach. Int. J. Simul. Process Model. 13(1), 57–72 (2018)

ElasTest: An Elastic Platform for E2E Testing Complex Distributed Large Software Systems

Juan Francisco Ribera Laszkowski[1], Andy Edmonds[1(✉)], Piyush Harsh[1], Francisco Gortazar[2], and Thomas Michael Bohnert[1]

[1] Zuerich University of Applied Sciences, Winterthur, Switzerland
{ribr,edmo,harh,bohe}@zhaw.ch
[2] University of Rey Juan Carlos, Madrid, Spain
francisco.gortazar@urjc.es

Abstract. As systems get more complex testing has also increased not only in complexity but in the total IT cost, which is estimated to increase even more by 2020. Testing large complex distributed applications is hard, time consuming and lacks tooling. Given that the digitisation of business has proved to be a key aspect for improving the productivity of developers in the delivery of the service to end-users, in this paper we present early results showing how these capabilities can also be provided to testers of software and services, by adopting standard interfaces and leveraging the tools provided by an early research open-source platform, capable of efficiently testing large scale systems, ElasTest.

Keywords: Cloud · Testing · E2E · Large scale · Distributed · Computing · Systems

1 Introduction

The demand for larger and more interconnected software systems is constantly rising, and recently more and more architectures opt for a microservices-oriented architecture [21], many of which are cloud native applications [20]. This increase has also caused that the development, operations and management, and complexity of such microservice-based systems to increase. However, the skills of software developers and testers must satisfy the rate at which these large systems are appearing [18], especially when, in this case, larger and more complex systems demand themselves more efficient testing processes.

The ElasTest project aims at significantly improving the efficiency and effectiveness of the testing process throughout the software development life cycle and, with it, the overall quality of large software systems. A set of required

This work is partially funded by the Swiss State Secretariat for Education, Research and Innovation (SBFI) in association with the European Union Horizon 2020 research and innovation programme via grant agreement #731535, for the ElasTest project [5].

tests that are modern and accepted, are defined by [17], who also shows that testing a full cloud native application is not a mean or small task. This is how the ElasTest platform comes to be, with the purpose of not only developing an open-source, modern test orchestration theory and toolbox, to allow the creation of complex test suites as the composition of simple testing units; but also, to create an impact in the community and become a worldwide reference in the field of large-scale software testing, providing sustainability of the project generated results.

In this context of testing and delivery of service, the challenging questions to be asked are:

1. How can a complete and large scale cloud native application be effectively tested and supported by a test platform?
2. How can the investments made in testing be minimised such that the organisation (e.g. SME, corporation) tasked with delivering the application can deliver the same reliability and assurance in the same or reduced time frame?

This paper attempts to tackle these questions and therefore, reports the work-in-progress of an efficient large scale system testing and open source research platform, ElasTest [7], which provides the means to test applications (or systems) "in-the-small" as well as the same systems deployed "in-the-large", through the support of industry standards.

We organize this paper by starting with an overview of the ElasTest Project, followed by the Architecture of the system which describes how services are composed and delivered to the tests that operate against an System under Test (SUT). Then, the current set of services offered by ElasTest are briefly described and we finalize with the Discussion and Future Work.

2   ElasTest Overview

The ElasTest project stands for Elastic Platform for Testing complex distributed large software systems. It is being developed by a consortium of European academic institutions, research centers, large industrial companies and also SMEs. The project began January 2017 and will run for 3 years. Its members are [6]:

- **Universidad Rey Juan Carlos**: is the project coordinator and has key involvements in overall plaform design, delivery of components related to test orchestration and implementing one of the key test support services.
- **Fraunhofer FOKUS**: provides their expertise both in telecommunication core networking systems and Industrial IoT (IIoT). For the telecommunications aspect, they provide a vertical demonstrator.
- **Technische Universitaet Berlin**: provide one of the core systems in ElasTest, specifically the system that provides all virtualised resources used by the platform and executed tests. Also provided is an emulated IIoT test support service. They also provide a vertical demonstrator.

- **Consiglio Nazionale delle Ricerche**: oversee and design the evaluation of the ElasTest platform based on their extensive experience of the theoretical foundations of Software Engineering for Testing.
- **IMDEA Software Institute**: provide two key test support services in ElasTest, namely the Security and Monitoring services.
- **ATOS Spain**: oversee the complete delivery of the cloud platform that ElasTest is built upon. Specifically this includes the components related to platform instrumentation.
- **Zuerich University of Applied Sciences**: deliver components related to the core ElasTest platform including Nexus for service delivery, Sentinel for system and service monitoring and a cost estimation engine.
- **Naevatec**: is a SME that provides a reliable continuous integration and delivery system and also provide one of the vertical demonstrators used to evaluate ElasTest.
- **IBM Ireland**: is the key partner providing the component related to test recommendations. These recommendations are based on the set of end-user provided tests and suggests new tests using machine learning.
- **Relational**: is a SME which delivers one of the test support services, the big data analysis service.

ElasTest is funded by the European Commission under the ICT-10-2016 topic of the Horizon 2020 programme [10]. ElasTest [5] is an open source platform with the objective to reduce the complexity of carrying out end-to-end tests of large scale distributed systems. The Systems under Tests (SUTs) can be applications and services. ElasTest gives developers and testers of systems the means to assess their tests in a way that is cost and performance sensitive. ElasTest's capabilities are built on common open source technologies, and ensures to provide elasticity and compatibility to integrate with multiple technologies.

Moreover, ElasTest supports both a lightweight deployment profile, suitable for laptops to be used for testing in the small, to a complete deployment profile, suitable for testing complete large scale systems in an automated fashion. Finally, ElasTest attempts to ease integration with existing continuous integration and deployment systems and currently has a custom Jenkins plugin.

Currently, the project having delivered its core open source platform is now improving and using it for the base line of research activities. Importantly, that platform will be enhanced not only by input from identified end-users but also by on-going evaluation activities of the platform. This evaluation will be based upon a set of vertical demonstrators. There are four of these demonstrators: an e-commerce demonstrator, a 5G carrier-grade network system implementation, a open online class course demonstrator focusing on real-time communication and an Industrial IoT demonstrator.

2.1 Elastest vs. Other Solutions

Elastest solves a variety of problems, but each individual feature has been solved by many different systems. Even though no single system delivers a solution that provides all the features that Elastest does, there are other options available to solve some of these problems. Testcraft[1] provides a codeless selenium testing framework with artificial intelligence. It provides a set of workflow creation tools for non-programmer to develop tests. Cypress[2] is a web service Javascript testing framework developed from the ground up, contrary to a selenium-based framework, which delivers a fast performing testing framework and a vast amount of information when a failure happens, for the problem to be fixed. Other examples include Robot Framework[3], which is a generic test automation framework written in Python which uses selenium to simplify the testing processs, Appium[4], which provides a testing framework written in NodeJS for iOS and Android, etc. That said, Elastest is not a replacement for other testing tools. Each developer has their own field or programming language where they feel comfortable. Nevertheless, where Elastest excels is at bringing together all the testing tools together and provide real End-to-End testing, starting from the deployment of the infrastructure of your applications, to deploying the Support Services to emulate other variables, and finally, providing a powerful Log Analyzer and a Recommendation System (among others).

3   ElasTest Architecture

ElasTest manages the full testing life cycle, deployment and monitoring of the SUT, execution of the end-to-end tests, all with the specified support services, and exposure of the results to the end-users. In order to use the ElasTest system, the user must first be granted access. Then, the user communicates the testing requirements through the concept of a "T-Job" (testing-job). A T-Job typically consists of a set of tests to be executed against a system endpoint and a set of estimated resources to execute those tests on. It is important to note that *services* are the ones that can be attached to the T-Jobs, whereas *engines* run irrespectively of the T-Jobs, collecting metrics, analyzing execution patterns, costs, etc.

Service delivery and composition is done through the ElasTest Service Manager (ESM), which manages the delivery (deployment, provisioning and execution, incl. destruction) of the Test Support Services (TSS). These TSSs are reusable services that are typically used by developers for creating their T-Jobs. These are deployed as part of the ElasTest infrastructure and shall autoscale to adapt to the tester needs. These TSS follow a Software as a Service (SaaS) delivery model in the sense that developers do not need to worry about how to deploy, provision or scale them.

Their capabilities are reachable through service-dependent APIs, defined by OpenAPI specification (as per ElasTest architectural principles).

---

[1] https://www.testcraft.io.

[2] https://www.cypress.io.

[3] http://robotframework.org.

[4] http://appium.io.

Currently the ESM provides all TSSs through an implementation of the Open Service Broker API specification [13], which is currently seen as an industry standard in delivering functionality as a service. It is used in platforms such as Cloud-Foundry [3], OpenShift [14] and Kubernetes [11]. Currently it is implemented against the 2.12 specification version and has specific ElasTest extensions.

The ElasTest Project currently provides five TSSs through the ESM. The motivations and also objectives of these TSS is as follows:

- Enable testers focus on their system's core functionality
- Simplify the creation of T-Jobs validating individual functions or SiS (i.e., deliver TSS capable of helping in the creation of T-Jobs)
- Increase reusability provide reusable capabilities for creating T-Jobs involving common testing tasks
- Decrease significantly the marginal (i.e. unit) cost of testing
- To be provided on-demand as cloud native services
- Provide access to capabilities/functionality through APIs that might be consumed by the T-Jobs or by the test orchestration engines.

In other words, these ElasTest Test Support Services are meant to act as SaaS services designed for helping developers in the creation of simple tests (called T-Jobs in this proposal) by providing capabilities commonly required for typical testing processes.

Each component within the microservice-based architecture of ElasTest has its own internal peculiar architecture and, for the sake of brevity, the internal architecture of these will not be detailed. Each of the components within the architecture are components that are implemented and developed by the ElasTest consortium. Below, we describe the macro architecture of ElasTest as shown in Fig. 1.

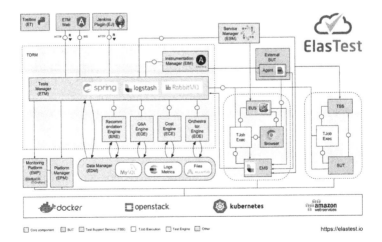

Fig. 1. ElasTest Architecture using the Fundamental Modelling Concept (FMC) notation [9].

- **Test Orchestration and Recommendation Manager (ETM):** provides access to a user through the user interface and/or the programmatic API. It manages all other components within a deployment of ElasTest.
- **ElasTest Service Manager (ESM):** allows the creation of on-demand instances delivered as services, which execute the specified T-Job. This component enables efficient testing and allow for the rapid creation of these tests. The TSS supported by the ESM are:
  - **User impersonation Service (EUS):** This service enables the impersonation of end-users' in their tests through GUI (Graphical User Interface) instrumentation and through mechanisms for QoS and QoE evaluation.
  - **Sensor, actuator and device impersonation Service (EDS):** This service is useful for enabling tests to emulate customized device behavior at the time of testing IoT (Internet of Things) applications.
  - **Monitoring Service (EMS):** This service leverages runtime verification ideas (in turn inspired by formal verification) to represent the system behavior as sequences of events that can be monitored in universal ways.
  - **Big Data Analysis Service (EBS):** enables the collection, analysis and visualization of large volumes of logs.
  - **Security Check Service (ESS):** for security vulnerability checking targeting specifically the problems of the main large scale deployed system
- **ElasTest Platform Manager (EPM):** The EPM is responsible for providing and managing the resources on which the various ElasTest components run on. The currently supported cloud infrastructures are: OpenStack [15], Amazon Web Services [2], Docker [4] and Kubernetes [11]. For orchestrating the SUT and the network services within the ElasTest platform, OpenBaton is used [19].
- **ElasTest Instrumentation Manager (EIM):** allows for dynamic modifications of the system under test and to inject real world behaviors over the system (e.g., connection latency or disconnects), while gathers information for the assessment at runtime as well as for later inspection.
- **ElasTest Data Management (EDM):** stores the logs and metrics which are generated during the execution of a T-Job. This component leverages the technologies of MySQL [12], Elasticsearch [8] as search engine, and Alluxio [1] as virtual distributed storage system.

Unlike the services described above, engines can run irrespectively of the T-Jobs, collecting metrics, analyzing execution patterns to report failures, costs, etc., and are described below:

- **ElasTest Cost Engine (ECE)** allows static estimation of test execution costs based on the estimated resource consumption matrix provided by the test developer. This module empowers test authors to optimize their test parameters iteratively and make the tests economical in the long term. ECE also tracks key lifecycle events and correlates them to actual resources consumed by a test execution to compute the true cost of the execution. The ECE utilizes the plan cost models registered by each support service in ESM in offering cost estimation and actual cost tracking for finished test executions.

- **ElasTest Recommendation Engine (ERE):** recommends new tests to the end-user based on the set of tests they have presented to the ETM. This component uses machine learning and artificial intelligence to generate a set of additional recommended tests that the end-user can choose to include in an updated version of their T-Job. This just like the use of external services through the ESM and cost estimation through the ECE are facilities that aid rapid system testing with the focus of cost and time-to-market.
- **ElasTest Test Orchestration Engine (EOE):** through the definition an orchestration notation for the graph of T-Jobs, where the edges provide the execution logic and the nodes act as checkpoints, it allows the synchronization of the T-Jobs and automatic verification on its incoming edges. Furthermore, it allows the test augmentation through custom operational conditions and the definition of sub-graphs basing on combinatorial techniques.
- **ElasTest Question&Answer Cognitive Engine (EQE):** enables the reuse of testing knowledge across software projects. Supports a dialog manager to support dynamic interaction between user and system, and generates answers for questions about designing new test cases. A GUI to enable conversation is also supported.

Furthermore, to complement, the **ElasTest Monitoring Platform (EMP)** is a general purpose monitoring framework that accords first class status to metrics and logs. It provides:

- advanced analytics and reporting/alerting functions which is used to monitor the health of service instances managed within the ElasTest Platform and therefore remediation of states based on red flags' alert.
- advanced queries such as *give me list of all hosts ordered by available RAM/CPU/Disk* which can be used by ESM's planner for scheduling.

In unison with the EMP some of the potential planned functionalities include online SLA monitoring, fault tracing and correlated queries over multiple metric streams. Finally, an Anomaly Detection Component is planned to integrate as well into these components to conjunctively allow ElasTest to achieve the smooth and fine grained life-cycle controlled execution of the test environments.

4   Discussion and Future Work

The work within the ElasTest platform has rapidly progressed yet there is still much work to be done. From the research perspective the following questions are seen to be answered by future work:

- Reviewing new stakeholders or evaluating existing competitors in order to provide ElasTest as SaaS;
- Evaluation of not only market conditions, but also the market positioning of ElasTest through a feature comparison with leading competitors;

- Near real-time service delivery and update with minimal wait times in having network-based access to a particular service. This will require the consideration of resource frameworks that far exceed the performance of current container-based technologies such as Docker;
- In order to make such services reliable and measurable suitable observability mechanisms will be needed and this work on observability tooling is being carried out by the EMP;
- With information collected on the running services of ElasTest, the question of how to leverage machine and deep learning arises. Such approaches can be used to detect anomalous behaviors that could indicate runtime errors and prompt remediation actions;
- One of the areas where a need has already been seen from the current five ElasTest TSSs is enhanced support for debugging of services. What is the best means to provide such capabilities: is logging sufficient or such approaches seen in OpenTracing [16] activities be investigated?
- From a business perspective, how can scaling of delivered services by the ESM be supported yet respect financial cost targets set by the end-user. Indeed how can SLAs of delivered services be defined in such a way to be self-validating?

The work in ElasTest, specifically on service delivery provides the impetus for further research in these areas and also provides not only an architecture but an implementation upon which new technologies can be applied against. Current efforts in test and quality assurance research and engineering still have to be furthered in order to address some of the needs of outlined here, within ElasTest and beyond it. Importantly for ElasTest will the evaluation of the platform with the previously noted vertical demonstrators.

References

1. Alluxio. https://www.alluxio.org/. Accessed 04 May 2018
2. Amazon Web Services. http://aws.amazon.com. Accessed 04 May 2018
3. CloudFoundry. https://cloudfoundry.org. Accessed 04 May 2018
4. Docker. https://www.docker.com. Accessed 04 May 2018
5. ElasTest. http://www.elastest.io. Accessed 04 May 2018
6. Elastest Consortium. https://elastest.eu/consortium.html. Accessed 23 July 2018
7. ElasTest Software Repositories. https://github.com/elastest. Accessed 04 May 2018
8. ElasticSearch. https://www.elastic.co/. Accessed: 04 May 2018
9. Fundamental Modeling Concepts. http://www.fmc-modeling.org. Accessed 04 May 2018
10. Horizon Programme. https://ec.europa.eu/programmes/horizon2020/en/what-horizon-2020. Accessed 23 July 2018
11. Kubernetes. https://kubernetes.io. Accessed 04 May 2018
12. MySQL. https://www.mysql.com/. Accessed 04 May 2018
13. Open Service Broker API Specification. https://github.com/openservicebrokerapi/. Accessed 04 May 2018
14. OpenShift. https://www.openshift.com. Accessed 04 May 2018

15. OpenStack. https://www.openstack.org/. Accessed 04 May 2018
16. OpenTracing. http://opentracing.io. Accessed 04 May 2018
17. Testing Strategies in a Microservice Architecture. https://martinfowler.com/articles/microservice-testing/. Accessed 04 May 2018
18. Top Trends for the Future of IT Procurement. https://www.gartner.com/smarterwithgartner/top-trends-for-the-future-of-it-procurement/. Accessed 23 July 2018
19. Carella, G.A., Magedanz, T.: Open baton: a framework for virtual network function management and orchestration for emerging software-based 5G networks. Newsletter **2016** (2015)
20. Gilbert, J.: Cloud Native Development Patterns and Best Practices. Packt Publishers, Birmingham (2018)
21. Newman, S.: Building Micro Services Designing Fine-Grained Systems. O'Reilly Media, Inc., Sebastopol (2014)

RECAP (Reliable Capacity Provisioning and Enhanced Remediation for Distributed Cloud Applications): The Simulation Approach

Patricia Takako Endo[1]([envelope]), Christos Filelis-Papadopoulos[2,3], Sergej Svorobej[1], Anna Gourinovitch[1], Konstantinos Giannoutakis[2], George Gravvanis[2,3], Dimitrios Tzovaras[2], Divyaa Manimaran Elango[1], James Byrne[1], and Theo Lynn[1]

[1] Irish Centre for Cloud Computing and Commerce (IC4),
Dublin City University (DCU), Dublin, Ireland
{patricia.endo,sergej.svorobej,anna.gourinovitch,divyaa.manimaranelango,
james.byrne,theo.lynn}@dcu.ie
[2] Information Technologies Institute, Centre for Research and Technology Hellas,
6th km Harilaou - Thermi, Thessaloniki, Greece
{cfilpapadop,kgiannou,gravvanis,Dimitrios.Tzovaras}@iti.gr
[3] Department of Electrical and Computer Engineering, School of Engineering,
Democritus University of Thrace, University Campus, Building A, Kimmeria,
Xanthi, Greece
{cpapad,ggravvan}@duth.gr

Abstract. In order to meet complexity, scalability and quality of service requirements in modern network infrastructures, resources need to be allocated and/or optimized along a Cloud-to-Thing (C2T) continuum using new paradigms. To accommodate the dynamism and address the variability, network operators and cloud systems will need to be able to pre-emptively take reconfiguration and remediation actions in a fully automatic fashion across the C2T continuum. In this work, we present the simulator approach in RECAP, an EU-funded research project, to develop the next generation of distributed cloud, edge and fog computing systems. Initial simulation experiments demonstrate that the RECAP Simulation Framework can run large-scale simulations of virtual content delivery networks and inform network optimisation decisions.

Keywords: Simulation · Cloud · Fog computing · Resource management

1 Introduction

The convergence and widespread adoption of mobile technologies, social media, cloud computing, and big data analytics are transforming the environment in

© Springer Nature Switzerland AG 2020
M. Fazio and W. Zimmermann (Eds.): ESOCC 2018 Workshops, CCIS 1115, pp. 219–225, 2020.
https://doi.org/10.1007/978-3-030-63161-1_21

which network operators conduct their business. The rapidly changing nature of both enterprise and consumer digital behavior and the variety, volume and velocity of the data being transferred across networks has resulted in dramatic shifts in the bandwidth, network infrastructure requirements and associated economic models that the traditional network operator approach cannot scale or adapt to easily. This situation is likely only to exacerbate as society moves towards the Internet of Everything and a networked society where people, processes, things, data and networks are interconnected.

The complexity, scalability, security, and quality of service requirements of the Internet of Everything represent significant technical challenges. In order to meet these requirements, resources need to be allocated and/or optimized along a Cloud-to-Thing (C2T) continuum using new paradigms such as fog and edge computing. Resource allocation and optimisation, however, is made more complex by greater dynamism and variability in quality of service (QoS) levels in IOE use scenarios. To accommodate the dynamism and address the variability, network operators and cloud systems will need to be able to pre-emptively take reconfiguration and remediation actions in a fully automatic fashion across the C2T continuum.

RECAP is a 3-year 4.6 m EU-funded research project to develop the next generation of distributed cloud, edge and fog computing systems. The project is developing a novel concept for the provisioning of cloud services, where services are automatically instantiated and elastically deployed close to the users that actually need them via self-configurable cloud computing systems. To accomplish this, RECAP addresses three key areas of cloud, edge and fog computing environments, namely: *(i)* deployment support for complex application components, *(ii)* infrastructure management support, and *(iii)* infrastructure operations support.

The remainder of this paper is organized as follows. The next section summarises the RECAP approach. Then, the RECAP Simulation Framework is presented and illustrated with reference to one of the RECAP use cases i.e. virtual content delivery networks (vCDNs). The paper concludes with a discussion of next steps with respect to work on the RECAP simulation framework and its integration with the wider RECAP project.

2   The RECAP Approach

The principal objective of RECAP project is to attempt to reverse the current common practice of providing cloud-based services by allocating data centre resources on a best-effort basis. Instead, RECAP seeks to incorporate a much more elastic model which delivers services and allocates resources in a dynamic manner tied to time-varying user requirements. In this manner, RECAP aims to develop the next generation of cloud/edge/fog computing capacity provisioning and remediation via targeted research advances in cloud infrastructure optimisation [2].

Pre-emption (and indeed remediation), as envisioned in RECAP, requires the modelling of complex applications and infrastructures using much more fine-grained and accurate application deployment and behavior models. Such models need to capture load and capacity requirements, variations over time, and most importantly the impact on infrastructure resources. RECAP seeks to achieve this through the concerted *(i)* prediction of the evolution of workload and application performance, *(ii)* simulation of different deployments across the C2T continuum, *(iii)* optimization of the deployment given the output of historic and real-time analysis, and *(iv)* relocation of services and application components to achieve the required QoS, as illustrated in Fig. 1. Different components in the RECAP architecture interact to achieve the optimal resource management required by the network operator (see Ostberg et al. [1] for further discussion).

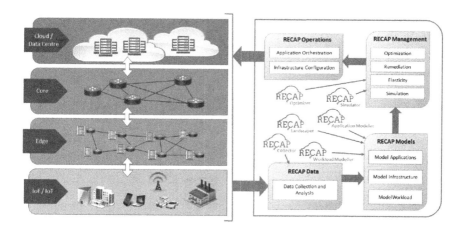

Fig. 1. The RECAP approach

In the context of this paper, two components in the RECAP approach are of specific interest. The RECAP Optimizer takes fully autonomous application placement and infrastructure management decisions throughout the network from the main data centers to the extreme edge. The RECAP Simulator, the focus of this paper, simulates the interactions of distributed cloud-application behaviors, emulates data center and connectivity networks systems, and feeds this data to the Optimizer to inform the resource placement and infrastructure management decisions.

To achieve this vision, RECAP evolves the state-of-the-art system software, simulation and modelling frameworks through the realization of different key uses cases compiled by the RECAP project partners. These use cases describe the challenges the industry faces today from both technical and business perspectives when adopting technological solutions spanning across fog, edge, and cloud layers. The project focuses on five such scenarios (see [2] for further details): *(a)* infrastructure and network management, *(b)* big data analytics engine, *(c)* fog and large scale IoT scenario for supporting smart cities, *(d)* virtual content distribution networks (vCDN), and *(e)* network function virtualisation (NFV).

3   The RECAP Simulation Framework

Due to the complexity and scale of the networks and systems in target use cases, the risk of adverse outcomes and cost of experimentation on live systems and full-scale deployment respectively are prohibitive. As such simulation presents itself as an appropriate alternative. The RECAP Simulator plays a key role in assisting the RECAP Optimizer in the evaluation of different deployment and infrastructure management alternatives against agreed parameters before actuation on real application deployments. The RECAP Simulation Framework utilises two different simulation approaches: *(i)* discrete time simulation (DTS) (also known as time-advancing simulation) and *(ii)* discrete event simulation (DES), as shown in Fig. 2.

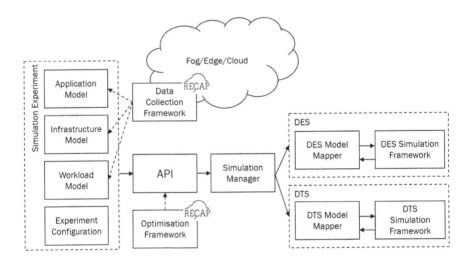

Fig. 2. RECAP simulation framework high level design

3.1   Simulating vCDNs

Content Distribution Network (CDN) providers offer a distribution service that puts content on caches closer to the end-users i.e. content consumers. vCDNs replace multiple customised physical caches with a standard server and storage running multiple virtual applications per CDN operator. To reduce costs associated with time and effort and maximize utilization of its network infrastructure, network operators need to identify the optimum location and amount of resources required to deploy vCDN systems and infrastructure just-in-time. In RECAP, this use case proposes to automate planning and operations, and improve veracity, thereby improving the efficiency of vCDN systems for a network operator. DTS-based Simulation is being used to support this use case. In order to evaluate the scalability of this approach, several experiments have been performed with a varying number of generated requests, measuring the elapsed time to complete the simulation. As time is critical, the RECAP simulator supports the execution of simulations sequentially or in parallel using multiple threads.

For the purpose of the vCDN use case, a 4-level hierarchical network topology composed of sites was used based on data provided by a network operator. The vCDN was modelled as a Directed Acyclic Graph (DAG), whereby sites were grouped per level not allowing inter-level communications. The most computationally demanding parts of the simulation are: *(i)* the update procedure for the state of the sites and *(ii)* the aggregation of metrics in specific timesteps. Each site is composed of nodes (servers) and virtual machines (VMs). Each VM, hosted on a specific node, retains a list of requests serving at a given timestep. Moreover, each site retains a list of requests that are forwarded, consuming only network resources, thus acting as a gateway for content. All requests are defined by their resource requirements (vCPU, memory, storage, and network) as well as their duration. At each timestep the prescribed duration of a request is reduced by an amount equal to the timestep, until it is considered finished (duration equals to zero) releasing the allocated resources.

The update procedure is performed per site thus allowing for efficient parallelization, without requiring synchronization points. The sites are enumerated in lexicographical order from top to bottom. Each available thread is assigned a site, cyclically, to update its state at each timestep. Furthermore, cyclic assignment in conjunction with lexicographical ordering has been chosen in order to reduce load imbalances during execution, since neighboring sites is more likely to have similar computational requirements. In order to further enhance performance the requirements of each request were modeled as a fraction of the available resources of a VM hosting a specific type of content. Thus, each VM retains a list of floating point numbers denoting the duration of the requests created by cache hits in a site. By retaining only one number per request, memory requirements and consequently memory transfers are reduced, simplifying the status update procedure and enhancing performance. Similarly, a list of duration variables is retained for requests created by cache misses in a site. Thus, an update procedure for a site is performed by updating duration variables for forwarding and cache hit/miss type request, followed by cleanup of finished requests and deallocation of respective resources and computation of energy consumption for active nodes in the current timestep.

The second computationally-demanding task in the simulation framework, namely the aggregation of metrics, concerns computation of collective (per level) metrics of sites and is performed based on user defined intervals. These metrics are aggregated in parallel through loop level parallelization, following the aforementioned lexicographical order for traversing sites and cyclic distribution to threads. Subsequently, the collected metrics are written to an output file.

If the interval for collecting metrics is small then the output size increases and performance decreases since the procedure of writing data to files is sequential. Selection of a large value for the interval results in under-sampling of the behavior, neglecting possible transient phenomena emerging during simulation.

Initially, an experiment was performed with a network topology composed of 509 sites with 3 levels (12 sites at level 1, 46 at level 2, and 451 at level 3). Requests were generated uniformly on the last level, and the average time duration of the requests varied between 300 to 1000 s. This experiment was run in a Xeon E5-2420-v2 (6 cores, 12 threads) with 48 GB RAM memory with the number of parallel threads varied from 1 to 12. In Fig. 3, the parallel performance for various values of incoming tasks and number of threads is presented. The parallel speedup of the scheme increases as the number of incoming requests and available threads increase, attaining a maximum of 5.92 (efficiency 49.37%) at 12 threads and 1602203 incoming tasks. It should be noted that the efficiency is reduced by inherently sequential parts of the code such as positioning of requests to VMs and storing outputs to a file.

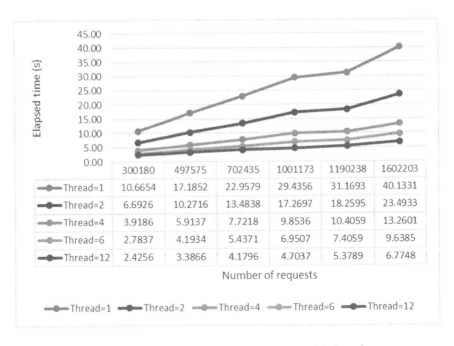

Fig. 3. Elapsed time of simulation using multi-threads

Currently, the RECAP Simulation Framework has the ability to measure the following metrics: cumulative accepted request per level, cumulative rejected request per level, cumulative cache hits per level, cumulative cache misses per level, average vCPU utilization per level, average network utilization per level, average storage utilization per level, energy consumption.

4   Next Steps

This work presents initial results regarding the RECAP Simulation Framework. From initial experiments, it has been shown that the DTS approach has the ability to run large-scale simulations of vCDN networks. However it should be noted that, to date, only a selection of assumptions were considered e.g. sites of the same level cannot communicate and the bandwidth was considered in a per site (as opposed to per link) granularity. Currently, the project is focused on the addition of a more detailed network model that will allow for the assessment of link congestion as well as same level communications.

Only one use case is presented above however the simulation application and network models are complete for other use cases. In the near term, further work is being carried out towards deeper simulation development and modelling of the edge and fog computing for smart cities use case through the use of DTS, and network function virtualization related use cases through the use of DES.

At the time of writing, the integration with the RECAP Optimiser is partially defined. The RECAP Simulation Framework has the capability to receive (a set of) JSON files containing a simulation configuration, execute it and provide the required output. In order to improve the integration between the RECAP Simulation Framework and the RECAP Optimizer, a web REST API-based approach is currently being implemented, and to validate the accuracy of the RECAP simulation models, real system data is currently being compared against simulation outputs.

Acknowledgment. This work is partly funded by the European Union's Horizon 2020 Research and Innovation Programme through RECAP (http://www.recap-project.eu) under Grant Agreement Number 732667 and the Irish Centre for Cloud Computing and Commerce, an Enterprise Ireland and IDA national technology centre.

References

1. Ostberg, P.-O., et al.: Reliable capacity provisioning for distributed cloud/edge/fog computing applications. In: 2017 European Conference on Networks and Communications (EuCNC). IEEE (2017)
2. Domaschka, J., et al.: RECAP Project Public Deliverable 3.1. Initial Requirements. https://recap-project.eu/news/initial-quality-of-service-metrics-and-models/

DevOps-Based Software Engineering for the Cloud

Andreas Christoforou[1](✉), Andreas Andreou[1], Luciano Baresi[2], and Michael Papazoglou[3]

[1] Cyprus University of Technology, 3036 Limassol, Cyprus
`andreas.christoforou@cut.ac.cy`
[2] Politecnico di Milano, 20133 Milan, MI, Italy
[3] Tilburg University, 5037 AB Tilburg, The Netherlands

Abstract. This paper describes briefly DOSSIER-Cloud, an ongoing H2020 project called that implements a series of coordination and support actions, aiming at promoting research in the area of Software Engineering for Distributed Systems development. According to the call, two internationally recognized scientific groups from the Netherlands (University of Tilburg – UvT) and Italy (Politecnico di Milano – POLIMI) collaborate with the Cyprus University of Technology (CUT) to facilitate transfer of scientific knowledge and expertise, as well as of best research practices from UvT and POLIMI to CUT, and ultimately strengthen the research and scientific profile of the partners in the relevant area.

Keywords: Twinning · Horizon2020 · Software engineering · DevOps

1 Project Description

DEVOPS-BASED SOFTWARE ENGINEERING FOR THE CLOUD (DOSSIER-Cloud) [1] is a 3-years project that proposes a series of coordination and support actions for promoting research in the area of Software Engineering for Distributed Systems development. It brings together two internationally recognized scientific groups from the Netherlands (UvT) and Italy (POLIMI) that collaborate with Cyprus University of Technology (CUT) so as to strengthen CUT's research and scientific profile in the relevant area. The aim of DOSSIER-Cloud is to facilitate transfer of scientific knowledge and expertise as well as of best research practices from UvT and POLIMI to CUT. The ultimate goal is that the research group of CUT increases its research capacity and prowess by investigating a number of significant and hot topics in the field of Distributed Systems development. We envisage that after the end of the project a number of high-quality research results will be produced enable its partners and especially CUT to significantly increase their international standing in the research community by both achieving related publications in the top-tier scientific journals and conferences of the relevant research area as well as by producing new tools that will benefit practitioners in the software industry. Close cooperation between the partners of DOSSIER-Cloud takes the form of

© Springer Nature Switzerland AG 2020
M. Fazio and W. Zimmermann (Eds.): ESOCC 2018 Workshops, CCIS 1115, pp. 226–232, 2020.
https://doi.org/10.1007/978-3-030-63161-1_22

knowledge acquisition and transfer through personnel exchanges organization of workshops and summer/winter schools with lectures delivered from UvT and POLIMI participation in international scientific conferences/workshops and establishment of strong links with the software industry.

The project is funded under the call "Coordination and Support Action – Twinning Horizon2020" - number: 692251. The duration of the project is 36 months (1/1/2016–31/12/2018) and the URL is http://dossier-cloud.eu/. The project is at the last quarter and the activities are now concentrated on strengthening the involvement of stakeholders and finalizing discussions on research topics for producing papers for publication in upcoming events.

The rest of the paper is organized as follows: Sect. 2 outlines the main objectives of the project while Sect. 3 describes briefly the research topics addressed and new challenges identified. Section 4 presents the results of the project thus far and Sect. 5 provides the summary and some conclusions.

2   Objectives

DOSSIER-Cloud revolves around three main objectives

- Objective#1: Acquire new and enhance existing knowledge on a set of research topics of interest that are sourced by the general themes of DevOps oriented software engineering processes and Tools for distributed software systems development
- Objective#2: Share research experiences and best practices with advanced scientific groups in the leading institutions. Change the research culture and scientific approach/philosophy of CUT's staff
- Objective#3: Form a collaboration basis with stakeholders and secure industrial involvement. Engage SMEs and practitioners to facilitate real-world experimentation and validation using real world feedback

The above objectives are closely related and intertwined with a variety of actions that were performed during the last 2.5 years each action serving one or more objectives. These actions involved

- Exchanging personnel and performing site visits to the leading institutions.
- Organizing summer schools in Cyprus and a number of workshops in the three participating countries with closed sessions dedicated only for the partners, as well as open sessions with industrial participation.
- Organizing meetings with stakeholders either one on one or in groups.
- Delivering special purpose/theme lectures and offering training on specific research methods and tools developed and used by members of UvT and POLIMI. The lectures and training were attended by graduate (master PhD postdoc) students at CUT often resulting in topics for theses or research problems to be addressed.
- Applying step-by-step problem-solving techniques in joint small-scale projects.
- Participating in conferences either by organizing workshops or presenting research work that was produced by the project.

3 Research Topics

The research topics investigated so far in the project were the following:

1. Introduction of a new, unified software process for developing distributed software applications under DevOps principles. This research topic describes a unified framework for developing distributed software systems where the phases of a new and dedicated DevOps-oriented life-cycle model is studied.
2. Definition of dedicated DevOps-oriented, Cloud-focused Metrics and Measurement activities. The subject of the second topic is the definition of a new, customized Monitoring and Control Mechanism (MCM) for DevOps oriented development of Cloud software and services.
3. Automation of build, deployment and operation activities in a DevOps environment. This topic focuses on automating the procedures for adjusting and reconfiguring the DevOps environment:

   - Automatic monitoring of service delivery, Cloud resource management and decision support/making and/or automatic re-configuration
   - Cloud Service Composition - Composing cross-layered Cloud services to build a service-based Cloud application

The above research topics triggered the lectures, discussions and exchange of knowledge between the partners and formulated the project's research plan for future publications. In addition, the collaboration between the partners enabled the identification of new research challenged, which are described in the next section.

3.1 New Research Challenges

Discussions and brainstorming between the partners on specific scientific topics in the areas of interest allowed the consortium to identify new research challenges that are also being addressed. More specifically:

- Social Software Engineering [2]: This challenge involved quite a few aspects. The first was the modeling and analysis of the organizational and social structures of teams aiming at investigating their impact on the software process for Cloud services. The second involved the improvement of teams' organizational and social structure targeting at optimizing the software process by decreasing waste (time, effort, code). Finally, the definition and analysis of the optimal organizational structure for DevOps strategies to results in a framework/guideline for better organizational configuration setups.
- Cloud Pricing [3]: Involved the two aspects. The first dealt with the development of solutions for optimizing pricing policies. The second focused on supporting Cloud providers to offer an attractive pricing scheme to their customers targeting to maximize their profit, while at the same time taking into account their services cost and market competition

- Cloud Resource Management [4]: Involved a proposition of a dedicated group of services that support resource management on the Cloud (workload prediction, dynamic provisioning, automatic resource management) and the utilization of CI/AI techniques to address Cloud optimization problems (e.g. workload prediction and balancing, management of physical or virtual resources, and others)
- Self-Adaptive Systems for the Cloud [5]: Included two aspects: First, the evolution and enhancement of MAPE (Monitor-Analyze-Planning-Execute) control loops to deal with complex scenarios of Cloud services and/or resource management by replacing conventional techniques (e.g. control theory) with Computational Intelligence/Artificial Intelligence models. Second, the development of recommendation systems for automatic software services/microservices synthesis
- Smart Manufacturing [6]: Optimization of concept generation, specification & design, monitoring of production lines and product transactions. Integration of all steps in the product fabrication process. Proposition a more harmonious development process utilizing data to develop intelligent technology to expedite new and higher quality goods.
- Smart Data Processing and Data Analytics [7]: Introduction of models and methods for managing and analyzing big volumes of data in a smart way and demonstrating how this data can be used to benefit various market sectors such as automotive, shipping and financial industry. These methods consist of techniques and descriptions for collecting, contextualizing, homogenizing and processing data with intelligent algorithms in such a way so as to highlight causes and results and predict future states to support decision making.

4 Project Results and Current State

Guided by the three main objectives mentioned in Sect. 2, the project produced the following results:

4.1 Scientific and Research Results

CUT, as the low RDI performing institution, has already started strengthening its scientific knowledge and expertise, which is anticipated to lead to improving its research position by increasing the number of high-quality published research papers in the relevant fields.

In the above context two workshops have already been organized and one is forthcoming:

- Workshop "Smart Data Systems and Applications" in the context of the 23rd ICE/IEEE International Conference on Engineering Technology and Innovation. Madeira, Portugal - June 2017.
- Workshop "Engineering Services Oriented Applications and Cloud Services (WESOACS) in the context of the International Conference on Service-Oriented Computing (ICSOC), Malaga, Spain – November 2017.

- Workshop on "Engineering Services Oriented Applications and Cloud Services (WESOACS) in the context of the 7th European Conference on Service Oriented and Cloud Computing (ECSOCC), Como, Italy – September 2018.

The collaboration with the leading institutions created the opportunity to meet and discuss with other research groups from universities and organizations in Europe, such as the Vrije University of Amsterdam, Technical University of Eindhoven, University of Gent, Fraunhoffer Germany, LIRIS/CNRS France, Universitat Politècnica de Catalunya, CSIRO Australia and University of Cairo.

Another result of the collaboration between the partners of DOSSIER-Cloud and the networking activities was the preparation and submission of several proposals in Horizon2020 calls.

As regards publications, the project has already produced two conference papers: In the first one, researchers from POLIMI and CUT introduced a novel model to support the decision of migrating to microservices architecture. This research work identified the key concepts and drivers related to the decision of migrating to microservices. These concepts and their interrelations were gathered by performing a literature review and then engaging a group of experts from the industry and academia that provided valuable feedback through questionnaires and interviews. The concepts identified were organized as a Multi-Layered Fuzzy Cognitive Map (ML-FCM), a graph-shaped computational intelligence model. The ML-FCM allows one to support decision-makers when considering the migration to microservices through automated reasoning, by means of (static) graph analysis and (dynamic) simulation over different and customizable scenarios. This paper was presented at the 15th International Conference on Service-Oriented Computing (ICSOC), in Malaga, Spain [8]. The second paper dealt with a proposed machine learning mechanism to improve the impact of cloud data sparsity in the context of session-based recommendations. To this end, introduced a way of improving the modeling capacity of Recommender Systems (RS) that utilize deep learning techniques with recurrently connected units and adopting concepts from the field of Bayesian statistics, namely variational inference. This paper was presented at the 2nd Workshop on Deep Learning for Recommender Systems (DLRS), in Como, Italy [9].

4.2 Industrial and Market Results

The CUT team was introduced to local organizations and companies in the Netherlands, such as the Municipality of Den Bosch and Philips Lighting, and presented part of its research work thus far, discussing also the possibility of collaboration for applying it to practical problems faced by these stakeholders (e.g. modeling and scenario analysis, automations, smart data processing, etc.).

During the stakeholder's meetings that were performed in the participating countries, the members of the DOSSIER-Cloud consortium emphasized on the improvements in software development productivity brought in by embracing DevOps and automations. Nineteen (19) companies/organizations were contacted thus far and the objectives of the project, as well as the potential of future collaboration were discussed with them.

A career day event was organized at the Jheronimus Academy of Data Science (JADS) in the Netherlands to bring together students and professionals working in the field of Data Science. Representatives of the project joined the event and distributed leaflets and newsletters to the companies and organizations that participated (e.g. Shell, Omron, Vivat, Hitachin, ABN-Amro, etc.) which disseminate the project results, and discussed with interested stakeholders about possible applied research collaborations.

CUT has established strong links with major industrial players in Cyprus for promoting further collaborations in the field of Industry 4.0 and Smart Manufacturing (Ministry of Energy, Commerce, Industry, and Tourism of Cyprus, Muskita Aluminum Industry Ltd., etc.).

4.3 Research Activity in Progress

CUT team members in close cooperation with researchers from project partners are currently performing research on the relevant research topics listed above. More specifically:

- Investigation of ways to optimize smart manufacturing by studying trends on process automations and data exchange (CUT and UvT).
- Utilization of Computational Intelligence techniques to model and analyze social aspects targeting at defining an optimum team organizational structure that leads to a better software development process (CUT and UvT).
- Processing of real-world data from the automotive industry aiming on one hand to identify and predict anomalies for supporting decision making in car maintenance, and on the other to facilitate predictive maintenance (CUT and UvT, in close collaboration with a Dutch company)
- Extend and enrich the research work conducted in [8] by applying and evaluating the proposed model on real world cases (CUT and POLIMI).
- Review of the main serverless computing providers, as well investigation of possible resource management approaches, to explore ways and their level of influence to the software development process (CUT).

5 Summary and Conclusions

DOSSIER-Cloud, a H2020 project, aims to increase CUT's research capacity and prowess through research collaboration with two internationally recognized scientific groups from the Netherlands and Italy, in the area of Software Engineering for Distributed Systems development. Knowledge transfer and acquisition are the main project objectives which rely on various actions and activities. These activities consist of personnel exchanges, site visits, organizations of workshops and summer schools and participation in international scientific conferences.

As the project comes to its end, one can easily conclude that the main targets of the project have been achieved to the greatest extent, with significant scientific results and establishment of cooperation with industrial stakeholders. The close cooperation between the three research institutions that was successfully developed through the project partnership will continue by working on common research topics of interest. At the same time, all communication channels that have been established with the industry will remain open for the benefit of both academia and industry.

References

1. DevOps-Based Software Engineering for the Cloud. http://dossier-cloud.eu/
2. Ahmadi, N., Jazayeri, M., Lelli, F., Nesic, S.: A survey of social software engineering. In: 2008 23rd IEEE/ACM International Conference on Automated Software Engineering – Workshops, pp. 1–12. IEEE (2008)
3. Al-Roomi, M., Al-Ebrahim, S., Buqrais, S., Ahmad, I.: Cloud computing pricing models: a survey. Int. J. Grid Distrib. Comput. **6**, 93–106 (2013). https://doi.org/10.14257/ijgdc.2013.6.5.09
4. Jennings, B., Stadler, R.: Resource management in clouds: survey and research challenges. J. Netw. Syst. Manage. **23**(3), 567–619 (2014). https://doi.org/10.1007/s10922-014-9307-7
5. de Lemos, R., et al.: Software engineering for self-adaptive systems: a second research roadmap. In: de Lemos, R., Giese, H., Müller, Hausi A., Shaw, M. (eds.) Software Engineering for Self-Adaptive Systems II. LNCS, vol. 7475, pp. 1–32. Springer, Heidelberg (2013). https://doi.org/10.1007/978-3-642-35813-5_1
6. Davis, J., Edgar, T., Porter, J., et al.: Smart manufacturing, manufacturing intelligence and demand-dynamic performance. Comput. Chem. Eng. **47**, 145–156 (2012)
7. Gandomi, A., Haider, M.: Beyond the hype: big data concepts, methods, and analytics. Int. J. Inf. Manage. **35**, 137–144 (2015). https://doi.org/10.1016/J.IJINFOMGT.2014.10.007
8. Christoforou, A., Garriga, M., Andreou, A.S., Baresi, L.: Supporting the decision of migrating to microservices through multi-layer fuzzy cognitive maps. In: Maximilien, M., Vallecillo, A., Wang, J., Oriol, M. (eds.) ICSOC 2017. LNCS, vol. 10601, pp. 471–480. Springer, Cham (2017). https://doi.org/10.1007/978-3-319-69035-3_34
9. Chatzis, S.P., Christodoulou, P., Andreou, A.S.: Recurrent latent variable networks for session-based recommendation. In: Proceedings of the 2nd Workshop on Deep Learning for Recommender Systems, pp. 38–45 (2017)

Author Index

Printed in the United States
By Bookmasters